Rethinking Disaster Recovery

Rethinking Disaster Recovery

A Hurricane Katrina Retrospective

Edited by
Jeannie Haubert

LEXINGTON BOOKS
Lanham • Boulder • New York • London

Published by Lexington Books
An imprint of The Rowman & Littlefield Publishing Group, Inc.
4501 Forbes Boulevard, Suite 200, Lanham, Maryland 20706
www.rowman.com

Unit A, Whitacre Mews, 26-34 Stannary Street, London SE11 4AB

British Library Cataloguing in Publication Information Available

Library of Congress Cataloging-in-Publication Data

Rethinking disaster recovery : a Hurricane Katrina retrospective / edited by Jeannie Haubert.
pages cm
Includes bibliographical references and index.
ISBN 978-1-4985-0120-0 (cloth : alk. paper) -- ISBN 978-1-4985-0121-7 (electronic)
1. Hurricane Katrina, 2005--Social aspects. 2. Disaster victims--Louisiana--New Orleans--Social conditions. 3. Disaster relief--Louisiana--New Orleans. 4. New Orleans (La.)--Social conditions. 5. New Orleans (La.)--Economic conditions. I. Haubert, Jeannie.
HV636 2005 .N4 R47 2015
976.3'35064--dc23
2014047005

∞ ™ The paper used in this publication meets the minimum requirements of American National Standard for Information Sciences Permanence of Paper for Printed Library Materials, ANSI/NISO Z39.48-1992.

Printed in the United States of America

Contents

Foreword: Ten Years Later vii
James R. Elliott

Acknowledgments xiii

1 Rethinking Disaster Recovery: Editor's Introduction 1
Jeannie Haubert

I: Gender and Sexuality in the Recovery Process

2 Trauma, Recovery, and Sexuality in Post-Katrina New Orleans 15
Mimi Schippers

3 It's Raining Men: Gender and Street Harassment in Post-Katrina New Orleans 27
Andrea Wilbon Hartman, Erica Dudas, and Jennifer Day-Sully

4 Rebuilding for Safety: Domestic Violence and Hurricane Katrina 39
Pamela Jenkins and Bethany Van Brown

5 Missing in the Storm: The Gender Gap in Hurricane Katrina Research and Disaster Management Efforts 53
Kristen Barber and Shiloh Deitz

II: Race and Class in the Recovery Process

6 On the Kindness of Strangers: Am I More Worthy of Your Sympathy Than Lakisha and Jamal? 71
Jeannie Haubert

7 Disaster, Reconstruction, and Racialization: Latinos in New Orleans after Hurricane Katrina 89
Elizabeth Fussell and Amy Bellone-Hite

8 Flourishing or Floundering?: Examining the Career Paths of African American Emerging Adults in Post-Katrina New Orleans 105
Farrah Gafford Cambrice

9 New Orleans's Katrina Recovery for Whom and What?: A Race, Gender, and Class Approach 121
Jean Ait Belkhir

III: Doing Academia through Disaster Recovery

10 Trauma Survivor as Author; Method as Recovery 139
Jessica W. Pardee

11 Housing Market Mayhem: Studying Discrimination Post-Disaster 153
Jeannie Haubert

12 "We're Still in the Trenches, Baby . . .": Navigating Academia in an Uncertain, Post-Katrina World 169
Danielle Antoinette Hidalgo and Dana M. Greene

13 Learning from Disaster: Post-Katrina New Orleans as a Sociological Classroom 185
Timothy J. Haney

PostScript: Notes on the Buildup to Katrina and the Future of the Gulf Coast 205
Dana M. Greene

References 211

Index 233

About the Authors 239

Foreword: Ten Years Later

James R. Elliott

A central claim of sociology is that natural disasters are social constructs, which is to say that natural disasters emerge through and reveal not just environmental processes but also pervasive and unequal social relations that take and (re)make places over time. This social fact became tragically evident in the case of Hurricane Katrina in a myriad of ways: from shoddy planning and infrastructure that left thousands of poor and disabled residents dead or stranded to uneven recoveries that continue to privilege the restoration of property over community and human rights. In the ten years since the disaster, sociologists have worked hard to reveal these dynamics and to uncover the social underpinnings of this historic "natural" disaster. Yet for a handful of them, the event was more than a social construct. It was a personal reality that spurred them to study the disaster while wrestling with their own place within it. This volume springs from these intersecting efforts—personal stories that emerged in and through the professional practice of sociologists living and working in New Orleans and the greater Gulf area when Katrina hit.

My own story started the day of the storm. After the city was nearly evacuated, I walked through abandoned streets to a local hospital where my wife worked as essential personnel. It was hot, and it was still. No wind. No cars. No pedestrians. No nothing. Just plywood on windows and a thick sense of uncertainty. A day later, after we rode out the storm and the winds finally subsided, the uncertainty only grew. Although the rains had stopped, flood waters began to creep—block by block—to the hospital's main entrance. Even with no outside communication, we knew that this was a bad sign. If water was reaching the upper lip of the proverbial bowl, the rest of the city was surely sunk. So we retreated back within the hospital, moved food and supplies to upper floors, cared for patients and each other, and waited for buses to arrive days later.

Once evacuated, news coverage confirmed what we already knew: this had been the big one that would change the region and its inhabitants for a long time to come. It was a stressful period, but there was comfort in connecting with others who had also been affected, hearing their stories, and knowing they were alright. One of those stories came from Jeannie Haubert, the editor of this volume. The storm had destroyed her house, but she was safe and—like many others in this volume—already thinking about how to help those in need, even as she wrestled with what the tragedy meant for her own personal and professional life. In these stories and connections resilience emerged, as did a reflexive commitment to turn the sociological gaze homeward to investigate New Orleans, its people, and their (and our) collective recovery.

Early on, most of this gaze focused on a pervasive and deep sense of failure, and rightly so. Connecting personal troubles to public issues, some sociologists illuminated how government agencies had become too complex, too detached, too corrupt to protect and serve their constituents, despite ample forecasts of storms such as Katrina. Others highlighted failures to stem institutional racism and a general lack of empathy for the poor. Others highlighted the hubris of thinking that we could control nature and contain risks created by our collective, large-scale transformation of it, often at great profit to a relative few. This side of the sociological brain sought answers to the important question of why the disaster turned out to be as devastating as it did and who was culpable. It is a line of inquiry that remains necessary. But, it is not sufficient. We need sociological research that focuses not just on who and what is to blame for the disaster but also on how people—including sociologists—put pieces of their fractured lives and communities back together in the face of underlying social problems and inequities that continue to operate long after the flood waters receded.

This volume is about those efforts. It is about social experiences and inequalities that simultaneously shaped different trajectories of recovery *and* how scholars came to study them the way they did. In this sense, the volume represents the dual labor of trained sociologists to make sense not only of the tragic event but also the role of the local sociologist within its long-term aftermath. It is, in professional parlance, a reflexive account that positions the researcher within the site of study as both survivor and scholar. This type of investigation requires more than sociological imagination. It requires thinking about how this imagination is situated and contextualized, not just in social spaces forged and reflective of race, class and gender, but in actual places where these dynamics interact with environmental forces, sometimes unforgivingly. In such settings, the sociological imagination transforms through the intertwining of personal and professional practice to become something different, something we might call the sociological determination.

As Tim Haney and I have discussed elsewhere, part of this sociological determination encourages sociologists to document and report as part of their methodology the personal, organizational, and political obstacles they encounter in conducting research on and in their respective recovery zone. This determination involves expressly revealing the visible and invisible work necessary to collect and process evidence that moves us from imagination through determination to analysis and interpretation. It illuminates how practitioners living and working in disaster zones maneuver through new institutional challenges that become part of their lives as well as the research sites in which they are embedded. Such conditions simultaneously invite and complicate empirical research for all investigators, but they are especially acute for those living and working in disaster zones defined by deep individual and collective liminality.

So, the question arises: Does this reflexivity and determination of survivor scholars make their sociological work better or more authentic than that produced by outside scholars who were not directly affected by the disaster in question? This is a complicated issue, and inevitably the question becomes, better or more authentic for whom? On the one hand, and from the standpoint of the discipline as a whole, the answer to the first question is probably no. In the academic world, research is ultimately judged by the usual yardsticks of theoretical contribution, methodological rigor, and original contribution. Being directly and lastingly affected by local tragedy can certainly provide motivation, access, and knowledge that is useful in meeting and exceeding these criteria, but it does not ensure them. Ultimately, reflexivity is an act, not a property, and thus can generate a full range of professional as well as personal outcomes.

On the other hand, and from the standpoint of the citizen sociologist, the work of survivor scholars is vital, meaning that the field would be the lesser if it did not occur and become part of wider conversation and discussion. One reason for this vitality is that it demonstrates and extends sociologists' calling, not just to professional practice but to communities of which we are parts. In this way, survivor scholarship pays witness to local recovery efforts while also becoming active parts of them. In the process, it strengthens local capacities and brings unique perspectives to those trying to understand the disaster and recovery from afar. Sometimes these perspectives can offer fresh insight into old problems of race, sex, and violence; other times it can illuminate how local disasters become national and international phenomena not just through short-lived media coverage but also and more meaningfully through longer term pedagogical projects of survivor scholars who have moved away.

This volume is a collection of windows onto such insights and contributions. Through them we can see what survivor scholars have seen and perhaps even catch our own reflection, spurring us to consider where one begins and the other ends. This is important, determined work, not just for the authors and editor of this volume but for you, the reader, as you continue to take and remake your own place within a world where future disasters are not only inevitable, but likely close to home.

Interstate 10 at Causeway Boulevard, Saturday, September 3, 2005. Staff photo by Eliot Kamenitz, *Times-Picayune/Landov.*

Interstate 10 at Causeway Boulevard, August 2014. Staff photo by Ted Jackson, *Times-Picayune/Landov.*

Acknowledgments

I have many people to thank, but first, a few acknowledgments regarding the contents and title of this volume. I want to thank Edwin Mellon Press for allowing me to reuse a portion of my chapter in *How Ethnically Marginalized Americans Cope with Catastrophic Disasters: Studies in Suffering and Resiliency* (see Weil 2010). Also, the phrase "rethinking disaster recovery" was inspired by Lee Miller's (2012) work and it is with great respect for her scholarship and with her permission that I recycle this phrase in my title. I am grateful also to Ted Jackson for his powerful photos.

This volume would not be possible without the tremendous support I've received from Winthrop University and from outside colleagues. Thank you to Debra Boyd, Karen Kedrowski, Jon Marx, and Adolphus Belk for helping to fund various portions of the writing and promotion of this volume, including funding a sabbatical, conference travel, a panel of speakers, and copyright acquisition for photographs. I am also grateful to Kai Erikson, Steven Kroll-Smith, and Lori Peek for their encouragement. Thank you also to my good friends and colleagues Richard Chacon, Jon Marx, Jennifer Solomon, Jim Elliott, Elizabeth Fussell, Kristen Barber, and Farrah Gafford Cambrice for your frequent feedback. Importantly, I am also very much indebted to the fourteen colleagues who contributed excellent chapters to this volume.

I also offer my deepest gratitude to Allison Morris whose intense dedication to proofreading each of the thirteen chapters was vital to the timely completion of this volume. I could not have asked for a better assistant. Lastly, but importantly, I extend my appreciation to my husband Jimmy Fitzpatrick, my son Ethan, and the rest of our family for keeping me motivated and for listening to hours of enthusiastic rambling about the contents of this book without ever looking bored. Thank you.

Chapter One

Rethinking Disaster Recovery

Editor's Introduction

Jeannie Haubert

I was kept out of my town, Pass Christian, Mississippi, for several weeks following Katrina's landfall on August 29, 2005. When finally permitted to return, we could only get our truck within four miles of the house. In the unforgiving heat of a southern September afternoon, my now ex-husband and I had no choice but to walk, and walk, and walk back to the place we once called home. The storm surge had been between twenty-five and thirty feet high where we lived. As we walked, we saw dead fish in the middle of the street. I passed a couch lodged in a treetop. It was surreal. I didn't take pictures or even cry. I just stared in disbelief. The streets were unrecognizable and in many cases, impassible. In our neighborhood, all of the old "shotgun" houses that were famed for having survived Hurricane Betsy in 1965 had not fared as well this time. They had been lifted up off of their foundations. They, and all their contents, had all floated around and were pushed to one side of the neighborhood like children's toys floating in a swimming pool. The houses were all there, but they were in the wrong places. Some were in the middle of the road; many were in the wrong lot. My place landed about seventy-five feet from where it was supposed to be. The only way I could tell where it was supposed to be was by using the concrete stairs that once led to the front porch and the mailbox stubbornly stuck in the ground as landmarks. Most of the other reference points had been similarly shuffled. One of the four exterior walls was missing revealing the soggy and rearranged former-life inside. Everything was gone, everything; all my possessions, all my books and schoolwork, all my pictures and mementos. I miss the pictures most of all. All I had was three days' worth of clothes, my folder of "important documents," my jewelry box, a truck and boat we took with us, my dogs, and some soggy gift cards we had precariously fished out of an overturned dresser through a broken window. My town in Mississippi and my university in New Orleans were devastated and my home was destroyed. The insurance company called it a "total loss."

Fast forward nine years and I am now sitting comfortably in my new home in Fort Mill, South Carolina, writing this book on my laptop while on sabbatical from my tenure-track job. There have been a lot of changes. My doggies, Max and Sammie, are still with me, but everything else is different. Different house, different job, different friends and family sitting beside me, everything, down to the furniture I'm sitting on. Most would say that I've been fortunate in my personal Katrina recovery; others would say that I've pulled myself up by my bootstraps. However, any sociologist will tell you, luck and hard work have a lot less to do with where we end up than we'd like to think. How then did I get from "total loss" to this nice new home, good job, and new life? How are others from the region faring nearly a decade later? What has happened to these areas since Katrina and what changes are still needed?

By now, most of us know the details of the disaster that befell the Gulf Coast in August 2005. The images are burned into our brains; those of bodies floating in the toxic waters that flooded the city and mothers stranded on the hot New Orleans's interstates with their babies clinging to them. We should never forget what happened in the days leading up to the storm and the gross neglect that left roughly 2,000 people dead and, with the help of Hurricane Rita weeks later, displaced two million others (Hsu 2006). Although I provide a few key facts below to contextualize the recovery for those who are too young to remember this storm and the destruction that followed, *Rethinking Disaster Recovery* is not about what happened *during* Hurricane Katrina or the emergency response period. There are many excellent books already out there about that (see, for example, Hartman and Squires 2006; Brunsma, Overfelt, and Picou 2010). Instead, this book is about what happened to people and social life *after* the cameras and the public interest moved on. It's about the slow and arduous process of putting the pieces back together as demonstrated through our analyses of everyday interactions and changes within organizations and key social institutions. While other books have examined some of these phenomena, time is a key component in gaining proper perspective on social change and now, a decade later, we are finally at the point of being able to meaningfully reflect on the long-term recovery.

A visit to the area or a glance at newspapers from the area might lead one to believe that the Gulf Coast is back and better than ever. The pictures chosen for this volume are a testament to the hard work and resolve of Gulf Coast residents, volunteers, and business owners to not only rebuild, but reinvigorate a wounded coast. Many people have worked hard performing grueling and exhausting work, and on the surface, a lot of neighborhoods look good—very good. But the contributors to this volume simply ask you to look closer. Who is missing from the pictures? What about the changes to culture, social life, work life, and the structure of institutions that are absent in the images? How might only touting the successes of the recovery serve the interests of a tourism-based economy and what/who might be left out of this narrative? Are we back and better than ever? Well that depends on who you ask and what you mean by better.

New Orleans, for example, has recovered over three quarters of its pre-Katrina population, has experienced economic growth in recent years despite the Great Recession, has much higher than average rates of entrepreneurship, and has seen a surge in the number of arts and culture nonprofits in the area; however, the benefits of the massive federal and private investments in New Orleans have been uneven, often leaving some segments of the population behind (Plyer et al. 2013).[1] The poor, for example, are particularly strapped in the increasingly costly housing market as more than a third of New Orleans renters pay over half their income in rent, a marked increase over pre-Katrina costs (Plyer 2014). Black men also are particularly struggling to achieve in the city. For example, in 2011, only 53 percent of black working age men were employed in the metro area compared to 73 percent and 78 percent for comparable non-Hispanic white men and Latinos. Those rates are very similar to pre-Katrina levels (54 percent of black men were employed in 2000), showing that, for this segment of the population, there has been little to no improvement in the quality of life despite the recovery money flowing into the city. In fact, income gaps by race have widened with African American households as they are making only *half* of what local white households make on average.[2] While crime rates are below pre-Katrina levels, they are still quite high as compared to the rest of the nation, and incarceration rates in Orleans Parish exceed pre-storm levels (Plyer et.al. 2013). Although nationally, men, women, whites, African Americans, and Latinos are more educated than ever, in New Orleans, educational attainment was stagnant for black men as compared to pre-Katrina levels and decreased for Latino men (ibid.). Domestic violence rates increased during the recovery period, putting women in particular at increased risk (see Jenkins, chapter 3). Many of the poor have either been shut out of public housing, or unable to fund rebuilding. Discrimination following negative stereotyping of some groups of evacuees also complicates the already difficult recovery process even further (see Schippers, chapter 2 and Haubert, chapter 6). The chapters in this book will expand on some of this and highlight the fact that the massive recovery effort needs to be more inclusive of the diversity of New Orleans's residents. However, it is important to realize that New Orleans's recovery is only part of the story.

Katrina was "only" a strong Category 3 storm when she hit U.S. soil, but she was massive with an unbelievably wide swath that heavily impacted Louisiana, Mississippi, and Alabama. As a result, Katrina was one of the five deadliest hurricanes in our nation's history and certainly the costliest hurricane to date, with the most severe property damage occurring in Mississippi. The eye of the storm skirted New Orleans with a last minute easterly turn, bringing it directly through southeastern Louisiana and the Mississippi coast. The beach towns of Waveland, Bay St. Louis, Pass Christian, Long Beach, Gulfport, Biloxi, Ocean Springs, Gautier, Pascagoula, and several other Mississippi towns were completely leveled by Katrina and suffered the brunt of her wrath. At first it appeared as if New Orleans, by far the most densely populated area, had been spared, until the levees were overtopped and eventually failed. Thus, in New Orleans, Katrina was a man-made disaster resulting from depletion of the natural wetland barriers that had protected the city in storms past and from poorly constructed/poorly maintained levees (Hartmann and Squires 2006). This man-made disaster resulted in a flood that left 80 percent of this major urban area underwater and roughly 1,000 people dead in Southeastern Louisiana alone (Plyer 2014). When we look at the human and physical toll across the region, the disaster was even worse: with around 2,000 dead from direct and indirect causes, 300,000 homes left uninhabitable (Weber and Peek 2012), and more than a million homes damaged (Plyer 2014). But it is population density and the human toll in terms of loss of life that puts New Orleans on center stage, and since this book is written by sociologists connected to New Orleans universities who study population, social organization, and social inequality, it necessarily focuses heavily on the Crescent City.[3] In this volume, we primarily highlight the particular struggles of historically marginalized groups in New Orleans, but that is not in any way meant to diminish the profound suffering of people—rich and poor, white and non-white, straight and gay, male, female, and transgender—all along the Louisiana, Mississippi, and Alabama coastlines.

In contextualizing the recovery from disaster, it is important to realize that Katrina was part of a series of tragedies that befell the Gulf Coast in a short period of time. Katrina hit the United States on August 29, 2005, and her sister Rita followed just weeks after in September 2005, wreaking much havoc on an already crippled coast with a staggering total of $150 billion dollars in damages (Plyer 2014). In 2009, the Great Recession was its own sort of disaster, one that deeply impacted this region containing the poorest states in the nation. As the coast was recovering, the BP oil spill in 2010 devastated Louisiana and Mississippi ecologically, economically, and emotionally as oil gushed for a relentless eighty-seven days into the waters that were the livelihoods of so many in the fishing and tourism industries. Thus, Katrina is in some ways shorthand for a series of disasters over the past decade.

What does it mean then to "rethink disaster recovery"? *Rethinking Disaster Recovery* is a compilation of reflective essays written primarily by sociologists affiliated with, or displaced from, Tulane University, University of New Orleans, Xavier University of New Orleans, and Loyola University of New Orleans. The contributors specialize in gender inequality, sexuality studies, racial and ethnic relations, immigration, class disparities, and disasters. Therefore, for us to borrow some terms from the table of contents, "rethinking" Katrina entails a critical evaluation of who is *flourishing* in post–Katrina New Orleans and who is *floundering*, who is still *in the trenches* and *missing in the storm*, what has been *reconstructed* and who has been *racialized,* who has benefited from the *kindness of strangers* and who has been demonized, and *recovery for whom.* In essence, rethinking and reflecting means drawing attention to the inequality embedded in the recovery of various social groups as well as examining how we, as current and former residents of the Gulf Coast, have been affected in our teaching, our research, and our careers. Everything was impacted, the production of knowledge and student learning included. Our reflections merge the existing research on the recovery with our own experiences and observations on the ground in the recovery zone. In this way, our Katrina stories are written with a sense of two-ness, to borrow from W. E. B. DuBois (1903): one, as scholars who are particularly attuned to inequalities, and two, as people who considered the Gulf Coast home. Each essay has at least one author who experienced Katrina firsthand and we believe that this two-ness makes this collection of essays unique.

FROM INSIDE KATRINA

Several of my local colleagues (who shall remain anonymous) have commented that the academic research on Katrina feels too detached, cold even. There are of course exceptions, but as a rule, some of us have felt the *verstehen* missing in the research we hear presented and read in books and journals.[4] For this reason, we've crafted chapters that are stylistically designed to personalize the knowledge.

Yes, much of the sociological cannon asserts that we are supposed to be detached and objective as social scientists, but for some of us, this detachment rings false and is a barrier to a fuller understanding of the recovery. It rings false not only because *all* research—quantitative, qualitative, historical, or contemporary—is influenced by the subjectivity of the researcher's choices in focus and method (whether or not those influences are made explicit); but it also rings false in that detached writing and research often misses the personal side of the story and misconstrues meaning. Awareness of what it means to put one's life back together following such a tragedy is perhaps best conveyed by someone who has firsthand experience with the loss, dislocation, and destabilization that followed in the years after the storm. At the very least, as some of the later chapters make clear, firsthand experience helps with rapport to better get at the experiences of other storm survivors. We write this volume then, not as detached academics, but as scholars writing from a unique standpoint, from inside Katrina.[5] As such we do not pretend to be the disembodied researcher; instead we embrace our local knowledge and combine our observations with a keen sociological eye on the rebuilding of the Gulf Coast.[6]

In making the argument that personally affected scholars have something unique to contribute, we don't mean to imply that our work is somehow better than what other scholars have produced. Many of these other works have brought the topics of disaster, race, class, and gender to a larger audience and have provided essential foundations for our own research. In fact, some of us were displaced, meaning that researchers who have come in since Katrina may even have had more time on the ground during the recovery than some of us; but for us, when Katrina hit, this was home and the loss was personal. That can be both a help and a hindrance in the production of knowledge as later chapters discuss, but certainly, in combination with work from outside researchers, the picture of life post–Katrina is more complete as we each stitch our various squares onto the quilt of post–Katrina knowledge and experience. Similarly, we need nonacademics to add their square to the quilt, particularly the poor, women, and racial and ethnic minorities. By taking seriously the lens through which these nonacademics view post–Katrina life, the overall body of knowledge (typically dominated by scholars, men, those in the middle and upper classes, heterosexuals, and non-Hispanic whites) is greatly enriched. Therefore, while this book should not be taken as the only authority on Katrina, it does add an important missing piece: the perspective of scholars writing from inside the Katrina experience—storm victims who also have the ability to place their personal troubles into a larger social context.

There will unfortunately be future disasters that parallel Katrina and they are likely to be more frequent and more intense as climate changes amplify storms, wildfires, and floods. Additionally, man-made disasters such as those associated with nuclear energy and oil spills present further threats. We use this case then to explore larger questions regarding some of the unique challenges that women face during disasters, to explore the way sexuality plays into recovery, to examine the impact of negative racial stereotyping on the level of assistance that displaced persons receive, and to consider how ethnic minorities are racialized in a post-disaster context. In other words, we use the case of Katrina to provide analyses of how various segments of the population are affected by disaster. Doing so could help lessen negative social impacts following future disasters while giving meaning to this experience so that it is not "a total loss."

TO COME IN THIS VOLUME

The chapters in this book are a mixture of scholarly reflections, empirical analyses of qualitative interviews and fieldwork, and syntheses of the existing literature. The aim of this volume then is to better understand the social impact of disasters on various groups in the U.S. population through a close examination of the Katrina case, and also to better understand the role of academics in studying and teaching about impacted groups. The first section of this book, "Sexuality and Gender in Disaster Recovery," is front and center precisely because gender and sexuality issues have received substantially less attention than race and class dynamics post–Katrina. Some reports have noted that sexually transmitted infections increased dramatically following the storm, but few analyses take the personal look at sexuality in recovery that Mimi Schippers takes in the opening chapter in this section. In a very personalized essay, Mimi Schippers explains that New Orleans has a long history of a public sexual culture, and as she argues in her piece, many people placed sexuality at the center of their trauma and recovery. The way they did so, she suggests, is inextricable from the history of sexuality in New Orleans. To illustrate the eroticized processes of trauma and recovery, she recounts specific phenomena that she witnessed and/or experienced, from the bar culture in New Orleans to the nonmonogamy—the phenomenon of "hurricane lovers." The following chapter blends gender and sexuality issues as three young female scholars discuss street harassment in post–Katrina New Orleans. In this essay, Andrea Wilbon Hartman, Erica Dudas, and Jennifer Day-Sully compare post–Katrina New Orleans to "the Wild West," in that women and children were kept out due to dangerous conditions and those few who were around were assumed to be for the entertainment of the men. From unease to perceived threat, the authors demonstrate the difficulties for women navigating everyday life in a post-disaster context. Next, Pam Jenkins expounds on the theme of violence against women, but evaluates it more from an organizational viewpoint as she assesses how agencies who assist domestic violence victims coped with the disorganization of life in a disaster zone. In many ways, advocates for victims of domestic violence are experts in displacement and trauma recovery, thus the organizational shifts that took place while these nonprofits were also in recovery-mode provide important general lessons for disaster management. The final chapter in this section provides a succinct review of the existing knowledge on women's experience post–Katrina. Barber and Dietz point to the dearth of literature on gender and disaster more generally and unpack the ways that research insights on Hurricane Katrina have both contributed to the body of literature on disaster and underestimated the impact of gender on individual experiences of disaster. Importantly, they also point to unique the contributions of women in successful disaster preparedness plans and in the subsequent recovery.

The second section of the volume highlights the importance of race and class in the recovery process as I begin with a primarily theoretical chapter that takes readers along with me through each of the six cities in my displacement period. Using a personal narrative and focusing on small group interactions, I point to racial and class privilege in disaster recovery. I show how it is manifested in sympathy exchanges between strangers and the gifting of key recovery resources such as housing. I conclude with a plea to rethink how we "do race" in daily interactions so as to begin to shift the racial discourse and balance the scales. The chapter that follows, by Elizabeth Fussell and Amy Bellone-Hite, provides a much needed focus on Hispanics following Katrina, as that population expanded in each of seven parishes from 2000 to 2012 (Mack and Ortiz 2013). They offer a literature review that traces the rapid demographic changes in the time period and the construction boom that brought many new brown faces to a largely black/white area. They provide a complex portrait of Latinos' labor market and living conditions and speculate on whether the influx of Latinos will result in a more permanent shift in the demographics of the city or whether the change was a temporary part of the reconstructing phase of the city. In their conclusion, they relate the Katrina case to a larger discussion of the impact of immigrants on racial dynamics in local labor markets. Shifting the focus from Latino(a) workers to African Americans, Farrah Gafford Cambrice points us toward the future of New Orleans, its young adults, and their outlooks on the local labor market. Based on thirty-one in-depth interviews with African Americans growing up in the wake of Katrina, Cambrice details the struggles that they, now eighteen to twenty-five year olds, are encountering as they plan for their future in a still damaged city. The narratives featured in this chapter demonstrate bifurcated experiences, in which some are on a clear path toward success while others struggle to find their place in the rebuilt city as they transition into adulthood. Opening with a very moving and descriptive personal Katrina story, Jean Ait Belkhir brings this race and class section to a close with his critical assessment of neoliberal reforms in education, healthcare, and public housing post–Katrina. He details troubling economic and social trends that continue to plague the city and suggests that the rebuilt New Orleans—now a whiter, wealthier, older city—is not necessarily better for the so-called reforms that have taken place.

One theme that is woven into the earlier sections is that of the difficulties a disaster context poses for academics attempting to practice their craft—meaning research, teaching, service, career advancement, and the like. The chapters in the final section, "Doing Academia through Disaster" focus on the lived experience of the academics working through disaster. This section considers methodological issues that arise in conducting research, difficulties in service learning, and the daunting career prospects for those displaced by the storms and university restructuring, all while navigating personal dislocation and emotional trauma. Starting off the discussion, Jessica Pardee—who interviewed many women displaced from New Orleans public housing projects—describes being forced to simultaneously deal with the trauma of her research subjects, and her own personal trauma. She argues that this is overlooked in methods textbooks, discussing how to work through trauma as a researcher who is also a survivor and the way she vacillated between "objective researcher" and "fellow hurricane survivor" at different points in the research process. Each role served different functions from self-protection to enhanced access to participants. Pardee discusses these roles and her struggle with them with unusual candor. In the next chapter, I too discuss research difficulties, but less from an emotional side than a practical one as a tight housing market shifted the nature of housing interactions, rendering discrimination audits largely ineffective. This indicates a need to rethink how we, as researchers, conduct housing discrimination research following a disaster. I also point to some gaping legal loopholes that have the potential to allow housing discrimination to run rampant in a post-disaster context indicating a dire need for federal policy changes. This is a chapter for anyone interested in housing market research and civil rights—from fair housing advocates to scholars. Next, turning from research concerns to career concerns, Danielle Hidalgo and Dana M. Greene look at the impact of Katrina on academic employment prospects in an already difficult job market. Hidalgo relates personal tales of academic life for underemployed adjunct professors on the post–Katrina, postfinancial crisis job market. Situating their experiences in a global and economic context, they explain how global social, political, and economic patterns have flooded the market with highly qualified workers vying for a limited number of jobs. This competition is exacerbated in a post-disaster context characterized by displacement and major institutional changes at affected universities. Lastly, Timothy J. Haney offers a compelling teaching piece that weaves his personal experience bringing Canadian students to New Orleans via a service-learning course. He uses journals to capture their thoughts and reactions to the slow pace of recovery in some of the neighborhoods. Through the eyes of students, readers are taken on a virtual tour of the Ninth Ward where the students feel the tension between volunteerism and disaster tourism as they help build houses. We also are given a taste of life in St. Tammany Parish and Plaquemines Parish, where the BP oil spill had a particularly heavy impact. Through his own reflections, Haney helps us understand what it's like to come back, to rebuild, and to teach about a place he once called home.

To close the volume, Dana M. Greene takes a step back and offers a few thoughts on the recovery and rebuilding of New Orleans as part of larger global, neoliberal development trends. In addition to the global contextualization, she provides fascinating background on the city's past and speculates on its future. Greene warns that, while New Orleans may feel a world away to some, disasters can and will strike in other places; therefore it serves us well to closely examine Katrina's lessons.

A NOTE ABOUT TERMINOLOGY

In an effort to make sociological conversations more public, we have tried to limit disciplinary jargon and offer explanations of less familiar terms in endnotes. With regard to terminology on racial categories, I have opted to treat *black* and *white* as uncapitalized adjectives because, for me, capitalization overemphasizes differences by skin color that, while socially important, are biologically irrelevant. While I respect differences of opinion on this, this stylistic choice stems from my desire not to reify skin color as a legitimate axis of difference. Because they are not adjectives and rather refer to culture and heritage, ethnic and pan-ethnic names such as African American and Hispanic remain capitalized throughout.[7]

NOTES

1. The recovery-focused investments in the area insulated New Orleans from the full effects of the recession. New Orleans employment levels dropped less during the Great Recession with only a –1 percent change in the percentage of jobs from 2008 to 2010 as compared to –5 percent nationally. The city also returned to prerecession levels faster than in the rest of the nation achieving parity with 2008 job levels in 2011 while the rest of the nation has yet to reach that mark. Additionally, New Orleans entrepreneurship rate is 56 percent higher than in the nation as a whole and the number of arts and culture focused nonprofits jumped from 81 to 122 despite the population decrease from 461,915 people in 2004 to 360,341 people in 2011 (Plyer et al. 2013).

2. In 1999, African Americans made 53 percent of what whites in New Orleans metro area earned on average and in 2011, they earned only 50 percent. This widening gap mirrored national data wherein percentages fell from 64 percent to 60 percent in the same time period. Latino households in contrast earned 77.3 percent of the average of the household income of non-Hispanic whites in 1999 and 77.7 percent in 2011 (nationally the percentages were 74.2 in 1999 and 71.6 in 2011). Importantly, median household income for all groups has declined in the past decade, but the racial and ethnic gaps have also widened both in New Orleans and in the United States generally (Plyer et al. 2013).

3. I lived in all three states post–Katrina and witnessed mass devastation throughout so I am particularly sensitive to the intense focus on New Orleans as if it were the only area affected. I discuss some of my experiences in other areas in chapters 6 and 11, but admit that the volume has a bias toward the New Orleans experience since the contributing scholars were affiliated with New Orleans institutions and much of this volume is about their observations.

4. *Verstehen* is a term used by classic sociologist Max Weber to mean a level of deep and true understanding that can and should be reached in social research.

5. A standpoint is a perspective through which one views the world. It influences what one focuses on as well as what we miss in our work. One's view of the world is influenced by one's social location—a combination of statuses such as race, class, gender, age, disability, etc. For example, feminist scholars have long claimed that women have a unique perspective to offer, that knowledge produced solely by men is partial because women may focus on different phenomena than male scholars and our blind spots also are different. Importantly, contemporary developments in standpoint theory acknowledge that social locations are multiple meaning that a Hispanic woman might view the social world from a somewhat different perspective than a black or white woman. As researchers our standpoint influences what we study, how we study it, and how we think and write about it.

6. Local knowledge refers to "knowledge situated in time, place, experience and relative power, as opposed to knowledge from nowhere that's supposedly value-free" (Griffin 2009, 446). It encompasses our recognition that it is impossible to have completely unbiased research because knowledge is constructed by researchers who have particular informational filters based on their past experiences and position in the social hierarchy.

7. There was one exception in a chapter wherein an author explicitly stated a preference to capitalize black and white. In this case, I deferred to the author's stylistic choice rather than impose my own.

I

Gender and Sexuality in the Recovery Process

Chapter Two

Trauma, Recovery, and Sexuality in Post-Katrina New Orleans

Mimi Schippers

It was my first night in New Orleans after living in Austin, Texas, for three months. Most of my neighborhood had flooded. The water came within inches of my floors, but didn't make it in. Everyone around me wasn't so lucky. Many of the houses on my block had already been gutted by the time I made it back, so there was debris strewn everywhere and my neighbors' belongings were piled high along the curb. Water-soaked and molding Teddy bears, nightgowns, mattresses, trophies, tables, and chairs were piled so high I couldn't see the street from the sidewalk. Patches of ground that used to be grass were now covered with a film of dark, brownish grey mud. The smell was overwhelming. Decay and loss hung like humidity in the Oak Trees that seemed to make it through relatively unscathed. At night, the street was dark because there were no overhead streetlights or stoplights, and the other houses were empty. Needless to say, I was deeply traumatized. It was not, however, simply a psychological trauma. This was a collective trauma, and as Ann Cvetkovich suggests, "trauma as a collective experience . . . generates collective responses" (Cvetkovich 2003, 19).

I had heard through the grapevine that Pal's, a corner pub three blocks from me, was open. There wasn't an operating gas station, grocery store, or stop light in the surrounding two to three square miles, but Pal's was open for business and offering a place for people to gather. In many ways, the flow of alcohol is the lifeblood of New Orleans, so I wasn't surprised that Pal's, the heart of our neighborhood, started beating long before other commerce or infrastructure were up and running.

I wouldn't go so far as to say I was a regular at Pal's before the storm, but it had always been one of my favorite bars. The crowd was always mixed in terms of race, class, and age. The drinks were inexpensive and served up strong, and there was a good selection on the Juke Box. The 1970's Playboy centerfolds on the walls of the "men's" bathroom—which was used by everyone regardless of gender—added a campy touch, and the really cute straight girl and even cuter butch lesbian behind the bar greeted everyone when they came through the door. That second night in the ruins of what used to be my neighborhood, my hurricane lover, Sam,[1] and I decided to hit Pal's, get our drink on, and see who was back in town.

You're probably wondering what I mean by "hurricane lover." Many people I knew partnered up and quickly fell in love with someone in the months after the storm. We called them our "hurricane lovers." For a few, these relationships lasted years and, in one case that I am aware of, resulted in marriage and children. For most, however, the relationships with hurricane lovers ended within a year. In my case, my relationship with Sam started right before the storm and ended within a few short months after returning to New Orleans. Despite its short longevity, I had fallen deeply in love with Sam and held on for dear life until the love and relationship, like steam rising as the city dried, dissipated with little notice. That was the way with hurricane lovers—short, emotionally and sexually intense, and bound to a few months in post–Katrina New Orleans.

I had met Sam a few months before the storm, and though we were lovers, our relationship was new and emotionally tepid when we evacuated to Texas. Assuming I was homeless, not knowing when, if ever, I could return to New Orleans or whether or not I still had a job at Tulane, I knew I had to travel light—emotionally and physically. At the same time, the weight of what was happening was too much to carry alone. Meanwhile, my life partner, Ken, with whom I was in an open relationship, was stuck in Chicago. I grew up in Chicago, and most of my family was there, so I briefly considered heading north to wait out my exile. This, however, wasn't an option. I was not "out" about being polyamorous, so seeing, let alone staying with family with Sam and Ken in tow was quickly crossed off my list of possibilities.

Much has been written about the effects of race, economic status, and, to a lesser extent gender on the experiences of evacuation and return. As far as I know, there has been no academic research published on the effects of the disaster on queer[2] New Orleanians. The Park Scholars of New Orleans, a group of academic researchers who visit New Orleans once per year to aid in recovery and report on their experiences, provide some information about how lesbian, gay, bisexual, transgender, genderqueer (LGBTQ) New Orleanians faired. A blog post written by Adam Polaski reports that many organizations that offered aid required that people present ID's in order to receive services (Polaski 2012). This meant that transgender men were required to stay in female-only shelters and transgender women in male-only shelters. Besides the reports by the Park Scholars of New Orleans, a handful of editorial mentions in the mainstream press, and an insightful article written by Charlotte D'ooge (2006), we don't know what evacuation, displacement, and return was like for queer people as a marginalized and vulnerable population. As D'ooge argues, it is more than likely that being queer compounded difficulties, especially for LGBTQ people of color and poor LGBTQ individuals. For many LGBTQ folks, relying on relatives or the kindness of strangers is complicated by strained familial relationships or homophobic, transphobic, and heterosexist discrimination. Because of heterosexism[3] and heteronormativity,[4] LGBTQ and nonmonogamous individuals are sometimes estranged from family or perceived as "deviant" or immoral by strangers, making family and strangers less likely to open their doors. Moreover, rooming or living with homophobic or heterosexist people would no doubt exacerbate the trauma of displacement. Unfortunately, researchers have not systematically studied housing or other forms of discrimination due to heteronormativity and/or heterosexism.

As a woman in a polyqueer[5] relationship with two men, going "home" to my family in Chicago was undesirable to me and my partners and probably unacceptable to most of my immediate and extended family. Though in a polyqueer relationship, being white, economically privileged, and a women's studies professor from Tulane opened up options that perhaps less privileged LGBTQ people who couldn't go "home" to their families of origin didn't have. I ended up in Austin, Texas, where a generous white, upper middle-class couple offered their garage apartment to me rent-free.

While in Austin, I was homesick and wanted connection, intimacy, and a sense of continuity with New Orleans. I could not be with Ken in Chicago, so I clung to Sam. I held on tightly because, in the stupefying trauma of losing New Orleans, he was a lifeline to my world before the storm, and yet he did not carry any of the baggage of "family." We never discussed plans for the future beyond when to return or where we might go next. My hurricane lover and I took each other for the moment, formed a deeply intimate and emotional bond, and didn't care how long it would last or where it would end up.

Judith Halberstam (2005) suggests that heteronormativity depends on "straight time." Straight time is the normative pace for relationship formation and development. A "successful" relationship, according to straight time, depends on longevity and a particular set of phases and outcomes like dating, followed by sexual and emotional intimacy, then sharing a household, and culminating in marriage and having children until finally "growing old together" and parting only in death. As Halberstam defines it, heteronormative straight time keeps everybody in line, privileges those who follow along, and stigmatizes people who live in queer time. Hurricane lovers, from what I could see, were not on "straight time" in this sense. No questions were asked about "where will this go" or about longevity and commitment. What mattered was feeling connected to each other and to New Orleans. In retrospect and as a sociologist, this isn't surprising to me. New Orleans is known for its sexual eccentricity and for not living by money or the clock. That I and many friends around me found community and a sense of belonging in the arms of lovers while queering time and what it means to be in a relationship makes perfectly perverse sense, but is in need of further theoretical and empirical exploration.

On that second night in New Orleans, like deer in the headlights, my hurricane lover Sam and I set out toward Pal's. We sauntered down the street stepping over and around my neighbors' coveted belongings, flooded cars, and trash as we made our way to a small sliver of yellow light spilling onto the dark sidewalk. Pal's sits on a corner and has plate glass windows that open up on to both streets at the intersection. The windows were still boarded up, but there was that sliver of light from the door and, in the darkness, it was like a beacon.

The patrons were gorging on the lifeblood flowing from bottles and taps, and for the most part, they were well on their way to intoxication. We bellied up to the bar to join them in every sense of the word. It wasn't long before a tipsy woman in her early twenties came over to chat with us. Chatting it up with strangers at a bar was the norm in pre-Katrina New Orleans, but after the flood, all conversations started with the same questions. "How did you fair?" "Did you lose your house?" After exchanging questions and answers about where we evacuated, when we came back, and where was the nearest place we could fill our tires with air, she leaned in, put her arm around me, and asked, "Wanna make out?" I looked at Sam, shrugged, and said, "Sure." We kissed for a few moments before she pulled away, smiled, and walked back to her husband, boyfriend, or hurricane lover sitting at the other end of the bar.

This wasn't the last time I was approached by an ostensibly straight woman and asked to kiss or make out. Though flirting in the bars of New Orleans was often playful and sometimes queer before the storm, in post–Katrina New Orleans, the rules for gender and sexual scripts, it seemed to me, had been suspended or shifted. The combination of a "broken" city with no rules and a sense of "we only have today because all can be lost" led to a sort of suspension of normal social structure. People didn't stop at stop signs, drove the wrong way up one-way streets, speeded, and parked anywhere and everywhere they could find open ground. All of these driving behaviors could be observed in pre-Katrina in New Orleans, but when I returned, it was the norm. In post–Katrina New Orleans, there were no real rules or anyone around to enforce them. The mainstream media focused on (and exaggerated) crime, and researchers and civil rights activists have documented the widespread brutal and sometimes deadly treatment of people, especially African American men, by police and other officials in post–Katrina New Orleans. That story was and should continue to be told.

But there was something else going on around this suspension of the rules, and unlike the behavior of populations targeted by the state, it went unnoticed by officials and by researchers.

A brief suspension of social structure meant that we didn't have to follow traffic laws, but it also meant that we didn't have to obey the rules for gender and sexuality. While all of these behaviors can be occasionally witnessed on the street or in certain bars during Mardi Gras or Southern Decadence, this seemed to be happening *everywhere* and all the time. It was as if the debauchery of Mardi Gras and Southern Decadence was carried through on the other side of the storm as a way to cope with trauma and to feel, ironically, normal. In her book, *An Archive of Feelings*, Ann Cvetkovich focuses on trauma as a cultural rather than clinical experience. Situating her work in trauma studies, Cvetkovich writes:

> Defined culturally rather than clinically, trauma studies becomes an interdisciplinary field for exploring the public cultures created around traumatic events. Trauma becomes a central category for looking at the intersections of emotional and social processes along with the intersections of memory and history. . . (Cvetkovich 2003, 18)

While Cvetkovich's focus is on how gendered, sexual trauma leads to lesbian public cultures, here I am interested in how the collective experience of geographically specific trauma gave rise to a public sexual culture of promiscuity in post–Katrina New Orleans. As a collective response to trauma *within the specific context of New Orleans*, a public sexual culture of promiscuity emerged as a strategy to form intimacies and a sense of community. Promiscuity, unlike long-term and committed relationships, opens a liminal space where one can form a bond that is at once intense and ephemeral. It is a form of intimacy that is embodied and embedded within a geographically specific history, yet, at the same time, mobile and temporary. All over the city, people were flirting and fucking, and they were doing it publicly. I had sex with Sam in broad daylight on the stoop in front of my house. I witnessed others doing the same in my and other neighborhoods. I was approached by people in ways that, in other circumstances, would be outside the norms of appropriate public behavior. One evening, at a bar uptown, a woman approached me and said, "Hi, my name is Meg. My husband is very attracted to you, and so am I." Rather than simply say "thank you," and turn back to my friends, which is what I would have done before Katrina, I asked, "Where is your husband?" She pointed to an attractive man at the end of the bar. I smiled and said, "Well, go get him." New Orleans has, in many ways, a long cultural history of nonmonogamy from the practice of placage,[6] to Storyville,[7] to the sex shops and strip joints on Bourbon Street and the private sex clubs in quieter, more discreet locations. At least one swingers' convention is held in New Orleans each year, and New Orleans is a major sex tourism destination, especially for non-monogamous couples. A heterosexual couple interested in dating a woman was not unusual. However, the bold and direct way in which she approached me in a very straight, uptown bar resonated with the other experiences I was having at the time. The husband, Edward, came over to introduce himself. They invited me out to dinner. I accepted, and over a couple of weeks, they wined and dined me and brought me to parties to meet their friends. Once in awhile, I would sleep at their place—a rented apartment for they had lost their house in the flood—or they would sleep at mine.

One night, they were staying at my house, and I woke to the sound of crying coming from my living room. Meg was still asleep next to me, but Edward was no longer in the bed. I got up and went to him. I sat next to him on my sofa while he cried, "We lost everything." He said, "I really haven't been able to cry because I feel like I have to be strong for Meg." Soon, Meg joined us on the sofa. As she, too, started to cry, they both slid to the floor and put their heads in my lap and sobbed. They talked about their home and how important it was to them and their relationship. As I write now, I wonder about my presence in their relationship at that time, and how a third person whom they trusted but who wasn't experiencing their loss opened space for them to grieve together. Did other people experience or turn to different forms of nonmonogamy to accommodate displacement, separation, trauma, and recovery? In a mononormative[8] world, most researchers don't think to ask questions about, let alone explore nonmonogamy as a possibility or strategy when separated from or, in this case, too close to lovers and partners.

All we know about sexuality in post–Katrina New Orleans is that there was an alarming and disturbing spike in the rate of sexually transmitted infections (STIs) (Greeley 2006). Researchers attribute the rise in STIs to inadequate sex education before the storm and lack of access to healthcare services in New Orleans after the storm (Clark 2006). Certainly this is a problematic outcome of the emergent sexual cultures after the storm, but this sole focus on the negative outcomes of sexual behavior in post–Katrina New Orleans renders invisible the positive role the erotic, sexual cultures, and promiscuity played in trauma recovery. This reflects and perpetuates what Gayle Rubin calls "sex negativity":

> This culture always treats sex with suspicion. It construes and judges almost any sexual practice in terms of its worst possible expression. Sex is presumed guilty until proven innocent. Virtually all erotic behavior is considered bad unless a specific reason to exempt it has been established. The most acceptable excuses are marriage, reproduction, and love. Sometimes scientific curiosity, aesthetic experience, or a long-term intimate relationship may serve. But the exercise of erotic capacity, intelligence, curiosity, or creativity all require pre-

> texts that are unnecessary for other pleasures, such as the enjoyment of food, fiction, or astronomy. (Rubin 1984, 278)

In post–Katrina New Orleans, there was so much more to sexuality and the erotic than the problematic spread of STIs. There was an opening up and celebration of the erotic that allowed some of us to form bonds with each other and heal collectively through erotic connection. For me, the erotic was a resource with which to feel a connection to public life in New Orleans before Katrina and connect with others who had returned after. I needed a sense of embodied belonging, not just to other people, but also to New Orleans. Here, I mean the erotic in the way Audre Lorde defines it:

> . . . the erotic offers a well of replenishing and provocative force to the woman who does not fear its revelation, nor succumb to the belief that sensation is enough. . . . The erotic is a measure between the beginnings of our sense of self and the chaos of our strongest feelings. It is an internal sense of satisfaction to which, once we have experienced it, we know we can aspire. For having experienced the fullness of this depth of feeling and recognizing its power, in honor and self-respect we can require no less of ourselves. (Lorde 1984, 54)

The erotic, in Lorde's sense, empowered me to stay and persevere. Audre Lorde also suggests that, once you know the erotic, you are empowered to refuse that which is not true to self and one's connection with others and refuse to participate in oppressive social relations. She writes:

> When we live outside ourselves, and by that I mean on external directives only rather than from our internal knowledge and needs, when we live away from those erotic guides from within ourselves, then our lives are limited by external and alien forms, and we conform to the needs of a structure that is not based on human need, let alone an individual's. But when we begin to live from within outward, in touch with the power of the erotic within ourselves, and allowing that power to inform and illuminate our actions upon the world around us, then we begin to be responsible to ourselves in the deepest sense. For as we begin to recognize our deepest feelings, we begin to give up, of necessity, being satisfied with suffering and self-negation, and with the numbness which so often seems like their only alternative in our society. Our acts against oppression become integral with self, motivated and empowered from within. (Lorde 1984, 58)

One sunny afternoon I was walking my dog in my neighborhood. I could hear hammers, saws, and other sounds of construction all around me. As I passed one house, there were five or six men working to repair the roof. When I approached, they stopped and gawked. I heard quiet banter, a chuckle, a laugh, and finally a whistle that sealed the definition of the situation as street sexual harassment.

The city had, for all intents and purposes, turned into a construction zone, and as all women know, a construction zone can be a hostile place for a woman pedestrian. Many women I know experienced severe and constant sexual harassment from the workers in New Orleans during that time (see Wilbon et al. in this volume). As is always the case when sexually harassed by a group of construction workers, I felt intense anger. This anger was, however, a result of more than just a feminist sense of personhood and its violation. This was *my* city. My home. It took a great deal of effort to get back, and no one, especially outsiders, were going to make me feel like I didn't belong or that my only purpose was to give them a sense of hetero-masculine privilege and power. I had been experiencing the erotic everywhere else, and this was jarringly dissonant and unacceptable. In an instant, my perspective shifted. *I'm not here for them, for their entertainment. They're here for me and for New Orleans.* Instead of lowering my head and hurrying my step or giving them the finger, I raised my hand to wave. I shouted, "Thanks so much for your help rebuilding my neighborhood!" The men's demeanor immediately changed. They smiled and waved, and as they went back to work, one man said, "No problem. Glad to do it."

In this instance, the social organization of gendered sexuality in the context of a construction site was momentarily suspended and transformed. My sense of the erotic was about connecting with people, and when the men began sexually harassing me, I felt a dehumanizing disconnect. In an effort to regain the erotic and that vital connection to others, I focused on my very real appreciation for the thousands of people who made their way to New Orleans to help us rebuild. Tapping into my now cultivated sense of the erotic, I unconsciously gender maneuvered to change the definition of the situation from one of street sexual harassment to one of helpfulness.[9] When I did so, what else could the workers do? Instead of being a sexual object, I was a New Orleanian in need of assistance. The workers dropped their aggressive, objectifying masculinity and picked up civility.

As a sociologist and New Orleanian, I see this experience, like hurricane lovers and public debauchery, as New Orleans culture and history carried through and surviving after the flood. New Orleans community happens in the street. Between our second line parades, Mardi Gras celebrations, and open container laws, the street is not just a passageway; it's a place to be. It's home. We sit on our porches and greet our neighbors *and* passing strangers. I have to imagine that construction workers were greeted often and perhaps thanked now and then. Certainly I, and perhaps those men on the roof, was familiar with this form of interaction on a New Orleans street. How did the construction workers experience their own sense of masculinity and sexuality in this strange situation? What was it like for other women, including the erotic laborers such as strippers and prostitutes often neglected as migrant workers, who had to live in an entire city that was under construction? We don't know because sociologists have not asked these questions.

Late spring, 2006, I was driving to campus and came to an intersection I had passed through many times since my return. The "temporary" stop sign that had been there for eight months had been removed and the stoplight flashed red. It wouldn't be long before the lights at the intersection would be fully operational. I remember first feeling surprised and then a small bit of relief. Grand reopenings at local grocery stores and gas stations meant that the city was recovering and everyday conveniences would return. It was a sign that things were getting back to "normal." The feeling of relief, however, was quickly swallowed up by a sense of sorrow and loss. After living in the chaos for months, I had grown accustomed to the disorganization. A part of me didn't want everything to go back to how it had been. The blinking stoplights, though safer, signaled, "stop," follow the rules, and ease back into normalcy. A more convenient life, it seemed to me, also meant a more conventional life.

Though relatively insignificant, that blinking stoplight signifies, in my memory, a transition from the sexual cultures of post–Katrina New Orleans to present-day New Orleans. Rather than live in the queer time of the present moment, I began looking forward to my and the city's future. I frequented the bars less, focused on my relationship with Ken, saw less of Sam, and eventually lost touch with him. Meg and Edward, like many who couldn't see a future in New Orleans, moved to another state. The social organization of sexuality is part and parcel to the social structure generally, and though we don't have research on this, my hypothesis is that the law-and-order crackdown on public culture that was deployed to get the city "back to normal" likely doused the erotic as much as any other part of street culture in New Orleans. As the infrastructure recovered, I saw the sexual organization of New Orleans gradually gel into something that resembled its debaucherous pre-Katrina self, but, at the same time, felt somewhat more conventional. One can still visit the strip clubs on Bourbon Street or attend a swingers' convention, but in some ways, there is hesitancy or, dare I say, prudishness about public sexual cultures in New Orleans now. The neoliberal project of "cleaning up" the city and its reputation to bring the tourist dollar back included an intolerance for public nudity and drunkenness. This has been especially oppressive to transgender individuals of color who are constantly harassed or arrested by police. Making the city "comfortable" and "safe" for outsiders meant "straightening out" New Orleanians.

In post–Katrina New Orleans, there was something more than the stench of decay and loss hanging in the air. In that dark and trying time, I could feel the erotic hanging like ghosts in the trees, caught by the history, culture, and humidity of New Orleans. In those first months after the storm I, along with many others, shook the trees to loosen the erotic and let it settle like a mist on our everyday interactions. Yes, there was street sexual harassment, other forms of sexual violence, and a rise in STIs. But there was something else, and no researcher, to my knowledge, has written about it. There is an important story here about the social organization of sexuality in New Orleans specifically, but that can inform understanding of the role of the erotic in disaster, trauma, and recovery more generally. What are the effects of collective trauma on the sexual practices and cultures of a population or geographic locations? What, if any, function does the erotic and sexual play in the collective experience of and recovery from trauma? While queer theorists grapple with trauma and focus on the psychological, these are empirical and sociological questions.

You might be asking yourself why I, a sociologist who studies gender and sexuality, have not done the research. When I returned to New Orleans in October 2005, I saw interesting, exciting, and sometimes horrifying things happening around sexuality. I remember thinking, "Someone should be studying this." This thought was invariably followed by a strong sense of guilt. I felt that I was falling down on the job as an ethnographic researcher and social theorist of sexuality. "Get your shit together," I would tell myself. "This story needs to be told. Get to work!" However, every time I thought about systematically observing the social world around me as a researcher, I would lose that sense of the erotic. It didn't feel right. When my researcher self came to the fore, I felt alienated from what I was witnessing and feeling. I could not, nor did I want to separate myself from the trauma of the disaster or the ugly and beautiful ways in which we were dealing with the ruins of our city and climbing out. At the same time, as all sociologists and especially ethnographers know, despite my need to not be the researcher, I couldn't suspend my sociological lens. Even though I couldn't bring up "researcher" as the most salient self during that time, I am always a sociologist.

While writing *Black Feminist Thought*, Patricia Hill Collins (1990) suggests that black women sociologists have a unique and special vantage point from which to understand the world. Black women academics have embodied experiences as black and as women in a racist and sexist world that gives them unique insight into social injustice and inequalities. With one foot in their communities and another in academia, black, feminist sociologists bring new knowledge to sociology and are, at the same time, capable of translating that knowledge to people in their communities. While I would never draw a comparison between my experiences of the emergent sexual cultures in post–Katrina New Orleans with those of black, woman academics, I find Hill Collins's perspective on specialized and subjugated knowledge useful. I am both a New Orleanian and a sociologist. I experienced the trauma of post–Katrina New Orleans, but did so as a sociologist of gender and sexuality. Though I suspended my work as an academic during that time—in every sense of the word, for I didn't teach, read, or write academic or scholarly work for six months—I never shed my specialized knowledge about gender, sexuality, and social organization. It manifested, not in academic ethnographic research, but instead as a journal of very personal, sometimes painful and sometimes joyful experiences. In Cvetkovich's terms, my journal was an archive of feelings rather than objective and systematic observations. "Trauma puts pressure on conventional forms of documentation, representation, and commemoration, giving rise to new genres of expression, such as testimony . . ." (Cvetkovich 2003, 7). Perhaps that is why this chapter takes the form that it does. I offer my own testimony to the erotic and sexual cultures in post–Katrina New Orleans as at once narrative and sociological analysis, and as an invitation to others, especially social scientists, to pick up the story where I have left off.

NOTES

1. All names have been changed to pseudonyms.
2. By "queer," I mean individuals whose sexual identities and practices and/or relationships fall outside the norm of heterosexual monogamy.
3. Heterosexism is the network of social, cultural, and political forces that systematically confer privilege to people who are or perceived to be heterosexual.
4. Heteronormativity refers to the cultural value placed on the monogamous heterosexual couple as the ideal, legitimate, and most desirable family structure.
5. Polyqueer refers to intimate and/or sexual relationships that include more than two people and are thus, outside the norm of heterosexual monogamy (see Schippers, forthcoming).
6. Placage refers to the common practice in nineteenth-century New Orleans where wealthy, white men would have intimate, committed, long-term relationships with and set up households for a free woman of color while maintaining a household elsewhere with a white wife (see Gould 1998; Martin 2000).
7. Storyville was the name given to a district in New Orleans where prostitution was legal from 1897 to 1917 (see Long 2004).
8. Mononormativity refers to the set of social arrangements and customs that reflect and perpetuate the idea that the only legitimate way to form intimate and sexual relationships is in monogamous couples.
9. Gender maneuvering refers to the interactional process by which an individual or group refuses to follow the rules or norms for gendered interaction, and by doing so, disrupt a hierarchical and complementary relationship between masculinity and femininity. In this case, I did not "play the part" of the sexual object and instead asserted my subjectivity as a citizen of New Orleans (see Schippers 2002).

Chapter Three

It's Raining Men

Gender and Street Harassment in Post-Katrina New Orleans

Andrea Wilbon Hartman, Erica Dudas, and Jennifer Day-Sully

In early January 2005, a fellow colleague and I were walking down Decatur Street in New Orleans's French Quarter. Our plan was to meet up with two friends downtown at a local bar. While crossing the busy street, two men approached in their automobile. The passenger in the truck rolled down his window while stopped at a streetlight and proclaimed "Hey! I want to lick your ass." Once we arrived, we saw our friends and gathered at the back end of the bar. As I was sitting on the stool near the edge of the group, I noticed an older white man probably in his mid-forties to late fifties staring as he leaned up against the wall next to me. At one point he leaned in and informed me, "You know, you have a great ass." I puckered my face and scoffed, speechless at his totally inappropriate comment. At this point another young woman came to my rescue, telling him that his comment was rude. We turned back to our conversation and tried to ignore him. About an hour later I rose from the stool to prepare to leave. As I stood up, the same man stepped forward, grabbed my buttocks commenting, "It looks even better when you stand up."[1]

The above story demonstrates the reality of sexual harassment immediately following Hurricane Katrina. This disaster, which struck and flooded the New Orleans area in late August of 2005 and remains one of the five deadliest hurricanes in the United States, had a tremendous impact on everyday life within the city. The demographic changes to the gender order in the fall months following the storm leads us to question how disaster affects the prevalence and occurrence of sexual harassment in public spaces.

The demographic changes resulting from the storm caused gender to become a salient identity for many in post–Katrina New Orleans. According to the U.S. Census and the *Times-Picayune*, New Orleans's total population dropped from 484,668 people in 2000 to 343,829 people by 2010 (a 29 percent drop). When the city "reopened" in October of 2005, men came back first. According to the U.S. Bureau of the Census, pre-Katrina New Orleans was comprised of a fairly even distribution of men and women, with 53 percent of the population being female and 47 percent male. When Hurricane Katrina struck New Orleans, the city ordered a mandatory evacuation—essentially flushing out the majority of residents. A Tulane University Newcomb College 2010 study reported that, from 2005–2008, whereas the total New Orleans population dropped 28.7 percent, the female population alone dropped 29.3 percent, the equivalent of approximately 68,000 fewer women (Newcomb College Center for Research on Women 2010). While most New Orleans residents were still in their Katrina-imposed exile, a few women dared to return to the city early. For the first few months of recovery, New Orleans was a whole new world.

UPON OUR RETURN

Returning to New Orleans in October 2005, two months after the storm, was simply unbelievable. We had never seen anything like it. A city that had once been filled with music, tourists, and never-ending parties for visitors and locals alike had been stopped in its tracks. Everywhere you looked, there were signs of destruction. The molding contents of gutted homes and lives were spilled onto the streets in massive piles of trash. What became signature blue tarps dotted countless damaged roofs. Stray dogs ran in packs. Entire neighborhoods sat dead and dark without power. The quiet of evening was eerie—it didn't feel like New Orleans. It was a warzone and the presence of military police that patrolled the French Quarter on foot with their automatic weapons or those cruising the streets in Humvees only amplified that feeling.

We were among the first of the Tulane sociology graduate students to return. Campus was closed for the fall 2005 semester but none of us could stay away any longer. We had to see it for ourselves. Erica and Jennifer, who had evacuated together, repacked Erica's little blue truck with their meager belongings and headed back south in October 2005. Andrea visited for an extended period in November and moved back to New Orleans the following January.

Upon our return, we immediately noticed the widespread destruction. The sheer amount of gutting, cleaning, and rebuilding that still needed to be done seemed insurmountable. But from across the country and even the globe came an army to keep peace and provide the muscle needed to get the job done—"man power" in every sense of the phrase. Amidst the post-apocalyptic scene, the rubble, the trash, and the unmistakable odor of decay was the undeniable energy of rebuilding. The city drew cleanup crews and demolition teams who filled the air with the nonstop hum of saws, the constant pop, pop, pop of nail guns hard at work—in those first few months of recovery, from morning till dusk, the city was buzzing with a distinct masculine energy. We felt this masculine energy the moment we returned home, as Jennifer recalls below:

> Journal Entry November 3, 2005: *Erica and I returned to New Orleans today. It's the same, but different. There are tons of construction men in the city. They creep me out. Two have moved into Trevin's old place across the hall from me. I just wish things could be like they used to be. But that New Orleans is a thing of the past. I'm on edge a little.*
>
> Journal Entry November 15, 2005: *Many people told me it was too early to go back—now I think maybe they were right. But I need to be here—this is my home. I won't be a prisoner in my own home—in my city . . . but I will watch my ass.*

GENDER AND FRONTIER CULTURES

This new world we encountered was mainly comprised of males working in the construction, rebuilding, and protecting (i.e., military) industries and they were disproportionately represented in comparison to those who initially returned to a post-disaster city. In order to understand the gendered implications of this kind of demographic shift, we searched for an empirical case similar to this new, masculine environment we (as women) faced as returnees. We found that literature on the American West frontier provided a useful framework for what we were experiencing: gender relations in environments where men comprise the majority of the population and its impact on our perceptions of safety on the street.

Frontier scholar, Murry Melbin, defines a frontier as "a new source of supply for resources that people want for subsistence or for more profit" (1987, 4). In this light, New Orleans was a frontier society. The subsequent levee failures and resulting devastation of Hurricane Katrina created a high demand in New Orleans for construction and manual labor and led to a sizable increase in employment opportunities for men in this sex-segregated industry. New Orleans was filled disproportionately with these new crews of male workers as they were the first inhabitants.

Research pertaining to the Old West highlights men as the primary demographic of frontier environments. Melbin explains, "[t]he demographic composition of the Western frontier was at first mostly young men. Many of them were unmarried. The West had a surplus of bachelors" (1987, 33). Further in her book, Julie Roy Jeffrey (1998) describes the White Pines silver mine in Nevada, 1867, as populated by "young men, for few women or family groups came during early boom times" (136). As a result of the gendered division of labor and the systematic exclusion of women from manual labor jobs, New Orleans saw a massive influx of a homogenous population, mainly comprised of men—many of them single—in which the female population is sparse.

Both cases—post-Katrina New Orleans and the Old West—exhibit economic opportunity for male-dominated occupations based on physical labor. In both cases, the environments are seen as unstable and dangerous, further exacerbating the lack of female and family presence. Jeffrey notes that men typically did not bring families west due to the characteristics of the mining frontier, which were deemed inappropriate for family life (1998, 145). In its first months post–Katrina, New Orleans was deemed unfit for vulnerable populations with re-entry permission underscored by an "enter at your own risk" policy. In addition to the myriad of possible health concerns due to contaminants, basic services were lacking such as grocery stores, hospitals, mental health facilities, and schools. Further, young women specifically, were noticeably absent with all colleges and universities closed for the remainder of the semester and Charity Hospital, a major local employer of women, shut down.

Thus, the frontier, and the process by which it was established, is a hyper-gendered space where men enter the environment first; women and families follow later. While most women who endured the move west arrived on the frontier a substantial time after men, some women arrived in frontier societies during the early stages of development. Some of the first women to appear, such as prostitutes, defied middle-class expectations and arrived for the same economic opportunity which motivated men. Jeffrey notes how "[p]rostitutes lost little time once they heard news of a strike. They did the best in those early days when competition was scarce and they could charge higher prices" (1998, 48).

New Orleans's immediate post–Katrina environment presents a new twist on the concept of frontier, where this disaster recovery environment created a new gendered paradigm in its streets. New Orleans has been a recognized settlement for hundreds of years and although it has always been a more sexually permissive culture, we weren't prostitutes or sex workers entering this new frontier. We were students trying to rebuild our lives in the wake of a major demographic shift immediately post-disaster, where the sexual energy became focused on a smaller, more concentrated population of women.

Frontier sites of the Old West shot up overnight, but New Orleans has been a long-established community and it created a situation where those returning home *early* were met with an evolving space where their gender identity became especially salient and brought on a new breed of necessary adjustments in this time of emotional trauma and shock. For example, the "new normal" for women living in the New Orleans frontier was one of avoiding certain streets that had once been traversed on an almost daily basis with relative ease:

> Journal Entry October 27, 2005: *I have to avoid walking down St. Charles Ave. now. This is wild since it's a major street. The men, they keep honking at me and whistling at me. Why do they keep waving at me? I have to remind myself to be careful!*

On the streets of the Old West frontier men stared, and women were avidly sought out for social occasions (Jeffrey 1998). Women realized their status as female held social implications and obligations. In New Orleans, much was the same. Jennifer recalls reuniting with a friend at a bar one night. When he saw her, he hugged her tightly exclaiming, "A woman! It's so good to see a woman!" It is also reported that women purposively secluded themselves at home to avoid street harassment and the potential for assault.

While men recognized women as valuable figures in traditional social settings, the culture of the Old West differed from that of "civilized society." Jeffrey notes that sexual mores were less rigid in this new environment, and that social standards and conventions broke down under rough and unstable conditions (1998, 137). Melbin (1987) argues that the absence of authority and other factors responsible for enforcing social control were lacking in these early developing societies, resulting in increased individualism. In other words, normal standards of conduct were loosened in transitioning communities where prostitution, gambling, drinking, and lawlessness were common.

Uncovering more about the experiences of *all* types of women is necessary in order to understand the relationship between demographic composition and gender relations. In the Old West, the lack of social order translated into violence and the threat of violence; however, minority women were the most likely to feel the effects of frontier communities. "While white women might well be caught up in the violence, it was Indian and Hispanic women who suffered most from the lack of order" (Jeffrey 1998, 139). This means that white women's racial status may have spared them the full effects of living in a frontier society.

Finally, in most modern societies, sexual harassment is very common. Obviously, sexual harassment in New Orleans existed well before Hurricane Katrina. However, upon return it noticeably increased to the point where it started to impact our daily routines and the routines of other female acquaintances. This was a complex environment deserving of a sociological interpretation.

STREET HARASSMENT AS SEXUAL HARASSMENT

In this chapter, we conceptualize street harassment as a social problem that takes the form of uninitiated verbal behavior (e.g., catcalls, verbal comments, whistling) and/or nonverbal behavior (e.g., intrusive glares, standing too close, stalking, indecent body exposure, blowing kisses, etc.) from an unknown person or group in a public space. While widely experienced by women globally, the occurrence of street harassment draws relatively little academic assessment. Eighty-five percent of women have reported experiencing some form of stranger harassment initiated by a man (or group of men) at some point in their life (Macmillan et al. 2000). Further, 90 percent of men have surprisingly admitted to having initiated some form of public harassment during the past five years (Gardner 1995).

In academic works, sexual harassment on the street level is often conflated with a brand of sexual harassment commonly found in the work environment. The term sexual harassment has become mistakenly synonymous with its popular culture definition as an inappropriate sexual act in the workplace or university, which usually expresses top-down power, and is bureaucratically punishable. In contrast, street harassment, a widely experienced social phenomenon with far reaching implications on women's perceptions of autonomy and safety, has received very little attention and therefore less opportunity for reform.

One of the earliest academic definitions of *street* harassment comes from Michaela di Leonardo, who argues that it:

> . . . occurs when one or more strange men accost one or more women whom they perceive as heterosexual in a public place which is not the woman's/women's worksite. Through looks, words, or gestures the man asserts his right to intrude on the woman's attention, defining her as a sexual object, and forcing her to interact with him. (1981, 51–52)

Additionally, Carol Brooks Gardner, a sociologist who studied public harassment on Indianapolis' streets in the late 1980s, defined public harassment as:

> . . . *that group of abuses, harrying, and annoyances characteristic of public places and uniquely facilitated by communication in public.* Public harassment includes pinching, slapping, hitting, shouted remarks, vulgarity, insults, sly innuendo, ogling, and stalking. Public harassment is on a continuum of possible events, beginning when customary civility among strangers is abrogated

> and ending with the transition to violent crime: assault, rape, or murder. (1995, 4; emphasis in original)

Although there is no universal definition of the term "street harassment," according to Holly Kearl, definitions commonly include terms such as "unwanted," "sexual," "uncomfortable," "touch," and "threat" (2010, 6).[2]

Post-disaster urban environments foster the presence of sites that are notorious for producing street harassment: construction zones. Here, a common technique of street harassment occurs when men call out to women, which evidently earns esteem and support from the other men within earshot (Gardner 1995, 106). Gardner notes that these types of interactions are something women frequently experience as abusive as it continues to signify male privilege in public spaces, reinforcing the gender hierarchy through women's physical vulnerability and the omnipresent threat of rape.

We find it surprising and unnerving that more attention has not been paid to street harassment. It has serious implications for the lives of women by limiting one's ability to enjoy public spaces and feel safe. In a post-disaster community where a gender imbalance exists and normal codes of conduct are loosened, it creates an environment whereby men coerce women into showing them deference. If women show no deference to their male harassers, the result is fearfulness (Leonardo 1981). Compounding the problem, those who return home immediately following a disaster—regardless of gender—are further impacted by post-traumatic stress, financial burdens, familial tensions, the loss of key networks, grief, increased risk of suicide, domestic abuse, and other trauma.

As of current writing, sexual harassment of women in public space is not a crime and thus not legally punishable. Although it is considered a civil rights violation in the United States and Canada, the absence of bureaucratic accountability could possibly serve to give offenders free reign over seemingly mute victims. Gardner notes, "Women . . . can currently experience shouted insults, determined trailing, and pinches and grabs by strange men and be fairly certain that no one—not the perpetrator and probably no official—will think anything of note has happened. Thus, public harassment is a sort of civic denial . . ." (1995, 4).

The overwhelming absence of legal accountability for those who publicly engage in harassment (outside of public masturbation, sexual touching, assault, and stalking) testifies to women's restricted civil rights. In this way, public sexual harassment is a "dripping tap" that occurs with such frequency that it is often unnoticed—by both women victims and male perpetrators—as an occurrence of sexual aggression and therefore not reported (Larkin 1997; Quinn 2002; Welsh 1999; Wise and Stanley 1987). Further, literature suggests that sexual harassment frames women's appearance standards and the presentation of femininity, interacts with class, and is influenced by racial meanings (Bordo 1993; Gleber 1998; Hill Collins 1990; Kissling and Kramarae 1991; Larkin 1997; MacKinnon 1989; Munson 2002).

Although we know we experienced the negative impact of increased street harassment as a result of the demographic shifts in rebuilding, we found it difficult to explain to those outside of our immediate circles. Duneier and Molotch (1999) note barriers or difficulties in studying public space interaction such as street harassment in that urban streets are full of sights and sounds that can obscure or cloud data collection. Another barrier is the fact that the individuals involved in the interactions are pedestrians and are in motion, resulting in fleeting encounters. These fleeting encounters are usually over in a matter of seconds, making them difficult to capture and analyze.

However, oftentimes, these types of "interactional vandalism" (Duneier and Molotch 1999) can be analyzed particularly when it happens right on your own doorstep. Jennifer recalls the means through which street harassment was not only perpetrated at her front door, but how these interactions can be racially charged. Once recovery commenced, New Orleans was flooded with Latino construction workers. They were pioneers in the city with regards to rebuilding.

> Journal Entry October 30, 2005: *I stepped outside one morning and heard singing in Spanish very, very close. But I couldn't figure out where it was coming from. It sounded so close! Searching my neighbor's yards, up and down the street . . . nothing. Then I looked up and realized I was being serenaded by the Hispanic roofers working on my neighbor's house. Harmless, yes, but another reminder that I am woman. I am different.*

For Jennifer, her interactions with some of the Hispanic men seemed almost flirtatious and less aggressive than other interactions. Nevertheless, paired with an underdevelopment in academic, social, and political realms, perpetrators of sexual harassment, in articulating the status quo, reproduce power dynamics that lead to the unequal distribution of resources, power, prestige and authority. A problem arises when academic underdevelopment is paired with the fact that, as public sexual harassment increases, women's fear of sexual assault and body victimization also increases (Bartky 1990; Hollander 2001; Macmillan et al. 2000; Madriz 1997). This includes ensuing problems managing feelings of vulnerability, depression, and anxiety (Macmillan et al. 2000; Stanko 1995; Welsh 1999).

In this way, the public sexual harassment of women by men establishes a symbolic relationship between actors that affirms gender stratification. It could be asserted that street harassment limits women's lives by fostering fear (Leonardo 1981; MacKinnon 1989) and therefore must be conceptualized as a form of social control affecting women's quality of life through the restriction of subjectivity in public space (Day 1994; Pain 2001; Rosewarne 2005) and access to social knowledge (Quinn 2002; Spain 1993). This is reinforced by the finding that men who sexually harass women in public do so in order to achieve specific control over material resources and authority (O'Leary-Kelly et al. 2000) while reinforcing their status as men (Benard and Schlaffer 1996). In this environment, it is difficult for a woman to walk down the street without being verbally or nonverbally accosted by strangers, thus reinforcing her sense of vulnerability and inferiority in public.

Returning to New Orleans was an eye-opening experience for the three of us. To return so soon after a natural disaster certainly had profound implications. Being women and returning to New Orleans "at our own risk" only a few months later, we saw just how few women resided in the city at that time. At times it felt like martial law and this is what makes our case so interesting. With the visible presence of police officers and the National Guard, we thought we would feel safe walking down the streets. We felt as though we would be protected in a myriad of contexts. But, in actuality, we were not. To return to the opening story of this chapter, we tell the story of Jennifer and her friends at a local bar. When the male customer commented on Jennifer's body, it took another customer, a female customer, to challenge this man and his sexist notions. It was not a situation where we could tell the cops, or tell the National Guard and expect something to be done about it. In the immediate post–Katrina environment, this was an unmet need.

WHERE DO WE GO FROM HERE?

Was it too early for us to return to New Orleans? That question should not be asked just because we are women. However, in a frontier culture, respectable women are expected to stay away and because of the heightened presence of street harassment characterizing this culture, our vulnerabilities were magnified. We rebuilt our lives in the midst of rampant sexism and street harassment and we did so with little to no respite. Our need to feel safe so that we could recover from the post-traumatic stress that we were dealing with as a part of seeing our city devastated was riddled with feelings of insecurity and inferiority simply because of our gender.

As compared to race and class analyses, few published reports on the aftermath of Hurricane Katrina have looked at gendered interactions in post-disaster societies. This chapter borrows from frontier and disaster literature to advance new and deeper conceptualizations of sexual harassment, public space, and gendered dynamics that occur immediately after a major catastrophe. Inspired by personal experiences, we examined how demographic shifts post-storm affected quality of life for women residents returning to their homes. This examination of the lived experiences of young women in post–Katrina New Orleans has implications for both disaster studies and the gender interaction literature, which frequently ignore this common and threatening form of male/female interaction.

The sexual harassment of women on the street should be taken up in further research as a relationship that is born out of demographic changes common to post-disaster cities and serves as a barrier that socially constructs women's ability to recover after a natural disaster takes place. The trend in natural disaster literature tends to rely on men's experiences as the universal experience—thereby ignoring experiences as told through the women's perspective (Enarson 1998; Fordham 1998). The available research that does look at women's roles approaches gender by adding "sex" as an analytical variable (Enarson 1998; Fothergill 1998) and tends to focus on other problems such as housing or childcare where women often serve as a mediator between the community and home spheres (Fothergill 1999; 2003). While these are certainly important roles, it may push our already marginalized personal concerns about street harassment and perceived violence to the furthest periphery. In contrast, we suggest that there exists a relationship between post-disaster social landscapes and women's vulnerability that gets expressed through concrete social and gendered interactions.

Disasters are social and political events that disproportionately affect marginal groups. The lack of resources—both social and economic—in marginal groups disturbs the individual's ability to bounce back/recover from the hurricane. Our narratives suggest that systematic street harassment impacts women's ability to recover emotionally, socially, and materially after a natural disaster.

For this reason, policy makers must also train themselves to see disaster through a gendered lens. Exposing racial, class, and gender inequalities are key for any successful post-disaster city planning. Common ways this can be addressed in realtime is through well-developed disaster recovery plans that ensure the immediate functioning of available street lights upon city re-opening, the immediate re-establishment of healthcare centers and mental health programs, and the investment in community organizations and centers that provide safe space facilities and meeting places to foster community ties. More attention in the media and academia should recognize women's lived experiences as they return to disaster-ruined cities. Perhaps construction sites and other public spaces seemingly prone to street harassment could institute worker training and display the contact information of the site's on-duty foreman or manager so that complaints may be more easily filed.

In the end, we hope this chapter acts as an instrument for broadening the scope of post-disaster research to get at the heart of women's quality of life starting from our conceptual framework. Challenging street harassment is possible especially considering that only a few decades ago women refused to be harassed in the workplace. Legal cases were won and harassers were held accountable. Sexual harassment in the workplace is, today, a serious legal issue. Perhaps street-level harassment is poised to do the same and will become a cornerstone issue in the fight for gender equity.

NOTES

1. The vignettes in this chapter come from Day-Sully's reflections on returning to New Orleans post–Hurricane Katrina.
2. In the fall of 2008, Kearl interviewed 900 people, including over 800 women, to glean a better understanding of how nonacademic individuals define street harassment. In her interviews she found the commonly used words above to describe street harassment.

Chapter Four

Rebuilding for Safety

Domestic Violence and Hurricane Katrina

Pamela Jenkins and Bethany Van Brown

Even those of us who spent our time thinking and writing about disaster were not prepared for Hurricane Katrina. Like many, I evacuated and waited for the storm to pass, and for the all clear to return home. I waited and waited, watching as the city I knew changed forever.[1]

On August 29, 2005, Hurricane Katrina made ground east of New Orleans. On the day after the storm, people who stayed woke up and thought that once again, the city had been spared. It did not take long for the cries of help from the Lower Ninth Ward and Lakeview to be heard. As the water poured over the levees, hundreds were stranded, others drowned. Finally, when the water in the city rose to meet the water in Lake Ponchartrain, 80 percent of the city flooded. Not long after the water began to recede, Hurricane Rita struck and pushed more water into some of the already flooded areas. After the water receded, the city, brought to its knees, began to rebuild. In its wake, nearly 2,000 lost their lives, nearly 1.5 million people evacuated, and much of the infrastructure of the city was destroyed (Peek and Erikson 2008). In addition, there was damage to the entire city:

> After the storm, New Orleans lost more than half of its population. More than 134,000 housing units (70 percent of all occupied units) suffered damage. Total monetary damages were 150 billion dollars (Rita and Katrina combined). Of the 120.5 billion in federal spending, most funding went to emergency relief. Charitable donations reached 6.5 billion. (Greater New Orleans 2013b)

It is nearly ten years after Hurricane Katrina, and much of the city looks as if the storm never happened. The streets are clean, the houses rebuilt, and businesses are open. But look more closely. In many neighborhoods, there are empty lots, still abandoned homes, and boarded up businesses and churches. The city is different, its citizens are different, and how we understand ourselves and our city has changed. In the ten years since Katrina, the understanding of violence against women in the context of disaster and its aftermath has changed. From the first days after the storm, with reports of rampant sexual assaults (much of which were later proven false), to the arduous and uneven rebuilding of the area, violence against women remains a social problem.

In this chapter, we explore how the context of violence and the response to violence changed in the decade since Hurricane Katrina. Comparisons of rates of violence against women pre- and post–Hurricane Katrina are not reliable, as the population altered significantly. In the immediate response, much of the population was displaced, and the return to the city included many newcomers. While the patterns of violence against women are similar, the context of violence changed considerably. Availability of housing, day care, healthcare, the criminal justice system and other services were limited for a time (from several months to years) after Hurricane Katrina. In addition, this chapter analyzes how the service provision responded to the post-disaster conditions. The stories of survivors and those of service providers combine to create a new understanding of violence against women in the context of disaster.

VULNERABILITY AND DISASTER

At first glance, disaster appears to affect everyone equally, not sorting out individuals or families by class, race, age, or gender. As we know, the effects of disaster are bounded by all of these factors and more. Victims and survivors of domestic violence can be at risk before, during, and after an event. And during a storm, certain kinds of risk may increase. In a context such as Hurricane Katrina, where the devastation is great and the recovery is long, the risk is unknown and uncertain. Similarly, all victims of domestic violence are not the same (Sokoloff and Dupont 2013). Some may be old, some may be disabled, others are homeless—vulnerability crosses many lines, and the threat of violence during and after a natural or man-made disaster changes.

Research indicates that women are especially disadvantaged during acute crisis events (Enarson 1998; Jenkins and Phillips 2008; Brown, Jenkins, and Wachtendorf 2010; World Health Organization 2002). During a disaster, social networks, transportation, employment opportunities, and household resources are severely impacted, intensifying an already dangerous household environment (Enarson 1998; 2002). In other words, when gender intersects with other areas of disadvantage during a disaster—in this case intimate partner violence—women are especially vulnerable (Institute for Women's Policy Research 2010; Jenkins and Phillips 2008).

The existing empirical research on the intersection of domestic violence and disaster indicates that there is an increase during the post-disaster period (Honeycombe 1993; Enarson 1998; 1999). Following the Saguenay floods and the 1998 ice storm in Quebec, battered women's organizations reported increased service demands (Enarson 1998). Battered women's agencies reported not only increased case management with existing clients, but also an increased number of new cases of domestic violence (Enarson 1998). Given the nearly complete evacuation of Orleans Parish after Hurricanes Katrina and Rita, it was difficult to compare pre- and post-incidents of domestic violence. However, Jenkins and Phillips (2008) found that intimate partner violence was reported as occurring more quickly and with more physical trauma. Harville et al. (2010) also showed that pregnant women after Katrina had heightened levels of stress and exposure to domestic violence.

Disasters are not static events; each disaster goes through stages: preparation, response, recovery, and mitigation. These are not discrete categories—vulnerable communities are often in recovery while they prepare and mitigate for the next storm. For victims and survivors of violence, each stage represents the possibility of violence and greater vulnerability. This vulnerability is reflected in events such as Hurricanes Rita and Katrina, because each phase of the disaster was longer and more complicated than the communities affected had ever experienced.

For those scholars who had studied disaster, Hurricane Katrina brought a clearer emphasis to the intersection of race, class, and gender (Boisseau et al. 2008; Jenkins, forthcoming 2015). In many ways, Hurricane Katrina was a catastrophe (Quarantelli 2005). This catastrophe had five disasters embedded in one event. The concept of five disasters includes pre-storm conditions, the storm itself, the levee break, the immediate response, and the long-term recovery. When a disaster happens, it is not over when the storm passes or even when the water recedes. After a disaster, the response and the recovery define, and in many ways, determine what a community becomes and how it responds to the most vulnerable.

LANDSCAPE BEFORE THE STORM

Before Hurricane Katrina, I worked alongside a range of providers and advocates on a number of issues around domestic violence. In 1994, newly elected Mayor Marc Morial formed a coordinated community response committee. The creation of this committee (Mayor's Domestic Violence Advisory

Committee) led to collaborations involving service provision and law enforcement. For example, the first Violence Against Women Act [VAWA] funding was received through the collaborative efforts with the city and the advisory group in 1997. The first changes in policing involved rewriting police procedures and creating police training in domestic violence. The change in police procedure was the first attempt to alter traditional ways of handling domestic violence cases.

New Orleans was a complex, unique city prior to the storm. High rates of poverty, interpersonal crime, flagging economy, failing schools, and other social problems defined the landscape. Yet, New Orleans as a community had many strengths: a complex culture, a rich sector of non-profit organizations, and a vibrant community life. Before the storm, there were five battered women services in the metro area; all but one had shelters attached to their program. Four programs came back after the storm, but one program did not re-open. Eventually, the empty flooded building that housed the program was torn down. Hurricane Katrina exposed the gendered vulnerabilities that were already present in the city of New Orleans. For example, prior to the storm, the rate of female-headed households was twice the national rate (Newcomb College Center for Research on Women 2010). Furthermore, 23 percent of all female-headed households with children in New Orleans lived below the poverty line and did not have cars (Institute for Women's Policy Research 2010).

Before the storm, there were eight domestic violence detectives, one for each police district. The rate of domestic violence before Hurricane Katrina was measured by police reports and protective orders. This was not a reflection of the actual rate, but of what data was available. In 2004, before Hurricane Katrina, the total number of protective orders registered with Louisiana Protective Order Registry was 23,244 (Jenkins and Phillips 2008). In 2005, the protective orders for the state was down to 18,544 with most decreases occurring in the areas hardest hit by Katrina.

DURING THE STORM

We left New Orleans to visit family in Iowa when the storm was still headed to Florida. When we got to Des Moines, we watched as the storm changed course and grew in size. We sat in a small town in Iowa and watched our city destroyed—watched as people cried for help. Years later, I still drive over the bridges and overpasses and think about who waited and waited for help to come.

During the immediate response to Hurricane Katrina, every level of government (federal, state, and local) failed to understand the depth of the levee failure and the needs of the people. The motto "on your own" describes how individuals and families made decisions to leave. The mandatory order to leave did not come from the mayor until Sunday afternoon, August 28, 2005 (Hauser and Lueck 2005). For the most vulnerable, the struggle to leave was difficult. As a result, thousands remained in the city. Some of those went to the Superdome, the shelter of last resort. Others remained in their homes while the waters rose and then, completely soaked by water, traumatized, and dehydrated since the water surrounding them was toxic, they made their way to the Superdome, and eventually the convention center.

The evacuation of 1.5 million people to nearly every state in the union created a context unfamiliar to most living Americans (Weber and Peek 2012). The evacuation occurred in a haphazard fashion as families attempted to leave ahead of the storm. For this group of displaced people, their lives were forever changed (Kroll-Smith, Baxter, and Jenkins, forthcoming 2015). For battered women, leaving was often complicated by their abusers. The director of a local shelter commandeered a bus herself and drove to Baton Rouge. Individual women had to gather their children, and sometimes evacuated with their abuser as there was little choice.

Marginalized groups are more vulnerable because they are less able to anticipate, cope with, resist, and recover from disaster (Fothergill 1999a; Blaikie et al. 2004). And after a disaster, not surprisingly, the traditional gender roles for women may increase their vulnerability. For example, disproportionately serving as the primary caregiver for children and elderly parents put some women in more vulnerable positions. Evacuating with young children and frail elderly often meant hours and days on highways jammed with others trying to outrun the storm. In addition, unequal access to resources makes women vulnerable to disaster in ways that differ from men (Fothergill 1996; Enarson and Morrow 1998; Enarson 1999). In the case of a prolonged event, the lack of resources grew throughout all phases of the disaster.

Hurricane Katrina exposed the gendered vulnerabilities that were already present in the city of New Orleans. Another aspect that created a vulnerable place was the fragmentation and separation of social networks. Social networks play critical protective roles, acting as buffers for victims to shield them from or reduce reoccurring violence, and impact a woman's opportunity for reaching safety. Evidence of the strength of the social networks appeared in the evacuation as huge caravans of families evacuated together. During disaster, women may be more vulnerable to abuse, because their traditional support networks are broken as people evacuate and become displaced (Enarson 1999; 2002; Litt, Skinner, and Robinson 2012). As 80 percent of the area was evacuated, leading to the separation of families and friends. Not only had the physical landscape changed, but also the informal social networks that helped to keep women safe were displaced.

Lack of resources, coupled with lack of transportation, complicate evacuation plans (Fordham et al. 2013). Due to power and control by the abusive partner, transportation is difficult for battered women, even under normal circumstances. Often, the abusive partner will not allow access to a vehicle to further isolate the survivor. In addition, traveling out of an area is not just objectively getting the ride, but involves navigating other issues of safety that may arise (Litt, Skinner, and Robinson 2012). Battered women reported issues of child custody during evacuation. Some of their children were with their former partners during evacuation, and normal exchanges were not possible. Thornton and Voigt (2010) document this dynamic with evidence of a woman who accepted a ride to leave town before Katrina made landfall, who was brutally raped by the two men who offered her help. Jenkins, Renne, and Keifer (2011) showed that after the evacuation for Hurricane Gustav in 2008, women who called the city were more likely to report that they did not have their own transportation and had to rely on others.

During the evacuation for Hurricane Katrina, women had to not only arrange and secure their transportation; they provided most of the caretaking of family members on the long journeys to many evacuee destinations. Statistics show that women head 55 percent of single parent households in New Orleans (Top 101 cities 2014). In addition, Louisiana ranks forty-ninth out of fifty for quality of life for children (Barrow 2010). As this evacuation occurred, women often traveled with children, formers spouses, elderly parents, neighbors, and friends (Jenkins 2012a). Survivors of the storm and domestic violence recount how difficult their evacuation was, as families often traveled together, which sometimes included a woman's former abusive spouse. The process of evacuation made women more vulnerable to the possibility of violence.

AFTER THE STORM

It is hard for anyone who was not here to imagine what life was like during the beginning of the rebuild. For much of the population, businesses, and nonprofits, it was a time to tear down, rebuild, and continue to work. As with many residents, I would work on the house, make phone calls about the house, visit the house, and go to work. This state of doing task after task did not last for a couple of months, but for some years. The work on our houses and organizations was not, for most of us, anything we had experienced. We hauled the soggy remnants of our lives to the curb and at the same time, called office after office trying to get our lights turned on, our FEMA trailer, or our water.

In 2005, social service organizations from around the world converged to help the people of New Orleans after Hurricane Katrina. For agencies, their landscape altered their work, staff, funding, and community. How these programs recovered shows their strengths and leadership in a catastrophe. Domestic violence programs faced some of the more serious challenges.

Immediately after Hurricane Katrina, much of the criminal justice system was not functional. The courts were closed down, the police were struggling, and the jail was not functional. At the same time, the service provision was seriously impacted. For a while after the storm, the main service provider, *Crescent House,* was defunded by the state. From *Crescent House's* self-study, Director Mary Claire Landry describes what happened:

> Imagine that in the midst of essentially redefining your entire perspective, you are informed by the State's Division of Administration that you no longer have a contract. You are no longer viable because your building and your city are devastated. But what about the people, what about the survivors who depend on you to be their safety net? You are exceedingly aware that a devastated building and a devastated city mean a devastated population. And you know that when a population is devastated that it is always the vulnerable that are hit the hardest. You know the vulnerable ones. The safety of domestic violence victims has been compromised because of confusion and dysfunction and batterers have already begun to take advantage. Survivors are calling you from all over the country. Your staff is providing what services they can over their cell phones. (Landry 2006)

Not only did the service providers talk on the phone, they created new ways to do outreach. The small number of returning staff to *Crescent House* found ways to find survivors of both abuse and Hurricane Katrina. They went to disaster relief centers to disseminate information, like the Jewish Community Center on St. Charles Avenue. They partnered with congregations and synagogues. In other words, they improvised and found alternative ways to reach victims (Jenkins and Phillips 2008). Survivors of domestic violence faced similar issues as other residents of the disaster stricken community, such as housing, transportation, limited access to healthcare, loss of community and employment. However, these issues were all intensified by the threat of violence in the midst of disaster recovery.

After the storm, the domestic violence community was fractured. But, because there was prior collaboration within the community, the group came together almost immediately. The group began by trying to assess what the need was and how to provide the basic of services for battered women. The difficulty, immediately after the storm, was connecting victims to services.

The storm meant that advocates had to do the work differently (Jenkins, Brown, and Mosby 2012). Advocates found victims and survivors at local disaster relief shelters, at FEMA centers, at the Salvation Army, or any other setting. The community of domestic violence providers began to think about the how to provide services differently. One local advocate described it in this way:

> What I was seeing at the FEMA centers were hundreds and hundreds of women dealing with domestic violence in their homes and not knowing how to navigate that. And that's what I knew what our mission was– we've got to create a safe place for people to come while they're staying in situations because they have no options and we've got to give them a place they can come [to] that they can feel safe, that they can get some respite, that they can get some support and that people aren't going to call them crazy or whatever. So that's where the concept of the *Crescent House* came from. It's not that I wanted to abandon the shelter model—but no way I was going to go back to shelter in the way we experienced it before [Katrina]. (anonymous interview 2006)

Both survivors connected to the programs before the hurricanes and those connected after had similar experiences. Reaching the programs was not straightforward. Asking for help about domestic violence was similar to receiving other aid; it was happenstance and often arbitrary (Kroll-Smith, Baxter, and Jenkins forthcoming 2015). Seeking help after Hurricane Katrina was a difficult, arduous process; for many, the information was incomplete and constantly changing. For battered women, this process was even more difficult. Battered women found help after the disaster in unique ways, not in the "routine way" of looking up an organization in the phone book and calling for an appointment. These survivors now had to seemingly stumble across the needed service, and programs began to understand that the work had to be different.

Providing temporary or permanent housing for survivors of domestic violence is difficult during normal times, but in the stages of response and recovery, housing problems are even more complex. And according to the Greater New Orleans Community Data Center (GNOCDC), rental rates skyrocketed as fair market rental units increased 46 percent from those before the storm (Greater New Orleans 2009). Most damaged housing units (80 percent) were made up of affordable to low-income housing. Moreover, the city's public housing units were declared uninhabitable and then demolished. Just before Christmas in 2007, the U.S. Department of Housing and Urban Development (HUD) received permission to demolish 4,500 public housing units to be replaced by mixed-income homes.

Housing and the availability of housing are central to the safety of victims living with violence, especially in the aftermath of Hurricane Katrina. Because disaster relief monies are typically awarded to the male head of household, receiving funds for housing (Louisiana Road Home program, FEMA trailers, non-profit housing vouchers, insurance) often involved dealing with their batterers directly. Survivors reported having to fight for the funds to repair their damaged homes. Insurance settlements became another strategy for power and control. The conditions and context of power and control shifted in the recovery. The housing options in a post-disaster recovery led to a greater risk of living with violence. Leaving in a non-disaster context is a process, as women often leave five or six times before they leave for good. A disaster context makes this process more complex and compounds these problems, as leaving then means finding a place to live in a situation of housing scarcity.

The issue of securing housing overlaps with the concept of the disaster, creating vulnerable spaces. The few victimization statistics that were collected on sexual assault after Hurricane Katrina by the National Sexual Violence Resource Center (NSVRC 2006) suggest that sexual assault did occur during all phases of the disaster. There are spaces that may make women especially vulnerable after a disaster. These spaces include evacuation sites, shelters, victims' homes, host homes, deserted streets and other open areas, vacant public buildings other than shelters, and other places such as hotels, perpetrators' homes, or cars.

During and after Katrina, the American Red Cross, faith-based organizations, city and community agencies, and other volunteer groups all organized emergency shelters. The need for shelters overwhelmed the state, and shelters sprung up quickly, without much ability to plan. In some of these local shelters, there was little or no intake process, and no way to know which families had a history of abuse.

Temporary housing, always an issue for battered women, became a problem as survivors found places to live after a storm. Hurricane Andrew illustrates how temporary housing sites are vulnerable spaces (Enarson 1999). Enarson (1997) documents one family who spent many months in a tent city in the outskirts of Miami, where the woman and her boyfriend lived after Hurricane Andrew destroyed their home, belongings, car, and workplace. Andrew hit everyone hard, especially low-income immigrant families. Even though much of the visible debris was cleaned up, displaced families still lived in disrepair (Enarson 1997). Spousal abuse calls to the local community helpline increased by 50 percent following Andrew, and over one-third of 1,400 surveyed reported that someone in their home had lost verbal or physical control in the two months since the hurricane (Laudisio 1993). The federally provided temporary housing, a FEMA trailer, is a 240 square foot living space; however, after the trailers were installed, reports of unhealthy levels of formaldehyde gas emissions from the trailers surfaced, making the trailers into a symbol of FEMA's botched post–Katrina efforts (Watson 2010). Additionally, adhoc FEMA trailer "neighborhoods" are often located in extremely isolated areas without security and lighting. Over 100,000 FEMA trailers were dispersed to affected residents of the Gulf Coast (NPR 2006). In New Orleans, this pattern emerged again, as trailers rested in open rural places, far from schools and bus routes. Trailers that were placed in front of individual homes were often far from other neighbors.

Recovery from disaster events, especially catastrophes, is uneven. Some families were able to rebuild their homes right away, while others' homes remained uninhabited for years after the flood. These unoccupied homes led to what was labeled as the "jack-o-lantern" effect, where only one house is lighted on an entire street, far from any other neighbor. This isolation can lead to situations where both community and intimate partner violence can more readily occur.

REBUILDING IN THE LIMINAL MOMENT

We continue to attend meetings, listen to advocates, talk to victims and survivors, and work on the ways in which victims and survivors enter the system. Not long ago, we did a set of focus groups with African American women who had been victims of domestic violence. The complexity of the situation both on an individual and structural level is still difficult to unravel. We heard stories of inadequate police response, stories of families who couldn't help, and systems that worked against the women's safety. Also, we heard more often than was comfortable that the women didn't want the relationship to end, just wanted the violence to end. These women are remarkable survivors—continually searching how to make themselves and their children safe. What remains impressive to us, even ten years after the storm, is the commitment by the local organizations to continue to provide services. Not only are the services back, but throughout the community, advocates are not only using national best practice but creating national best practices.

Disasters can provide an opportunity for change (Smith 2012). The domestic violence programs in New Orleans certainly took this opportunity to change how they imagined and carried out their work. Beginning in 2007, the community, especially Catholic Charities, *Crescent House*, and other community leaders, worked to bring a family justice center to New Orleans. There were community meetings, planning meetings, conference calls, and even more meetings. Within five months after we began the discussion (it often takes eighteen months), the New Orleans community opened the Family Justice Center (New Orleans Family Justice Center Alliance 2014). This center, now operating as its own non-profit, has thrived in the aftermath of Hurricane Katrina.

The New Orleans Family Justice Center (NOFJC) is the best-known example of how the community worked to change the service provision, but there are others. After Hurricane Katrina, the issue of domestic violence became less separated from other programs. Other local community groups, such as Women with a Vision and the Institute for Women and Ethnic Studies, began participating in the discussion of domestic violence bringing their own unique perspectives to the issues. Another integral part of this process is the Blueprint for Safety Project, a project that audits the law enforcement response to domestic violence and recommends policy changes. This program led to an examination of the disparate impact of domestic violence on African American women.

Hurricane Katrina is the touchstone for what we, as a nation, got wrong about disaster. The recovery for victims of domestic violence changed service provision and law enforcement. Much will be written of the recovery of the city, and of the brain gain, the influx of young talented individuals to the area following the storm. In many ways, the city in has recovered. In 2012, the New Orleans metro area recovered from the recession and reached 1 percent employment above the 2008 job level (GNODC 2013). The New Orleans area continues to diversify its industries by increasing knowledge-based industries and business start-ups. For example, in 2012 New Orleans has thirty-four arts and culture nonprofits per 100,000, twice the national rate (ibid.). Yet, in many ways, economic growth declined, and educational attainment, especially among African American men, did not advance. In New Orleans, fewer black men are working as compared to other parts of the country (ibid.). While the incarceration rates have decreased, the rate of incarceration continues to be higher than the national rate (ibid.).

However, inside of that recovery, inequality remains. The persistent high rate of violent crime rates, incarceration, and lack of good jobs are all still part of the landscape of New Orleans. One of the major post–Katrina events was the release of a 158-page report documenting the operational practices and conduct of the New Orleans Police Department by the U.S. Department of Justice (NOPD 2014). After years of crisis and the many problems that surfaced during Hurricane Katrina, the Department of Justice filed a lawsuit, which was settled on July 24, 2012 (NOPD 2014). The settlement incorporated all the changes in the federal report. A part of this report detailed the ways in which the response to domestic violence and sexual assault was inadequate. The NOPD was required to work with the NOFJC to increase safety and improve practices for victims. As a result of the consent decree, the NOPD, the Family Justice Center, and the Blueprint for Safety Project have been involved in rewriting NOPD policy, and developing training for law enforcement.

Louisiana remains a dangerous place for women. The Family Justice Center provides services on an annual basis for about 1,500 women. NOPD receives 11,000 calls for service a year, with 4,000 arrests (Woodward 2013). The city has changed as well. Homelessness increased after the storm, not just because of the lack of affordable housing, but also because of the influx of workers (UNITY 2011). A part of that homeless population is women and children. Yet, the women seeking services at the Family Justice Center are overwhelmingly African American (72 percent), 10 percent are Latin and another 4 percent are Asian or other non-white ethnicities (NOFJC 2013).

Planning for the next disaster involves understanding the dynamics of domestic violence. The intimate and ongoing nature of the violent relationship puts victims at risk. Additionally, the effects of Hurricane Katrina are still part of the long-term recovery of New Orleans. Housing, medical care, schools, government, non-profit organizations, and families have all been changed by the events.

The United States is experiencing a marked increase in billion dollar disasters. In the 1980s, we averaged two a year. In the 2000s we averaged six a year. In 2011, we had fourteen (NCDC 2014). With each disaster, government at all levels reviews the response efforts and attempts to improve how disasters are handled in the immediate aftermath. However, less attention has been paid to long-term recovery efforts. Since Hurricanes Katrina and Rita, the region has faced a number of storms (Ike, Gustav, Isaac), plus the BP oil spill, which created more uncertainty and risk. In the face of cascading disasters, communities continue to go forward. Throughout, there is a continuous tension between being prepared for the next storm and recovering from the last one. In the midst of this, domestic violence programs continue to plan and respond to the issues of domestic violence.

Violence is repetitive, but the patterns of behavior are altered by the social context. In the aftermath of Hurricane Katrina, the institutional response, battered women programs, community advocacy programs, and criminal justice programs are responding in a more coordinated fashion to domestic violence. Can this knowledge be transferable?

Specifically, the response to domestic violence and the response to disaster share the commonalities of crisis and recovery. How do we get victims to safety? How do we treat their injuries? Then, how do we provide for long-term housing, employment, childcare, and schools? And, finally, how do we keep them safe? In New Orleans, ten years later, domestic violence advocates have created both a crisis and long-term response plan to this pandemic social problem. Organizational efforts to assist victims and reform policing have been innovative, coordinated, and largely effective. Given the massive and highly publicized failures of the city, state, and federal response to Katrina, it seems that there is much that emergency managers could learn from domestic violence providers in fashioning a program for long-term safety.

NOTE

1. In many ways, this essay reflects our collective personal experience (in italics throughout the text). Pam Jenkins has worked in domestic violence programs in Louisiana for twenty-five years, while Bethany Brown's involvement began after the storm in 2006. When "we" is used in the text, it refers to our collective experiences. However "I" refers to Pam's particular Katrina experience.

Chapter Five

Missing in the Storm

The Gender Gap in Hurricane Katrina Research and Disaster Management Efforts

Kristen Barber and Shiloh Deitz

I had been evacuated for three months when I returned to New Orleans. It was late December, and I was returning to the city to complete my Master's degree. During my post–Hurricane Katrina exodus I had stayed with family in Michigan, and for Christmas that year my mom asked me whether I wanted a water filter or a handgun. She was nervous for me to return to a city that was a disaster zone. After all, she had seen the television coverage of the storm, with dead bodies floating down the streets and women shown as "pregnant in sweltering shelters, anguishing mothers searching for their children, and exhausted older women wading through filthy water" (David and Enarson 2012, xvii). There was a sense that women were particularly at risk in the aftermath of Hurricane Katrina; but I assured my mom a water filter would do, and that I would be fine navigating my life in this battered city.[1]

As Sociologist Elaine Enarson (2012a; 2012b) notes, women are among the most vulnerable in disaster; yet they are often overlooked in both scholarly work and emergency response efforts (see also David and Enarson 2012; Enarson 2009; Ross-Sheriff 2007; Willinger 2008). She asserts that, "In over fifty years of research on emergencies, disasters, and catastrophes in the United States, a conspicuous silence around gender has been maintained—a looking away, perhaps a calculated blindness" (Enarson 2012a, 2). Research instead focuses largely on how class stratification and the historical marginalization of racial and ethnic minorities place some groups of people at more risk than others during disasters (Bullard and Wright 2009; Hartman and Squires 2006; Levitt and Whitaker 2009; Potter 2007). When women are considered, it's usually in terms of "sex" rather than "gender," with researchers comparing numerical rates of poverty between males and females, instead of looking at how gender differently shapes men and women's perspectives of and experiences with disaster (see also Fothergill 1996; 1998). As a result, the distinct needs of women are often ignored, with local and federal emergency response agencies doing little to mitigate the severe effects of gender during disasters like Hurricane Katrina.

Looking back ten years since Hurricane Katrina, we investigate what we know about women's experiences with the storm and what scholars say about the needs of women, children, and entire families in such a disaster. We ask: What does research teach us about women's lives during and after Hurricane Katrina? What are the consequences of overlooking women in disaster management? How have women served, and continue to serve, as operatives in the recovery and rebuilding of their communities? And what sort of policy changes might mitigate the vulnerability of women in disaster more generally? To answer these questions, we evaluated the literature on Hurricane Katrina with a particular focus on what this work has unearthed about women's experiences, needs, and contributions during and after the storm. We find that this research revolves around five main areas: scholarly prescriptions to prioritize a gendered lens in disaster research; sexual and domestic assault; reproductive health needs; decision-making responsibilities of female heads of households; and women's ongoing roles in rebuilding their communities. While this work reaches across various topics, only a handful of scholars have focused on women post-storm. An August 2014 Google Scholar search reveals 4,300 sources with "Hurricane Katrina" in the title, and only seventy-four of these also contain "women," "woman," "gender," "female," "sex," or "girl." Drawing from both systematic studies and personal narrative case studies of women in Katrina, this scholarship highlights how important it is for disaster scholars and management professionals to consider women's vulnerability, roles as caregivers, and agents in rebuilding.

WHERE ARE THE WOMEN?: RACE AND CLASS IN HURRICANE KATRINA RESEARCH

I attended the 2006 American Sociological Association conference a year after Hurricane Katrina caused rising waters to topple over New Orleans's levees. As I made my way through the book exhibit, I noticed a slew of freshly printed books on Hurricane Katrina. There had been a race by scholars to publish on this new hot topic. The covers of the books showcased images of black New Orleanians outside of the Superdome, wading through deep, dank water flooding the city streets. Flipping through the tables of contents, researchers were writing about the sociologically salient issues of race and class as structures that unequally shaped people's experiences with the storm. Conspicuously absent were chapters focused on the nuanced experiences and struggles of women during and after Katrina.

Class divisions drastically shaped the realities and opportunities of people in New Orleans as they prepared for and dealt with the aftermath of Hurricane Katrina. Financially needy citizens could not necessarily afford to evacuate, whether because they did not own a vehicle (Seager 2012; Willinger and Knight 2012), could not take time off from work (Fussell 2006; Pardee 2014), or had similarly situated social networks of friends and family who were local and without means (Weber and Peek 2012). And while police patrolled city streets to urge evacuation in the final hours before the storm, the city made little effort to mobilize available resources—such as school buses—to help relocate those most vulnerable (Butterbaugh 2005; Raines 2005; Sullivan 2005). To add insult to injury, the needy were popularly criticized for not taking the initiative to evacuate.

It is not a coincidence that the frightened and desperate faces stranded at the Superdome were black. Suffering long-standing economic inequalities, African American New Orleanians made up the majority of low-income residents, and this disadvantage has geohistorical roots. Scholarship shows that an "ethnic geography" shaped settlement in New Orleans after the Louisiana Purchase, with mostly wealthy whites living in higher-elevated and less risky areas: "Areas that lay farthest from sources of nuisance and risk *and* closest to amenities and opportunities commanded the highest prices and attracted the best infrastructure and housing" (Campanella 2007, 706). After the Civil War, "Destitute and the target of racial prejudice, the freedmen settled mostly in the least desirable, highest-risk areas in the back-of-town" (708). These inequalities had not disappeared in 2005, as the levees broke along and washed away the lowest-lying and predominantly poor black neighborhoods.

Deep-seeded racial and class inequalities rose to the forefront of post–Katrina experiences, as well as both public and academic debates of how historical discrimination and contemporary systematic neglect placed some at higher risk than others. Yet, analyses of how gender operated through class and race to shape people's experiences of the disaster were largely missing in media conversations, and academic research that informs emergency preparedness and response policies has been slow to take up gender as a major organizing principle of disaster vulnerability. Enarson (2012a) notes that generalizations about the effects of race and poverty on disaster experiences gloss over the fact that "women more often live below the poverty line, work part-time, are elderly, primary caregivers, disabled, in need of reproductive health services; and they less often have pensions, college degrees, and stable housing" (Barber 2013, 764; Enarson 2012a).

In her groundbreaking work on the "feminization of poverty," Diana Pearce (1978) showed that women make up the bulk of those living below the poverty line. Even before Hurricane Katrina made landfall, New Orleans exemplified this with high numbers of poor women, particularly single mothers. In 2005, 14.8 percent of U.S. women were low-income, but 26.5 percent of the women of New Orleans, and nearly one-third of New Orleans's black female residents, were in poverty (U.S. Census Bureau 2005). Due to their low social positions and lack of powerful networks, these women had little choice in the conditions of their displacement and few resources to shelter their children from the trauma following the storm (Peek and Fothergill 2008). While gender was clearly an issue mediating disaster vulnerability, these women "were described simply by their race . . . the gendering of the storm and its effects do not make headlines" (Belkhir and Charlemaine 2007, 138). Reporters and scholars have neglected women's unique experiences and needs in discussions of post-storm recovery; yet as we discuss later, women are often the unsung heroes of rebuilding efforts.

Additionally, gender matters for better understanding the effects of race and class on experiences of disaster, for example, it was black *women* who were often in desperate need of low-income, affordable housing after the storm. City planners decided to demolish the Big Four public housing projects, leaving many residents little opportunity to return home. "Thousands of poorer women of color and their families were forced to leave their homes because the levees failed, but actually lost their homes to city planning" (Henrici, Helmuth, and Carlberg 2012, 145). This destruction allowed planners to push forward an unpopular but previously scheduled agenda. As Sociologist Jessica Pardee (2012) notes, "Public housing residents were unwanted in a recovering New Orleans. Within weeks of the storm, [the Housing Authority of New Orleans] HANO announced plans to demolish four large-scale public housing projects because of "flood damage," including units with no water intrusion at all. Many of these undamaged apartments were slated for demolition previously, making Katrina an opportunity to move the plans along faster . . ." (63). Overlooked or disregarded as citizens important to the fabric of New Orleans, poor black women have not necessarily found living in new, often racially and socioeconomically homogeneous host cities any easier. The triple disadvantage of being poor, black, and female is a socially marginalized position that differently and unequally structured these women's opportunities, choices, and (ongoing) experiences with the aftermath of Katrina.

A CITY OF MEN: SEXUAL AND DOMESTIC ASSAULT

I became acutely aware of what it meant to be a woman living in a disaster zone shortly after returning to New Orleans. My mom, who helped me to move back, decided to stay through New Year's Eve, and we made our way to the French Quarter to celebrate with locals who reveled in being home. We shuffled down the dark streets, weaving through crowds of people who were drinking and dancing. With caution and angst, we walked past military police peppering the old cobblestoned streets. They wore sand-washed camouflage, carried automatic weapons, and drove around in armored vehicles. These daunting and serious men stood in stark contrast to the resilient New Orleanians attempting to reclaim their city with boisterous celebration. Their presence also struck me as a sign that New Orleans had become not just a militarized space but also a masculinized space.

Men were everywhere in New Orleans following the storm. They occupied the city as military and construction workers who migrated (and immigrated) in because of the enormous opportunity for rebuilding work (Ross 2012; Willinger and Gerson 2008). Local residents trickled slowly back into the city, while many never returned. And because entire families evacuated, women were scarcer than before the storm (Willinger 2008). With streetlamps inoperable, police slow to respond, and men dominating public spaces, New Orleans became an exceptionally unfriendly place for women (Barber et al. 2007; Batlan 2008; Gehman 2012; INCITE! 2012). This post-disaster environment constrained the freedoms of women, who experienced high rates of sexual harassment and assault (SARA 2006). Media reports of sexual assault emerged first with stories about the horrendous environment of the Superdome, where people reported witnessing the rape of women and girls (Brown and Jenkins 2011; Hafiz 2005; Lawson 2010; Pardee 2014; Stockemer 2006; Strange 2006).

Local and federal authorities utilized the Superdome to shelter those unable to evacuate the city. Opened Sunday night as the hurricane neared the Gulf Coast and the National Hurricane Center declared Katrina "potentially catastrophic," the Superdome housed approximately 20,000 people (Treaster 2005). Photos of crowds funneling into the stadium show clearly that the bulk of those in need were poor blacks; but they were also likely to be single mothers, children, and the elderly (Peek and Fothergill 2008; Spence, Lachlan, and Burke 2007; Weber and Peek 2012). A far cry from the refuge people were seeking, the Superdome became a site of interpersonal and institutional violence, especially for women. The military reportedly exercised indifferent governance over citizens, threatening to shoot into the crowd in order to control people (Idakula 2007) and separating mothers from their children when evacuating them from the city. Reports of sexual violence proliferated, with Pardee (2014) noting that the lack of privacy for women, little formal safety for children, and dearth of basic needs and sanitation contributed to and exacerbated women's experiences of assault. Ruth Idakula (2007) found herself with no other option than to paddle down flooded streets in a small boat to the Superdome for safety. She describes hearing that girls were being assaulted, "I stopped a man who was walking by . . . and he told me a little girl had been raped and killed in the bathroom . . ." (39). People were packed into the Superdome, and emergency response operated on the ground without attention to or mitigation of these immediate dangers facing women.

There are disputes about how high the murder and rape rates were in the Superdome those days following Hurricane Katrina; police, local authorities, and the media questioned women's reports of assault (Butterbaugh 2005; Pardee 2014). What is certain, however, is that New Orleans saw a 45 percent increase in women's reports of sexual assault (SARA 2006), and that this threat emerged in an environment where men occupied "hyper-masculinized . . . roles as protectors and first responders" (Pardee 2014, 124) with power and control of spaces, bodies, and resources. Women who returned to the city encountered aggressive interactions with men even months after the storm. Graduate student Jennifer Day, for example, experienced more than usual amounts of sexual harassment, with men grabbing and making sexual remarks about her body (Barber et al. 2007). And women who did not report suffering sexual harassment or assault still felt uncomfortable living in an otherwise male-dominated, post-disaster space. Historian Mary Gehman worried about being a potentially vulnerable woman after weathering the storm. "The prospect of being the only person on the block, and a lone woman at that, bothered me a bit, given reports of looting, potshots at police, a general sense of lawlessness . . ." (2012, 29). At the same time, protection by police was racialized, with white women at times occupying a "status as protected" and black women (and men) experiencing continued suspicion and hostility (Batlan 2008).

In addition to the rise in sexual assault, women also experienced higher rates of domestic violence. Before Hurricane Katrina, 33.6 percent of women in the city reported intimate partner psychological victimization; this number rose to 42.5 percent after the storm (Schumacher et al. 2010). And post–Katrina intimate partner violence rates were three times higher (Anastario, Larrance, and Lawry 2008). The lack of access to basic financial, public, and social network resources after Katrina compounded already vulnerable women's risk to violence and forced many into life-threatening situations without the means to escape (Jenkins and Phillips 2008). Criminologist Bethany Brown (2012) argues that people face a sense of disempowerment in the aftermath of disaster, and that men are likely to use domestic assault to retain a sense of control in their lives.

With city infrastructure collapsed and people dispersed, previously important resources including women's shelters and crisis hotlines were closed immediately after Hurricane Katrina. There are, however, stories of some local advocates—working for the New Orleans Battered Women's Shelter, for example—who did not evacuate but instead stayed to help victimized women (Brown 2012). These advocates, largely women, were prepared to aid disaster victims and victims of domestic violence, but they were "systematically excluded from emergency planning and policy . . . their resources are not identified as valuable" (Brown 2012, 187; see also Brown, Jenkins, and Wachtendorf 2010). Such women are inspiring agents of change and recovery, and their skills could have more broadly aided local women if mitigating agencies had incorporated them into official disaster management strategies.

Women's fears of being harassed and assaulted by men in a newly masculinized and militarized city infringes on their ability to feel safe during disaster, and when they are otherwise seeking help. The threat of harm by men who dominated the city might have accounted partly for the low repopulation rates of women, and thus of entire families headed by women—from 2005 to 2007, New Orleans saw a 45.2 percent drop in the female population (U.S. Census Bureau 2005; 2006; 2007). Women's experiences of sexual and domestic assault, however, have been much overlooked in the study of Hurricane Katrina. Out of the seventy-four sources mentioned above that reference gender and Hurricane Katrina in the title, only five titles include "gender based violence," "domestic violence," "domestic abuse," or "sexual assault." While this is not a perfect count of work that considers assault during and after Katrina, it gives us an idea of just how under-researched the topic is. There were no real efforts by local or federal response organizations to protect women from assault during Hurricane Katrina, to encourage report of assault, or to track the predominance of assault. This lack of consideration for women's safety during disaster reflects a longtime marginalization of women's experiences with male violence.

WOMEN'S REPRODUCTIVE HEALTH NEEDS

As I write this, my spouse and I are expecting our first child. Living in St. Louis now, we have access to much needed prenatal and postnatal healthcare, and we can be assured that our pregnancy is healthy. I can only imagine what it is like to bear the weight of pregnancy in disaster, having to consider mobility and displacement, prescription refills, prenatal health, and worries about health complications for mom and baby or where to deliver. Often serving as primary caregivers, women also have to worry about the healthcare of their young children; and their reproductive health depends on access to affordable care and birth control to help prevent both unwanted pregnancies and the contraction of sexually transmitted diseases. Women's unique health needs, however, are rarely or insufficiently met in the wake of disaster, having dire consequences on many women's overall well-being.

After the storm, Governor Kathleen Blanco controversially closed Charity, New Orleans's leading hospital in the care of the poor and indigent, with flooding and mold supposedly serving as deterrents to renovating the historical and wide-serving hospital. In a retrospective editorial, Roberta Brandes Gratz (2011) laments, "The abandonment of the old Charity Hospital stands as a potent symbol of the many disappointments and betrayals experienced by the residents of New Orleans after Katrina. The loss has been a huge blow to the poor African-American community Charity served." Like the public housing projects, many locals saw the closure of Charity Hospital as an unnecessary waste propelled by urban planning agendas rather than the actual damage or community needs. Inadequate triage centers emerged in empty parking lots to compensate for the lack of hospital care, but overall very little replaced the services Charity had provided to many of New Orleans's poorest. For example, doctors practiced medicine in the Lord & Taylor department store downtown, where "[c]linicians see patients in doorless 'rooms' framed by temporary cubicle walls. In a former merchandise loading dock, patients undergo CT scans in a trailer. Upstairs is dental care, a steep walk up the long-silent escalator" (Molpus and Baldwin 2006). And while providing basic emergent and preventative care to those stranded in or returning to the city, they did not adequately, if at all, address the reproductive health needs of many women.

The Federal Emergency Management Agency worked with the department of Health and Human Services to assure the safety of food, water, and the environment to treat the severely ill and injured, and to identify the dead (Lister 2005). Yet they all but ignored the specific medical needs of women struggling through pregnancies and postpartum recovery in the disaster zone and in nearby cities, and who were often without insurance and vital information about where they could receive affordable medical treatment (Peek and Fothergill 2008; Tobin-Gurley and Peek 2010; Zotti et al. 2012). According to the Centers for Disease Control (2013), disasters increase the risk of low birth weight, preterm birth, early pregnancy loss, spontaneous abortion, intrauterine growth restriction, and decreases in infant head circumference. Pregnant women are more susceptible to infections during disaster, and many of the medications used to treat the infections are teratogenic toward pregnant women. They also need particular immunizations, and disaster-related stress like living without running water, being stranded in the hot and humid Superdome, evacuating the city on overcrowded buses, or being stranded on highway overpasses could have more serious repercussions for the health of pregnant women and fetuses (Zotti and Williams 2011). After Hurricane

Katrina, many women found themselves in new locations without prenatal care or other medical resources.

For community well-being, healthcare professionals need to prioritize emergency pediatric and preventative care as well as long-term healthcare solutions. For example, newborn screening makes it possible to identify and treat serious illnesses in babies that could otherwise result in life-threatening conditions or mental retardation. However, the functioning of pediatric care in New Orleans after the storm was disrupted, and important resources like The Louisiana Newborn Screening and Follow-up Program halted altogether. Without newborn screening and other routine checks, as well as accessible hospitals like Charity, babies and their mothers can suffer from serious yet preventable illnesses (Callaghan et al. 2007).

Rates of teen pregnancy and sexually transmitted diseases, including HIV/AIDS, were also particularly high in New Orleans and Louisiana before the storm, and continued to be an issue afterwards as many women's health centers, including Planned Parenthood, were destroyed in or abandoned after the flood (Greeley 2008). With lack of access to doctors and pharmacies for birth control prescriptions, New Orleans experienced a baby boom nine-months after Hurricane Katrina—producing what Willinger and Gerson (2008) refer to as "Katrina Babies." With a 4.3 percent increase in births among women twenty to thirty-four years old in 2006, it is clear that women lacked access to basic reproductive medical attention and access to birth control, and that there is an ongoing need for obstetric and pediatric care in the city.

A dearth of reproductive care jeopardized the health of women post–Katrina, especially as the city saw an increase in prostitution. Owing to the influx of men in the city, there was a boom in the underground sexual trafficking of women and children (Ross 2012). With a largely poor local female population and a suspended service economy, many previously and newly destitute women had few other options than prostitution to support themselves. With this sexual economy comes the vulnerability of women, who experienced a rise in unwanted pregnancies and sexually transmitted diseases such as HIV/AIDS. Indeed, Louisiana reported the seventh highest national rate of new HIV/AIDS cases in 2005, and in 2006 29 percent of all new HIV cases in the United States were reported in New Orleans (Greeley 2008; LDHH 2004; 2007). Black women were particularly susceptible as they made up an estimated 81 percent of all women living with HIV/AIDS in New Orleans (ibid.).

HEADS OF HOUSEHOLDS AND DECISION MAKERS

I was lucky. My apartment building did not shift off of its cinderblock foundation, and many of my belongings were salvageable. Most importantly, my friends and I were safe. I had the financial means and geographically dispersed social networks necessary to evacuate the evening before the storm rolled in. I had no children or elderly parents who were dependent on me, and I had a safely located family in the Midwest who could afford to support me while I was not receiving a paycheck and had no access to my bank account. I also didn't have to worry about losing my job for evacuating, finding housing and a job in a new location, placing my children in school elsewhere, or figuring out how to access public assistance on which my family and I depended. This was not the case for many women living in New Orleans during Hurricane Katrina; women who bore the burden of making decisions and navigating local and federal bureaucracies post-storm for both themselves and others.

Police driving through low-income areas announcing mandatory evacuation via megaphones did little to facilitate the evacuation of women and their families. The New Orleans city government was publicly criticized for not mobilizing resources to evacuate residents without means for transportation. This criticism points to the issue of poverty in disaster risk and management but also ignores how gender intersects with class to create a myriad of barriers for the safe and successful evacuation of many families.

In New Orleans, women headed 56 percent of households before the storm, and 41 percent of those female-headed households lived in poverty (Gault et al. 2005). These women were responsible for navigating disaster preparedness and evacuation decisions for their entire families—often with few options to take leave from already low paying jobs, limited access to transportation, and little savings for gas, bus tickets, hotel stays, and other necessities for evacuating (Pardee 2014; Willinger 2008; Willinger and Knight 2012). For example, while Idakula (2007) considered evacuating her young son and herself for Hurricane Katrina, she lacked access to a car and "couldn't contribute for gas and didn't want to financially burden anyone" (34). As Hurricane Katrina whipped across the Gulf, these women not only occupied the most financially vulnerable of locations, they also had to navigate the physical, psychological, financial, and bureaucratic effects of disaster for others.

Elizabeth Davis and Kelly Rouba (2012) found that women often made decisions about whether or not to evacuate for Hurricane Katrina based on the needs of children, disabled family members, and elderly kin (also see Croom, Jenkins, and Eddy 2007). And because many New Orleanians had extensive previous experience with hurricanes and did not see Katrina as particularly more dangerous, women had to decide whether they should take children out of school and to consider how they would arrange accommodations for kin with special needs (Pardee 2014; Zotti et al. 2012). Perhaps most importantly, they had to decide whether evacuating for a maybe-disaster was worth risking their jobs. After all, employers can easily replace low-skilled, low-paid workers and do not often provide their employees with leave policies or vacations. In 2005, 53.9 percent of New Orleans's service workers were women working in jobs like healthcare support, food preparation, grounds cleaning, and personal care workers.

What research shows us is that we do not know a whole lot about women's experience of relocation from New Orleans, even ten years after the event. Some work suggests that women who evacuated had family members encouraging them to leave New Orleans before the storm rolled in and had access to "caravans of kin" that shared the costs of evacuation and provided emotional support (Pardee 2014; also see Litt 2008; Zotti et al. 2012). Although many women lacked the dispersed social networks helpful for evacuation, they also tended to have more familial support than men, which both aided women's struggles in caring for dependents after the storm but also created stress for them (Reid and Reczek 2011). Personal narratives suggest women who did evacuate their families went to nearby cities that built at least some infrastructure to deal with the Hurricane Katrina diaspora, such as Houston and San Antonio.

Due to the material destruction caused by the flood, and compounded by interpersonal and organizational discrimination, New Orleans became inhospitable for many. Although "returning home was judged to be an important measure of the recovery process" (Willinger and Knight 2012, 59), many women could not return to New Orleans because of a dearth of affordable housing and government support. In many new locations, single mothers reported encountering barriers to accessing government support and stable housing, finding flexible employment, obtaining reliable childcare, providing their children with stability, and accessing healthcare for themselves and their children (Tobin-Gurley and Peek 2010). Capricious housing policies in host cities, for example, included the confiscation of vouchers, government failure to adjust voucher values to local rental costs, and inadequate or absent moving assistance (Pardee 2012).

In host cities many women faced a quadruple stigma as single mothers, Southerners, racial minorities, and low-income evacuees of Hurricane Katrina. Due to the multiple burdens of caretaking while struggling with poverty and racial discrimination, these mothers suffered higher levels of psychological distress after the hurricane (Paxson et al. 2012; Vigil et al. 2009). At the same time, they may have seen New Orleans as a disaster zone even before the levees broke, having long struggled to find decent-paying jobs, good public schooling for their kids, and safe and affordable housing. Extended kin networks guarded many black women in New Orleans against poverty pre-Katrina. Yet, this support was sometimes lost when families were scattered across the country as part of the Hurricane Katrina diaspora (Litt et al. 2012). These women did not have the same support to encourage them to return; and for those who did return to New Orleans, social networks were often missing or less stable.

WOMEN IN RECOVERY AND REBUILDING

After the storm, people were reeling from the tragedy of Hurricane Katrina, having lost homes, family and friends, and personal mementos, as well as their general way of life. Yet, as many of the women I knew settled into a "new normal" post-storm, they also began to set their sights on rebuilding their city and communities. I watched as strong, intelligent women bravely shifted their career trajectories to preserve the artistic, musical, and cinematic culture of New Orleans. They worked for the city government or for non-profit organizations, and they both developed and revealed an inspiring commitment to place. Women like these are integral to the vibrancy that continues on in the streets of the French Quarter and in the hearts of new and old New Orleanians.

Despite the particular vulnerability many women faced in the aftermath of Hurricane Katrina, they have also shown great resilience, creativity, and hope in rebuilding their lives and communities. From interviews with women disaster survivors, Ophera Davis and Marie Land (2007) note the "resoluteness" of women, who "have shown amazing strength" (85). While men occupy most state and federal level decision-making positions, local women have been, and continue to be, key in the rebuilding of New Orleans. Without formal recognition or representation in high-level organizations, women have created and participated in grassroots movements to "Bring New Orleans Back" (e.g., Randall 2006) socially, culturally, and economically.

Women are often on the forefront of grassroots movements. Building on Patricia Hill Collins's (1990) concept of "motherwork," Sociologist Pamela Jenkins (2012b) explores how women work to transform and aid in the recovery of their neighborhoods after Hurricane Katrina. The social expectation that women perform care work means they are practiced in providing for families, and as Brenda Robichaux (2012), former Principal Chief of the United Houma Nations, explains, "this devotion" has inspired more international grassroots work, such as the establishment of the United Houma National Relief Fund to aid in subsequent disaster relief.

Women have also been key to preserving homes, memories, and local businesses in New Orleans's ethnic and religious enclaves (Peterson and

Krajeski 2012). Women of the Vietnamese community in Versailles, for example, created collations with other marginalized groups to resist the presence of a dumpsite in their neighborhood (Nguyen 2012). "Both women and men of this community actively struggled to close the Chef Menteur landfill, but Vietnamese American women . . . sought to find commonality in multiple points of oppression with others dealing with similar environmental and social issues during the recovery efforts . . ." (198). Women in the local Jewish community used their organizational skills and social networks to build alliances and to halt rebuilding efforts that were unhealthy for their neighborhoods (Rosenbaum 2012). In one particularly poignant example, a local woman by the name of Ms. Rose fought for environmental justice in the city and in the federal treatment of her community (White 2012). She called upon and worked with other environmental organizations to protect her and her neighbors' homes; and she understood this protection effort as a gendered process, with women as guardians of "memory and place" (166).

While non-local relief efforts are essential to disaster recovery, long-term recovery is not possible unless community members are active in the process. Victims of disaster are uniquely attuned to the character and needs of their own neighborhoods and families, and their visions might differ from outside relief organizations (Roderick 2010). These perspectives are crucial in rebuilding not only material homes but also a sense of culture and community after disaster. Grassroots movements have helped to put power in the hands of those individuals who are part of and thus invested in communities that are rebuilt, and women are generally the foot soldiers in local change (e.g., Gaarder 2011). Social work professor, Fariyal Ross-Sheriff (2007) draws attention to the seemingly mundane efforts of homemakers in rebuilding communities:

> Women's creativity in finding resources to prepare meals; in consoling children, relatives, and friends; and in mediating the conflicts that stress and deprivation engender are seldom deemed newsworthy events. These quiet actions, including prayers and encouragement, hidden in the recesses of shelters or in the solitude of late nights and early mornings, do not embody spirit-stirring photo opportunities. These are, however, the actions that mend the soul and weave the fabric of culture and home. (6)

It is common for women to work to keep their neighborhoods safe and healthy for their children and families, and these efforts are more salient post-disaster.

Now ten years after the storm, as non-local volunteer efforts have faded and left, it is local New Orleanians who continue to dedicate themselves to rebuilding the city. The population has not fully returned, but the proportion of women (52 percent) to men (48 percent) approximates pre-storm levels, when 53.4 percent of the population was female (U.S. Census Bureau 2005;

2012). And it is these women who are instrumental in rebuilding New Orleans through everyday grounded efforts.

ADDRESSING WOMEN'S NEEDS IN AND AFTER DISASTER

The vulnerability and hardships women faced during and after Hurricane Katrina could be mitigated in future disasters with smart, gender-sensitive policies. The above research suggests that we focus on issues of assault, reproductive health, transportation, employment, and childcare, as well as on prioritizing the tracking and location of dispersed family members. This research also suggests that because they are resilient, structured support for women would aid the recovery of children, the elderly, and local communities. Preliminary research on women in grassroots movements reveals their effectiveness in helping to repair the city (e.g., Scott and Katz-Fishman 2007). And so advocates and responders might support women's roles in building coalitions between organizations (community centers, churches, city/federal agencies) to help expand services and to reach more people. Natural disaster rebuilding efforts need to prioritize women's community leadership and representation; pulling women from underrepresented positions to the forefront of planning for future disasters.

ASSAULT MITIGATION AND HEALTHCARE

Domestic violence advocates should be included as routine emergency responders who are trained to reach out to and create easily accessible safe zones for women and their children. Rebuilding needs to prioritize the fixing of streetlights, implementation of emergency phones, and erection of diverse community triage centers. Policing agencies must consider distributing resources that focus not only on petty crime, but also on sexual and domestic assault. In the Superdome, for example, a careful evaluation of space and patrolling of dark corners and restrooms could have exponentially increased the safety of women and girls. In stressed situations, it is women who are asked to wait until other, "more important" issues are addressed, and thus it is women's immediate needs which are compromised. An active effort needs to be made to ensure that women's rights and safety are preserved.

State-funded healthcare for low-income residents should be prioritized in rebuilding efforts post-disaster. While triage centers sprung up to address urgent care issues, women's sexual and reproductive health went largely unaddressed by local and federal medical efforts. The unique health needs of pregnant, birthing, and postpartum women are particularly important, with these women needing easily accessable obstetric and gynecological care. Birth control and sanitary pads should be distributed to women, and made available in sexual and domestic assault triage centers. In the event of a disaster, women of childbearing age (particularly pregnant and post-partum women) need to be thought of as family caregivers within their larger family units. The distribution of resources to healthcare facilities, such as the Reproductive Health Assessment After Disaster (RHAD) toolkit, could help to assess and meet some women's health needs (Zotti and Williams 2011).

EMPLOYMENT AND CHILDCARE

In order to diminish the debilitating effects of disaster on families, the government should place caseworkers in shelters to provide job counseling and job placement support to single women who are heads of households. While women should be considered for higher-paying employment, such as construction, they should also receive skills education that makes them marketable in both the post-disaster economy as well as in other locations to which they might evacuate and rehome. Given the difficulty many single mothers face juggling work and family, easily accessible and free daycare should be a priority in local relief efforts. Agencies could establish or reestablish latchkey programs for after school so that some mothers can complete their evening shifts. And to help compensate for the gender pay gap and discrimination that especially low-income women of color face in getting jobs, the federal government might visit welfare policies to consider stipends for women who are supporting children, parents, and other kin. Many of these recommendations address long-standing issues that existed before the storm, but which are compounded in women's experiences and in the struggle to support entire families during disaster. Mentoring and job training that help residents to find better paying jobs could lead to safer and more resilient communities.

SOCIAL NETWORKS

Housing policies currently ignore non-nuclear family structures, but should account for the ways that housing locations determine public transportation, school districts, social networks, and job markets for women and their families. The Urban Land Institute proposed zoning the lowest lying areas of New Orleans for green spaces rather than rebuilding because of the risk of being destroyed by another storm (Henrici et al. 2012; Pardee 2012). This means destroying the homes of some of New Orleans's poorest residents, and of many single mothers. Promises to rebuild public housing in less risky areas of the city have not been upheld (Laska 2007) and social networks important to supporting families are dispersed. Pardee's (2014) work shows the importance women's local networks made in their survival before the storm, the likelihood they would evacuate, their ability to sustain evacuation, and their efforts to rebuild lives. At the same time, people reported being carelessly separated by military at the Superdome (Idakula 2007), and frontline community responders were not prepared with people databases to help connect family members who had evacuated (or been evacuated) to diverse cities (Weber and Peek 2012). The reestablishment of social networks via the careful study of local neighborhoods, community organizations, and churches might help us to better understand how these support networks operate and how they can be maintained during and after disaster.

CONCLUSION

In 1996, Sociologist Alice Fothergill wrote that women are underrepresented in disaster research, although gender dramatically and differently shapes the disaster experience for men and women. Taking a gender-neutral lens in studying and responding to disasters such as Hurricane Katrina results in inadequate management efforts that ignore the unique experiences of women, who disproportionately confront risk, have unique needs during disaster, are responsible for entire families, and are integral to rebuilding communities. It has been eighteen years since Fothergill wrote her article and ten years since Katrina swept across the Gulf of Mexico; yet, race and class continue to dominate sociological work on disaster and analyses of how gender shapes human experiences and responses to disaster fall to the wayside. We join gender sensitive disaster scholars in their call for researchers to analyze the race and class of disaster through a gendered lens. A purposeful effort to recover women's experiences from the margins can help scholars, emergency responders, and rebuilding strategists to better mitigate hierarchies of vulnerability, to mobilize women as agents of recovery, and to make sure women are no longer "missing in the storm."

NOTE

1. The vignettes in this chapter come from Barber's reflections on returning to New Orleans post–Hurricane Katrina.

II

Race and Class in the Recovery Process

Chapter Six

On the Kindness of Strangers

Am I More Worthy of Your Sympathy Than Lakisha and Jamal?

Jeannie Haubert

On August 27, 2005, I began my year-long journey of displacement. At the time, I thought it would be a three-day trip from coastal Mississippi to Northern Mississippi and I'd just come home to some broken windows. I had no idea that, when I finally was allowed to come home, it would be to an utterly demolished house that had floated off of its foundation and landed in another yard—mashed up against other apparently buoyant houses. The neighborhood was unrecognizable. The concrete entranceway that now led to nothing was half a block away from the shell of my house. The missing front wall revealed the mass destruction inside. Needless to say, I was homeless for a bit. The narrative below details my homeless story and my recovery as I tell it through a sociological lens that connects my recovery to my privileged social status. I tell this tale of privilege not to make myself feel good, because recognizing privilege does the opposite, but instead to call attention to how race and class continue to structure interactions in daily life in ways that channel important resources toward dominant groups and away from marginalized groups.

The outpouring of kindness and generosity following Hurricane Katrina was unprecedented and truly uplifting for survivors. Families and friends provided emotional support, shelter, and help rebuilding, but what was truly astounding was the assistance that complete strangers from around the country showered on those who were displaced. There are thousands of images of volunteers saving strangers with boats, tearing out moldy walls, constructing new homes, and feeding and sheltering the masses left homeless by Katrina. This aid was essential in filling in gaps left by inadequate planning and response at the local and federal levels of government. Americans were so moved to do something that shelters across the country had to turn away volunteers and donations because they were so overwhelmed with generosity. Americans, often stereotyped as solely self-interested, forcefully challenged that label in Katrina's aftermath as thousands sacrificed to help people they had never even met.

The personal narrative that follows will inevitably read as conflicted because I write it both as a hurricane survivor who is extremely grateful for the help so many of us received from benevolent strangers, but also as a sociologist who is concerned about the unequal recoveries of certain groups of Katrina survivors. Throughout this chapter, I contrast the Katrina stories I've read of working-class African Americans to mine as a white, middle-class survivor, but I also discuss intersecting inequalities and acknowledge the marginalization of other social groups such as Latinos, LGBT, and women. I argue that exchanges of sympathy and assistance post–Katrina were tainted by unfair assumptions about the biography of hurricane survivors which, in turn, impacts the ability of minority group members to recover at the same rate and to the same extent as those in privileged social categories.

As C. Wright Mills famously pointed out, the sociological imagination is a perspective that combines *history*, or social forces present at a particular historical moment, and *biography*, understood as an individual's personal experiences (Mills 1959). This chapter then is a reflection on my biography, given the larger social context. In what ways did my social position influence my experiences following the storm? In what ways did social position and the larger context matter for others? My central argument is that African Americans from New Orleans were assumed to have a deviant biography and were therefore afforded less sympathy and diminished access to key recovery resources freely given to white evacuees like myself. Admittedly, my personal narrative is not systematic evidence nor can it be said to be generalizable; however, post-disaster analyses rarely meet these criteria as large-scale data sets are unavailable and researchers more often rely on ground-up observations to build theory. Thus, I do not argue that my experience is representative of all similarly situated survivors, only that there are compelling reasons to believe that race matters in recovery as do other axes of oppression like class, sexual orientation, and sex.

This chapter is unique in that it is written from a place of social privilege whereas other post–Katrina researchers have, and rightfully so, highlighted the marginalized voices of poor racial minorities. Privilege narratives provide a useful counterpoint to the marginalization narratives, thereby enriching our understanding of post–Katrina recovery processes. Moreover, this discussion is unique in that I discuss the longer-term displacement period whereas most race scholars have focused on the inequalities evident prior to the storm and in its immediate wake (some excellent examples are Hartman and Squires 2006; Potter 2007; Bullard and Wright 2009). Lastly, this chapter differs from many racial analyses post–Katrina in that it focuses attention on everyday interactions rather than the organizational and institutional failures that disproportionately disadvantaged people of color on the Gulf Coast. Of course these larger-level analyses are indispensable, but micro level racial analyses are sparser and are also important in understanding the totality of experiences post–Katrina. Theoretically, the major contributions here are to show how 1) combining privilege narratives with discrimination narratives—two sides of the same coin—and 2) combining race theory with the sociology of emotions tells us much about race and racism in the twenty-first century.

SOCIOLOGICAL UNDERSTANDINGS OF SYMPATHY AND RACE

Candace Clark's work "Sympathy Biography and Sympathy Margins" (1987) is one of the most influential in the sociology of emotions and was among the first pieces of scholarship to explore sympathy interactions in depth. In her work, Clark outlines the unwritten rules for the exchange of sympathy between individuals. As with a bank account, individuals can make deposits when they give sympathy to others or withdrawals when they claim that they need sympathy in a given situation, and how much is in one's sympathy account at any given time—called his or her "sympathy margin." If an individual receives sympathy, for example after the death of a loved one, he or she is expected to repay that sympathy in a reciprocal manner should the original giver experience a loss. How much sympathy one can claim or one gives is largely a function of the depth of the relationship between the individuals; for example, one's boss may be less sympathetic to the death of a grandmother than one's best friend. It is also a function of how often one claims sympathy and whether those claims are deemed legitimate; for example, the boss may be less sympathetic if the employee has had to miss work for family emergency on multiple occasions in a short period of time. He or she may have been very sympathetic in the beginning, but what was once a wide sympathy margin can quickly become used up if an individual claims too much sympathy or breaks some of the other rules Clark outlines, such as not displaying gratitude for the sympathy given (Clark 1987).

As many Katrina evacuees found out, sympathy margins are also time delimited, meaning that individuals only have so much sympathy to give before our willingness to give becomes exhausted. In the case of Katrina, these depleted sympathy accounts became known as "Katrina fatigue," as individual volunteers and even whole communities hosting evacuees eventually grew tired of tending to the needs of Katrina evacuees. Volunteers reached a point after which they seemingly thought that evacuees were claiming sympathy for too long, that they should already have it together or have tried harder to improve their situation (Peek 2012). As Clark notes, "long-term problems, while they may be worth more sympathy, may call for greater emotional expenditures than others can or will put forth," meaning that those who do not recover "in a timely fashion" from disaster will find that sympathy simply runs out (Clark 1987, 305). Moreover, evacuees typically were strangers to the volunteers, meaning the depth of their relationship required very little display of sympathy in the first place. One would certainly be obligated to take in a family member or friend after a disaster, but volunteers who were helping were going above and beyond what was required with very little likelihood that they could ever call on evacuees for reciprocal sympathy if they should need it.

Clark focuses almost exclusively on relationships between friends, family, and acquaintances and makes little mention of race, class, gender, or sexuality; however, when strangers are involved, status in the social hierarchies matters. Social position matters because, in the absence of actual knowledge about an individual, people look for cues (manner of dress, skin color, accents, whether someone is in a wheelchair, etc.) to quickly size up strangers and more often than not, those in dominant groups are treated as individuals who are "down on their luck" whereas those in subordinate groups are often lumped together, negatively stereotyped, and blamed either for causing their plight or not recovering quickly enough.

A key component of Clark's theory is that sympathy margins are influenced by one's "sympathy biography" or record of past adherence to sympathy rules. 1. Has he/she made unwarranted claims to sympathy in the past? For example, I had a student once who wanted out of a test because of allergies. When I explained that the girl on chemo showed up for the test, he quickly repealed his sympathy claim. 2. Has he/she claimed *too much* sympathy in the past or accepted sympathy too readily? Everyone has an overly dramatic friend for example who seems to have a new crisis every week. This concept of sympathy biography, one's record of past sympathy claims, makes sense between friends or acquaintances that have a relationship history, but strangers have no insight as to an individual's sympathy biography. I argue instead that in the case of strangers, group position is used as an indicator of one's sympathy biography. For example, homeless children are afforded more sympathy than working-age adults or the elderly. Women with a flat tire are given assistance more often than men. Someone with a visible disability may receive more accommodations in the workplace more readily than someone with a less visible disability like post-traumatic stress disorder (PTSD). In the absence of truly knowing an individual, we fill in the gaps for what we don't know about the individual by relying on assumptions about race, ethnicity, class, gender, disability, age, religion, or sexual orientation (group position). Strangers are forced to make a split-second decision on whether or not to give sympathy. In deciding, he/she will weigh 1. whether the plight seemingly warrants sympathy—in the case of Katrina there was no doubt that sympathy was warranted 2. the other's complicity in the plight—those who didn't evacuate were sometimes blamed or afforded less sympathy for not getting themselves out of harm's way, and 3. the moral worth of the other—meaning is he/she a good person. The last two, as I will explain, are where race and class come in.

Most sociologists who study race conceptualize racism not simply as prejudice based on the skin color of an individual, but instead as a sense of group position (Blumer 1958). Often, this is said to encompass perceived competition for scarce resources (Bobo and Hutchings 1996). These more sociological understanding of race view it as a socially constructed category that funnels opportunities and resources toward dominant groups while denying access to subordinate groups. By extension, racism is not an individual pathology or even a collection of bigoted individuals; rather it is a system of power, a set of norms and practices that support the existing social hierarchy. In this view, race is less about biology and more about social norms. Racism is found "in behavior as well as in attitudes and in culturally and economically produced systems of advantage and exclusion that generate privilege for one racially defined group at the expense of another" (Brown et al. 2003, 43). Importantly, this "sense of group position" view also means that racial understandings are dynamic rather than fixed. In other words, they can vary from place to place and over time meaning, for example, that understandings of what it means to be black in New Orleans (or black and from New Orleans) may be somewhat different than what it means to be black in California.

Interestingly, Clark barely mentions social status or group position as defining features of sympathy exchange. In a quick side note, Clark mentions that, "perhaps the middle class elicit more (sympathy) than either the wealthy or the destitute" (1987, 298), but she never mentions race. To her credit, Clark admits that space does not allow her to focus on *all* of the factors that affect sympathy exchange and she calls for more research, saying, "a multitude of such norms await further empirical specification" (1987, 298). Admittedly, Clark accomplishes a lot in her thirty-three pages, but her omission of race is glaring, leaving much room for theoretical development particularly as we expand beyond exchanges between intimates. In the stories below, strangers assumed that I, a middle-class white Katrina survivor, was worthy of sympathy and afforded me a wider sympathy margin than others. As the stories show, this advantage translated into key resources that led to a relatively speedy personal recovery.

OLIVE BRANCH, MISSISSIPPI: VICTIM-BLAMING POST–KATRINA

"New Orleans was a sin-filled city. God gave 'em what they had coming" said the innkeeper unapologetically. So much for extending an "olive branch" to those in need! Stunned is the only way to describe the look on our faces as she said this to the seven of us who had just evacuated together from New Orleans, LA, Pass Christian, MS, and Long Beach, MS, two days before. We had just learned that the levees had breached in the "city that care forgot" and we were already mourning what we knew would be a tremendous loss of life. Upon seeing our faces, the innkeeper backtracked a little explaining that, "of course there were some good people, but overall, that city was asking for the wrath of God with all of the gays and prostitution and sin going on there." We were appalled at her cold view of our neighbors. Needless to say, we only spent a couple of days in Olive Branch and avoided that innkeeper like the plague. We talked to people who had stayed to operate shelters in our towns and quickly learned of the total devastation of not just our homes, but our entire towns and workplaces. We also learned that we would not be allowed back in for a while, and the bill from that inn was adding up. We cried, but also counted our blessings as we knew others who hadn't gotten out and were suffering physically in a way that we were not. We watched as much news as we could stomach until we had to turn it off. To distract ourselves, we played board games, and told funny stories from the past as we tried to enjoy each other's company. We cooked and ate all of the food we had pulled from our freezers so it wouldn't go bad. We ate like kings and drank a good bit too. But reality was there waiting for us, it was time for a new plan.

Clark's research on sympathy says little about social status and nothing about heterosexism or prejudice, but she does discuss victim-blaming. Victim-blaming encompasses a belief that the victim was responsible for bringing about their plight; therefore, they are not deemed worthy of sympathy (1987). If, for example, a man was drinking and driving and got in a car accident he would be afforded less sympathy than someone who was hit by a drunk driver. Unfortunately, the victim-blaming displayed by the innkeeper was not isolated. In the days and weeks after the storm, there was a good bit of dinner table and media chatter about the idiocy of those who "chose" not to evacuate. The assumption that they were just too headstrong to leave reduced the sympathy margins of those who stayed as they were assumed to be at least partially responsible for their plight. But it wasn't idiocy that kept so many people from evacuating. As numerous social scientists have documented, for most, it was social class. It was much less about *choice* than about barriers to evacuation such as lack of transportation, lack of funds for costly evacuation expenses, and the concentrated social networks of the poor that left them nowhere to go (powell et al. 2006; Haney et al. 2010; Barnshaw and Trainor 2010; Fussell 2012). Shortly after Katrina, Jones-Deweever and Hartmann succinctly described the reality of poverty in words worth reiterating:

> For many, being poor means being trapped in failing school districts, unable to ensure a quality education and thus a way out for their children. It means being relegated to a place where no one else wants to live, isolated, and disjointed from the rest of society . . . in New Orleans that meant being trapped on low ground. . . . Poverty means frequently juggling [pressing expenses] because there is simply not enough to fulfill every need. That is the reality of poverty in America, a reality that has become increasingly difficult to escape. (2006, 87)

In other words, being poor, as more than a quarter of New Orleanians were, means sometimes having to choose between food in your stomach or evacuating for a *potential* hurricane hit, one of many such threats that come each year. This is really no choice at all; yet the dominant narrative post–Katrina framed evacuation as a decision smart people made. Rather than viewing the poor as trapped in failing schools, isolated from decent jobs, transportation, and quality neighborhoods, Americans are quick to assume that poverty, especially black poverty, is instead attributable to a poor work ethic and frivolous spending habits—in other words, that these folks are to blame for their situation. The reality however is that, in America, one can work a full-time job and still fall below the poverty line and that race and gender correlate with earnings. For example, black women working full-time earned an average annual income of only $19,400 in Louisiana and $19,900 in Mississippi—right at the poverty line for a family of four in 2005 and below it for 2006.[1] In contrast, the median earnings for white women in the same areas were roughly $6,000 higher, but still well below those of white men.[2] The individualistic perspective of poverty ignores important social forces that constrain both opportunity and choice, and it is just as shortsighted when used to explain how the middle and upper classes made "the right choice" to leave.

Let's consider for a moment how social class impacted my evacuation story. Jason, (my husband at the time) and I lost everything. That was related to the fact that we bought a home in a racially integrated, working-class neighborhood that, not coincidentally, was in a flood zone. Beyond Katrina's physical impact, it is clear that the picture I paint above of my first few days post–Katrina starkly contrasts with the images on televisions across the country of thousands of people trapped in the Superdome and Morial Convention Center. The irony in the name of Olive Branch, Mississippi, was not lost on us, but we also knew that our ability to evacuate to Olive Branch in the first place was influenced by our "good jobs," which gave us sufficient funds for travel and weekends off (Katrina hit over the weekend). Moreover, consistent access to the Internet meant that we had no trouble finding a place that would allow us to bring our pets and pretend that this trip was a little get away with friends.

In 2004, one in five men and one in four women in the city of New Orleans lived below the poverty line (Jones-DeWeever and Hartmann 2006). For black women, one in three lived below the poverty line and their increased likelihood of being poor extended well beyond the city boundaries. Access to personal transportation was limited in New Orleans, yet there were no citywide plans to evacuate those without transportation (Haney et al. 2010). Shelters were the only option for the poorest residents. Thus a car and discretionary travel funds, time off work, and the ability to quickly find suitable accommodations were luxuries that a large proportion of people in New Orleans and along the Gulf Coast could not afford.

To the untrained eye, it may have seemed ridiculous that those "stubborn people in New Orleans" stayed only to be trapped on roofs and in the Superdome and convention center. And yes, there were some who thought themselves invincible after surviving storm season after storm season, there were many who were fatigued from a number of costly false alarms the year before, and others simply waited too long to leave and got caught in gridlock. But for a great many, the costs of leaving were simply too high. Evacuation was not an option.

Most people said to me in response to my evacuation story, "Oh, you were so lucky to have gotten out beforehand," but luck had very little to do with it. My household's social class—defined as occupation, assets, and education—was what got us, our friends, and our pets out. Our social class helped us live in relative comfort while we tried to figure out what to do next. And those who did not evacuate were no more deserving of their plight than I was lucky.

SHREVEPORT, LOUISIANA: RACE AS SOCIAL CAPITAL

We came to the realization a few days after Katrina that we were going to need longer-term accommodations. We could have either headed to Shreveport to stay with Grandpa or Charlotte to stay with Mom. Shreveport was closer and we wanted to be ready to go when we were allowed back. In Shreveport, we stayed in the relative comfort of a family member's home for two weeks with our own room, Internet access, electricity, and we were spoiled by frequent dinners out. Of course Grandpa still had trouble comprehending the enormity of the disaster and wanted to know why we didn't have any dress-up clothes for synagogue. Are you kidding, Grandpa? But we simply went shopping for new clothes, which I would have needed anyway after all of this eating out! It did get expensive to buy all new stuff and it did put some strain on our finances to be on this "involuntary vacation," but in the end, we were able to absorb those rebuilding costs and the fact that he let us stay rent-free for as long as we needed helped a lot.

Bourdieu (1986) conceptualized social capital as relationship ties that can facilitate upward mobility. Certainly all people have relationship ties, but the strength of those ties in facilitating upward mobility (or in this case, basic stability) is not equal. On the Gulf Coast and in New Orleans in particular, those of higher social class were much more likely to have family and friends who lived outside the disaster zone and who had considerable resources to share. In contrast, the poor in particular in New Orleans tended to have more concentrated social networks. Most of the poor and working class in the affected areas had lived there for generations and knew very few people outside of the disaster-affected area (Haney et al. 2010; Barnshaw and Trainor 2010; Fussell 2012).

As Katrina research has clearly demonstrated, African Americans with concentrated social networks were less likely to be able to evacuate, were more likely to die, and were more likely to have family and friends that were similarly devastated by the storm, thereby severely limiting the value of those ties in helping them recover (Bevc et al. 2010). Katrina's impact on African Americans was disproportionate in terms of displacement and the emotional, physical, and financial toll in the immediate aftermath (Haney et al. 2010),[3] but recovery has also been stratified by race and class. Having family and friends to lean on outside of the disaster zone made meeting one's basic needs easier, made finding a new place to live, getting a job, and getting "back on ones feet" easier. Race does not "determine" social networks as there were middle-class African Americans who had family outside of the disaster zone and were able to recover quickly, but the close interconnection between race and class on the Gulf Coast meant that African Americans were more likely to be poor, socially isolated, and have social networks filled with people in a similar economic position and concentrated on the Gulf Coast. This means that, on average, African Americans were less likely to be able to transform social networks into recovery resources, and when they did, those networks could only take them so far (Fussell 2012).

For example, in *Displaced: Life in the Katrina Diaspora*, Jaquelyn Litt (2012) tells the story of a mother in Baton Rouge who took fifty-four evacuees into her two-bedroom home, most of them strangers to her, while she and her husband slept on the floor. Neighbors never complained and, in fact, some, having nothing else to give, gave their food stamps to help her feed the massive group. So it is not that poor folks did not receive help; the literature shows that they did, but they often received help from volunteer institutions (i.e., churches, emergency shelters, etc.) or from similarly situated others who also had limited means. Volunteer institutions were necessarily short-term remedies and, as I will discuss later, Katrina evacuees needed recovery assistance for longer than volunteers were able to give.

Housing wasn't the only thing I got for free in Shreveport. It was my interactions with strangers that I remember most from this part of my Katrina story. I was not charged for haircuts, and multiple dinners were "comped" by owners of small family businesses all because the Katrina tragedy had stirred complete strangers to help in any way they could. Sadly, it was from those same benevolent strangers that I heard the most prejudiced remarks. The hairdresser confessed to me (with her black coworker not too far away) that she was probably going to have to move out of Shreveport because of the racial transition in the town. She said that the mall where she grew up had already "turned dark" and that things were sure to get worse now after Katrina. She might go to West Virginia. "They have pretty much only whites there." Days later, the owner of a local restaurant took care of the bill for our table upon learning that we were evacuees, but then he began to editorialize about Katrina. He explained that he was not racist, but there was a difference between "regular black people" and the (N-words) coming out of New Orleans. Wow. Just wow. These people had been through exactly what I had been through . . . well not exactly, many were not able to evacuate and suffered tremendous discomfort and witnessed atrocities in person that I only had to watch on TV. But they were like me. They were my neighbors from the Gulf Coast who had just been through a horrific and traumatizing ordeal. How dare he call them that! How dare that hairdresser say what she did! They didn't know anything about them, but they didn't have to. Their skin color and the fact that they were from New Orleans meant that they must be thugs, criminals, immoral and unsavory elements, while my skin color signaled to him that I was worth helping. I was heartbroken and utterly disgusted.

By this time, the media had done a great job of distorting what was happening in the city with a sensationalistic and racialized focus on looters, violence, and gang activity (Dynes and Rodríguez 2010). For white evacuees like me, skin color plus evacuee status became a form of social capital that could be cashed in for tangible resources and services. For black evacuees, there was an initial burst of sympathy, but the reception in communities that received large numbers of evacuees changed quickly from welcome to mistrust and sometimes to hostility (Miller 2012; Peek 2012; Weber 2012). These changing contexts were found not only in Louisiana, Texas, and South Carolina, but in Denver too, confirming that these reactions to evacuees were not attributable to the default stereotype of a "backward" South. In fact, some Denver evacuees noted that they were more accustomed to "southern style racism because it was more obvious than the more covert, but still damaging discrimination that they suffered there" (Peek 2012, 36). Black evacuees who had been sheltered in Denver reported numerous encounters with individuals who, "assumed they were violent, illiterate, poor, engaged in criminal activities, or were abusing drugs. These are stereotypes that African Americans regularly face during non-disaster times, of course, but the evacuees believed that their status as victims of Katrina and former residents of New Orleans led to additional resentment and mistrust" (Peek 2012, 36). As a result, black evacuees reported bullying in schools, workplace discrimination, harassment from neighbors who wanted them to leave, and social and residential isolation (Peek 2012; Weber 2012). All of this was a result of the stereotypes associated with poor blacks who would somehow contaminate these "perfect" places. These negative reactions were detrimental not only to their physical and emotional health, but also compromised their ability to find stable housing and employment.[4]

GULF SHORES, ALABAMA: TESTING THE SYMPATHY MARGINS FOR KATRINA EVACUEES

Grandpa would have housed us for much longer I'm sure, but we didn't like being a burden on family. And frankly, having this Depression-era guy follow us around the house to switch off lights and lecture us about electricity usage got a little old, as did that funky thick coffee he would make and leave sitting in the pot for a week! Bless his heart. The overt prejudice I was assumed to share due to my skin color had really soured me on Shreveport, too. We began searching for a place to start over . . . on our own. Again, I hit the vacation websites that I'd made it my hobby to peruse. I went to VRBO (vacation rentals by owner) because my obsessive vacation searching on the Internet in my spare time had taught me that those were fully furnished and were often cheaper than going through a rental agency. To my delight, I discovered that many owners were offering a "Katrina discount" to any evacuees in need. There were hundreds of discount housing offers for Katrina evacuees. Score! I contacted a woman with a gorgeous place in Arizona just because Arizona seemed cool and hey, being shut out of my town and my university, I had nowhere else to be. I also contacted a couple in Gulf Shores, Alabama, with a condo walking distance from the beach. I told each that my home had been demolished by Katrina and that I was staying with family, but that it was wearing thin. To my surprise, both offered their fully furnished homes to me for FREE for as long as I needed. The one in Arizona was stunning and had even been featured on the cover of a travel magazine! The one in Gulf Shores was also lovely. It was a two-story condo two blocks from the beach with a washer/dryer, full kitchen, and beautiful beach decor. Gulf

Shores was closer and it made sense to be ready if and when school and/or work reopened, so we headed to Alabama and stayed there for a month and a half, rent-free. Under any other circumstances, that rental would have cost us $1,500 a week. It was not just physical comfort that place provided. It gave us a chance to get ourselves together, to figure out our next move. We didn't know when Tulane would reopen. We didn't know if we'd rebuild in Mississippi or relocate. We needed time for the dust to settle and that is what this Alabama couple's gift gave us. They gave us time in a comfortable and beautiful setting which made it admittedly easier to forget for five minutes all of the loss and upheaval we were experiencing. As my stepfather put it when he came for a visit in Gulf Shores, "You do homeless really well!"

Readers of this chapter, now several pages in, may find themselves wondering, who are Lakisha and Jamal? They are in the title, so where are they in this story? Well, they are not physically in this story, but they were in my head quite a bit during this time. Lakisha and Jamal are the names from a 2004 field experiment in which fictitious resumes were sent in response to want ads to test for racial discrimination in hiring (Bertrand and Mullainathan 2004). In this experiment, all other variables on the resume were held constant so that only the names of the applicants varied. "Are Emily and Greg more Employable Than Lakisha and Jamal: A Field Experiment on Labor Market Discrimination" was published in the *American Economic Review* and according to Google Scholar had been cited 1,646 times at the time of this writing, meaning that this is an article of tremendous importance in both race and economic studies. Its viral impact is attributable to the authors' disturbing findings that white-sounding names receive 50 percent more callbacks for interviews than black-sounding names. This heartbreaking finding confirmed what black parents all across the country have been telling their children for decades now, that "you have to work twice as hard to be just as good," as black applicants would have to send out twice as many applications as their equally qualified white counterparts to acquire the same number of interviews. In their study, this gap held across industry, employer-size and occupation providing irrefutable evidence that race still affects opportunities in employment. Might the same be true in housing?

Upon receiving multiple offers for free luxury housing, I had to wonder, what if my email had been signed by Lakisha and not Jeannie? Consequently, I began an investigation to find out if race was affecting opportunities for housing for black evacuees. Findings revealed that a website sponsored—but apparently not screened—by FEMA and the Red Cross did contain racially discriminatory ads, the overt nature of which was truly astonishing (Weil 2007b). The proportion of discriminatory ads was thankfully quite small, but the overt racism in the ones that did discriminate was telling as these examples from the website demonstrate:

1. "Due to the town we live in it has to be a white couple or a white single mom with no more than two children. We live near schools and I am also a nurse." (Urania, LA)
2. "We are a rural family of five and have limited rooms available; however we have a spacious home and could partition off areas. We can provide possible job opportunities and transportation. We would prefer a middle class white family." (Jasper, AL)
3. "We do have a 32-foot motor home equipped with all adminities such as fridge, ac, shower, bathroom one full size bed and two single beds, closet space etc. . . . We do apologize but we are requesting only white or Chinese families. Sorry." (type-os unedited; Kansas City, MO)

I also found evidence of religious "must be Christian" and heterosexist "sorry but no gays" discrimination. Determined to get these revealing findings beyond academic circles, I contacted the *New York Times* and several television shows, but couldn't get a return call despite the rare "smoking gun" that I had found. I did however get the attention of James Perry at the Greater New Orleans Fair Housing Center who subsequently filed complaints with the U.S. Department of Housing and Urban Development against the five websites and presented an expanded version of the data before Congress.

Clearly race and class privilege allowed me access to key recovery resources that were being denied to others. In contrast to the suspicious-eye Lakisha and Jamal may have been greeted with, I was viewed as what Clark would call a "sympathetic character," a good/respectable person who had obviously fallen on hard times. To make matters worse, there is some evidence that these privileges also extended beyond free housing offers to the rental housing market. For example, Latino renters in Mississippi following the hurricane were significantly more likely than Anglos to be required to pay for and complete credit and criminal background checks before being permitted to rent an available unit (Weil 2010).

MOBILE, ALABAMA: THE IMPORTANCE OF RACE AND CLASS IN THE RENTAL HOUSING MARKET

We didn't want to overstay our welcome in Gulf Shores. By October 2005, we knew more from our workplaces about when we could go back and the search for rental housing began. I was done with my Tulane coursework so I was able to teach as a visiting instructor at Tulane's satellite campus in Biloxi. Still, so much housing had been destroyed. The closest we could find to our jobs in Biloxi was a small rental in Mobile, Alabama, roughly an hour and a half away. We signed papers for the town of Pass Christian to bulldoze our Katrina-damaged home and we attempted to start fresh.

Prices were crazy and you had to be fast! A two-bedroom apartment that would have cost $600 before Katrina easily went for $1,000 or more at that time. And even at those inflated prices, available units were gone as soon as the paper came out. For one house, we called at 8 a.m. for a rental ad that had just been placed that morning. It was already rented, so we moved our search to craigslist.com. When we found an available cottage that would allow dogs and had a small fenced yard, we bent over backwards to get it! We agreed to $750/month with a $750 deposit and a $750 pet deposit ($375 refundable). To seal the deal, we paid seven months up-front, a whopping total of $6,750 at once.

With so many evacuees added to the rental market and clamoring for a few available units, rental agents or homeowners (the vast majority of whom were white) could and did exercise preferences (Weil 2010) and middle- and upper-class evacuees used financial capital to acquire housing. Even if racial discrimination was non-existent, prices in the post–Katrina market were exorbitant, more than twice the pre-Katrina rentals during this time period (Weil 2010). While one might argue that this was simply supply and demand capitalism, the media portrayals equating New Orleans's blacks with both poverty and criminality meant that housing was necessarily more difficult for black evacuees to come by (see Haubert, chapter 11 in this volume). As a result, many remained in shelters for an extended period of time; however, the welcome quickly wore thin. Around the time I would have been outbidding the competition in Mobile, sympathy for shelter occupants was already waning (Peek 2012; Miller 2012). Within only three weeks of their arrival, those in shelters began to be seen as a dependent population who were not interested in standing up on their own two feet. Moreover, there were some racial minorities who were excluded even from emergency shelters, such as when Latino Katrina victims were denied access to Red Cross shelters because they were wrongly assumed to be workers who had arrived to the area to take advantage of the cleanup work (Weil 2009). Thus, for racial minorities, finding stable housing—an important first step in recovery—likely took longer and America's feelings of goodwill were time-delimited, leaving many non-white survivors without housing or sympathy for their plight. The second step—finding a steady source of income—was not much easier.

ROCK HILL, SOUTH CAROLINA: KATRINA SURVIVORS ON THE JOB MARKET

In the fall of 2006, one year after Katrina, I started my first full-time teaching job at Winthrop University in Rock Hill. We bought a home and filled it with all new furniture. The location was perfect. My parents were preparing to retire and were a short thirty-minute drive away in Charlotte, NC. The long journey of displacement that began years earlier had ended. We had settled.

Now I will admit to a little bit of luck in Rock Hill. It just so happened that a university near where I grew up was beginning a hiring search in fall 2005, and I just happened to see the job posting as I was trying to figure out my next move. I wasn't planning to go on the job market yet, but I did want desperately to finish my PhD and I needed a year of student teaching as part of the degree. In September 2005, I emailed Winthrop's chair and asked if I could help them out with a course while they were searching for a new hire. The fall courses had begun so he didn't need me that semester, but he encouraged me to apply for the vacancy. Focused on completing my requirement and assuming he was just being nice, I ignored him and went about my search for another student teaching opportunity. When months had gone by and I still had not applied, he sent me another email to encourage me to submit an application. I did apply and I got the job.

For many viewing Katrina from the outside, successful disaster recovery meant getting a job and when evacuees did not get one in what outsiders saw as an appropriate amount of time, frustration set in (Peek 2012; Miller 2012). For example, Lori Peek quotes a social worker who directed the Katrina long-term recovery program in Denver. This social worker says, "It's not Coloradans that were affected, it was people from Louisiana and Mississippi. So I think on a community level, what we've seen a lot of is: 'Isn't that over yet?' 'Haven't you moved on?' 'Do you have a job?'" (2012, 34). Of her study of volunteers in Huntsville, Texas, Lee Miller says, "Recipients of disaster assistance were supposed to leave the system and become self-sufficient. Locally, responders and volunteers assumed that evacuees would either return to New Orleans or get back on their feet and become autonomous residents. When neither of those outcomes seemed possible, people were encouraged to go elsewhere" (2012, 115–16). Why didn't either of those outcomes seem possible? Because 1. research has shown that the rebuilding of New Orleans provided little access to affordable housing and other necessary amenities that would enable evacuees of lower socioeconomic status to return (Crowley 2006) and 2. because people of color, who face discrimination in hiring processes and acquiring housing under normal circumstances, were doubly stigmatized post–Katrina as race and place stereotypes combined to the exclusion of this particular group (Peek 2012).[5]

Interviews with black New Orleanians post–Katrina revealed that they learned to hide their evacuee status on the job market (Peek 2012). While white evacuees living outside the South also struggled with negative stereotypes of Southerners, black evacuees faced the added layer of racial discrimination. Black survivors reported being told there were no open positions while "We're Hiring" signs sat in store windows, and they spoke of shaking hands with potential employers only to have them wipe their hands on their clothes afterwards.[6] Whereas being hired in my trained occupation a year after Katrina signaled the last step in displacement and recovery to me, other researchers note that the typical Katrina recovery cycle stalled in the search for housing phase and that the search for stability was still ongoing as late as the fall of 2008 (Miller 2012, 116).

I personally did not encounter this so-called Katrina-fatigue and perhaps it was because my race and class privilege allowed me to garner some key recovery resources before the Katrina-fatigue set in, or perhaps it's that I was permitted a wider sympathy margin in the first place. Did sympathy for my plight as a Katrina survivor help me land this job and reach that final stage? I'm not sure. It may have. Thousands of people wanted to help post–Katrina any way they could, and in weighing one qualified candidate over the other, this hiring committee could certainly feel good about doing their small part to help a Katrina victim, and it *was* a big help. At the very least, my unusual story certainly made me stand out from the other applicants and gave me a reason to email the chair. Sometimes those intangibles give an applicant an important edge in even getting to the interview stage. I certainly never felt I had to hide my status as a hurricane victim, and that in itself may be a manifestation of racial privilege given the very different stories evacuees in Texas told (Peek 2012). And rather than disadvantaging me on the job market, my evacuee status, combined with class privilege and social networks, allowed me to transform my Katrina disaster into scholarship, tenure, promotion, and even this book.

CONCLUSION: RACE AND SYMPATHY MARGINS

Although the destruction of both my home and entire coastal town represents a worst-case scenario in terms of property-loss, my recovery story represents a best case scenario—one in which privileged social status played a key role. Even in this best-case scenario, recovery in terms of full housing and employment stability took a year. For most Katrina survivors, it is taking much longer, and this chapter provides some clues as to why. While I was afforded sympathy and lent helping hands throughout my five-city journey, black survivors who were initially shown sympathy saw it dwindle and shift to feelings of hostility surrounding their slower recovery.

Clark says that, whether individuals are afforded sympathy, "can make the difference between getting fired and not getting fired, between going to prison and going free" (1987, 300). For Katrina evacuees, it meant either being seen as a looter or as a survivor gathering needed supplies (Dynes and Rodríguez 2010). It meant being seen as a "sympathetic character" that shouldn't be charged for services immediately following a disaster, or as an invader who could threaten the stability of the community. It meant offers to "work with" potential renters on exorbitant housing costs, or being subject to a criminal background and credit check (Weil 2010). It meant being encouraged to apply for a job or being steered away.

Sympathy exchange between strangers is entirely dependent on social statuses. Based on their real or perceived social statuses, individuals are assessed in terms of their respectability or moral worth. Particularly important in acquiring a wide sympathy margin are assumptions about respectability in work and family. Long periods of unemployment in particular can drain sympathy accounts (Clark 1987, 303). This can disproportionately impact African Americans who are overrepresented in terms of single parent households and who experience higher rates and lengthier periods of unemployment. Even though more whites are on government assistance than African Americans, black women in particular are often labeled with the negative stereotype of welfare queens—a slight to the morality of both their work and family statuses. African American men from New Orleans were assumed to engage in criminality rather than traditional employment, further reducing sympathy margins for this group when all are lumped together.

In the case of Katrina, black and from New Orleans signaled "poor, deviant, and system dependent" individuals, negatively impacting sympathy margins. Unfair media portrayals reinforced this pre-existing stereotype and heightened fears, but media cannot shoulder all of the blame as the narrative they brought to the public about African Americans post–Katrina resonated with the pre-existing stereotypes of race in this country and therefore largely went unquestioned (Dynes and Rodríguez 2010). White Katrina survivors, on the other hand, were assumed to be worthy of sympathy. We were not viewed as abusers of the system and therefore were not necessarily assumed to be poor (even though many white evacuees were poor), were not thought to have been responsible for our predicament, and were not assumed to have criminal tendencies as demonstrated by strangers' willingness to open up their homes. Instead, we were assumed to have respectable family and work histories that just so happened to be disrupted by a massive disaster.

Americans are generally critiqued for being self-involved, apathetic, aloof, and greedy. There are cases in which that label may be deserved, but Katrina showed a very different side, an America that was truly moved to action. Many gave freely of their time and possessions to help, some for quite a long time. While the grassroots response was arguably more effective than the local and federal governments' responses, racial discourses structured who was deemed worthy of help and for how long. As a nation we showed generosity, selflessness, and compassion after Katrina, but we must be ever vigilant not to let cultural assumptions about race taint our good works. The cultural messages Americans are sent daily about race—via movies, TV shows, news, song lyrics, music videos, and other cultural outlets—write the script for us on how we are to judge the moral worth of various groups. We must recognize that marginalized groups typically have a negative biography unfairly ascribed to them simply because of the social category they happen to fall into. We as individuals have a choice to blindly follow that cultural script *or* to question it and push back against it, as did the homeowner who advertised this free Katrina housing: "We are a white family with 3 kids. 5, 3, and 9mos looking to open our home and our hearts to a black family, any kind, preferably with kids. We want to teach our kids that love is colorblind" (Weil 2007b). In a subsequent phone interview, the woman who placed this ad clarified that she made this targeted offer because she felt that black people had been portrayed so negatively in the media and she thought they might be having a harder time finding housing as a result. As we make ourselves more racially conscious and we act as this homeowner did, we *change* the racial script slightly and encourage others to do the same. Such acts of resistance can and do alter the structure of race in America and help us work toward a world where, in times of crisis, Lakisha and Jamal receive just as many helping hands.

NOTES

1. Ibid.
2. Ibid.
3. Ibid.
4. Ibid.
5. For more on labor market discrimination under normal circumstances, see Kirschenmen and Neckerman (1991); Moss and Tilly (1996); and Bertrand and Mullainathan (2004) as a few examples.
6. Ibid.

Chapter Seven

Disaster, Reconstruction, and Racialization

Latinos in New Orleans after Hurricane Katrina

Elizabeth Fussell and Amy Bellone-Hite

Elizabeth Fussell: Hurricane Katrina sent my research, and my life, on a detour. I shifted from studying the factors pushing migrants to the United States from Latin America to studying the economic, social, and political forces pulling Latin American migrants to New Orleans. Watching these migratory dynamics unfold in people's lives was intellectually challenging and emotionally wrenching. At the same time, these dynamics were playing out in my own life and my family and I decided that New Orleans was not the best home for us (Fussell 2008). I've returned to New Orleans every summer since leaving in 2007 to continue my research, and Amy and I have had occasion to share our observations over that time. Now, almost a decade after the disaster, I see Hurricane Katrina's impact on New Orleans as a model of how climate-related disasters may impact major urban areas. This is a major concern as climate change science predicts more intense and frequent coastal storms, and my "Katrina detour" provides me with insight on how climate change may impact societies.

Amy Bellone-Hite: Prior to Hurricane Katrina, I studied impacts of rapid change on Amazon Basin boomtowns. In one case, I examined how economic crisis resulted in a massive relocation of former Bolivian tin miners to a small frontier town, creating a massive population boom for which the host city was ill-equipped. In another case, I studied how Venezuela's state-led development policies during its oil-boom had led coastal, cosmopolitan Venezuelans inland to massive state-owned basic metals industries, and how a reversal of these policies later dismantled these industries through privatiza-

tion. In both cases, the state shaped populations' responses to crises. Little did I know that New Orleans would be another example of an external shock leading to rapid population shifts and alterations of the city's social and economic fabric. Katrina offered a new, much more personal lens for my research; not only was New Orleans my adopted hometown, but it was my own nation's response and, as Beth mentions above, one we should not expect to be anomalistic given climate change's impacts.

Well before Hurricane Katrina's landfall, the mosaic of North and South American, African, and European cultures that made New Orleans a cosmopolitan city in the eighteenth and nineteenth centuries had faded into the black-white dichotomy typical of Southern cities in the United States. New Orleans was not among the "new destinations" for Latino and Latina immigrants in the late twentieth century (Zuñiga and Hernández-León 2005). It had a small Central American and Caribbean population that included immigrants and their descendants, with diverse social class backgrounds and levels of acculturation, settled throughout the metropolitan area. Hurricane Katrina changed this cultural landscape by creating a construction boom that attracted tens of thousands of workers, many of whom were unauthorized Latin American immigrants (Donato et al. 2007; Fussell and Elliott 2009; Fussell 2009a; Trujillo-Pagan 2007). Teaching at Tulane and Xavier Universities with specializations in the Sociology of Latin America, we were each compelled to study these Latin American immigrants as they arrived to a New Orleans in recovery and in social flux.

Initially, the media and the public speculated about how the Latino immigrants would be received in this majority African American city, particularly since most observers expected members of both groups to compete for the plentiful construction jobs. Newspaper and television headlines stated "Hispanics rush in to rebuild New Orleans; fears raised about city's makeup" (Taylor 2006) and "Big Easy uneasy about migrant wave" (Martinez 2005). In a highly publicized meeting with business leaders in October 2005, Mayor C. Ray Nagin stated, "How do I ensure that New Orleans is not overrun by Mexican workers?" although he later clarified that he only meant that New Orleans residents should be hired first (Campo-Flores 2005). In the year after the disaster, each of us received press inquiries from highly regarded national journalists wanting expert commentary confirming heightened racial tensions in our city. Without empirical support for this narrative, neither of us commented. For the media, New Orleans was an opportunity to hash out the American publics' anxiety about immigration and race relations between African Americans and Latinos, which was especially acute as Congress was debating, and failing to find consensus, on comprehensive immigration reform.

Interest was local as well. After Tulane and Xavier Universities reopened in January 2006, returning students sought out our classes and began research projects focused on studying the workers. Such research always required face-to-face interviews since there were few data sources about New Orleans's population as a whole, much less this highly mobile segment. Despite the many demands facing us at work and home as we coped with life after a disaster, we joined our students in the field, conducting interviews on worksites, day labor pick-up sites, bars, churches, or any public gathering place. It was difficult to interview these men and women who were working extremely long hours doing difficult and dangerous work and using their time off to recuperate for the next days' work. Soon, advocates established medical and legal clinics, workers' rights groups, and even discussion groups to promote intergroup understanding for the workers, especially the unauthorized immigrants and day laborers who were subject to employer abuse and criminal victimization. These organizations also provided research sites for studying the arrival and reception of Latino and Latina immigrants in post–Katrina New Orleans. Using both systematic data collection and circumstantial observation, we investigated the labor and living conditions of the Latin American immigrants in New Orleans.

In this chapter, we reflect on what we have learned about the arrival of the Latino population and their reception by non-Hispanic residents that we have observed over the last decade. First, we describe the disaster and the governments' and construction industries' responses. We go on to argue that the structural conditions established in the immediate aftermath of the disaster produced a rapid response labor force, the bulk of which was working-age Latino men present in the country without authorization. We discuss research documenting the dirty, dangerous, and demeaning jobs that were essential to cleaning up the city that were well remunerated compared to what they could earn in other places in the United States or their home countries. Then, we discuss how these conditions combined with the slow recovery of the affordable housing market and the prolonged displacement of African American and low-income residents to fan the flames of what has been called "black exclusion, brown exploitation." We relate this case to the social science literature on the impact of immigrants on local labor markets and their racial dynamics. Finally, we conclude by discussing the state of knowledge about Latino immigrants in New Orleans specifically, and its relevance to broader sociological questions about labor markets, race, and ethnicity.

THE DISASTER AND RECONSTRUCTION

On August 29, 2005, Hurricane Katrina's storm surge breached New Orleans's levee system, flooding 80 percent of this below-sea-level city. "Dewatering" took six weeks, prolonged by Hurricane Rita adding rain to the floodwaters on September 25 (Kates et al. 2006). After residents were allowed to return, the City's population recovered gradually, reaching only about half its pre-Katrina size by mid-year 2006 and about three-quarters by mid-year 2012 (Frey, Singer, and Park 2007; U.S. Census Bureau 2014). Widespread housing damage delayed residents' returns; 71.5 percent of the 188,251 housing units in Orleans were damaged, with 55.9 percent having major or severe damage (U.S. Department of Homeland Security 2006). This unprecedented destruction demanded a massive labor force; many workers came to participate in the cleanup, most notably the mobile, Latino labor force already present in the United States (Fussell 2009a, 2009b).

Construction employment spiked after Hurricane Katrina, even as the population in the New Orleans metropolitan area shrank (figure 7.1). Figures from the U.S. Bureau of Labor Statistics's Current Employment Statistics program tell the story: In the months preceding Hurricane Katrina, about 29,200 of the 609,700 nonfarm employees, or about 4.9 percent of this labor force, worked in construction. The Hurricane Katrina disaster displaced nearly all residents of the city, but by December 2005, even though the total number of nonfarm employees fell to 454,300, there were 29,400 construction workers in the area. The number of construction workers peaked in June 2006 at 33,700 and, while gradually falling from this peak, has to date remained above pre-Katrina levels, with the exception of a few winter months (U.S. Bureau of Labor Statistics 2014). Because these numbers exclude proprietors, self-employed, and domestic workers, they certainly understate actual construction employment since many workers in the construction sector are self-employed, off-the-books employees, or day laborers. This informality in the labor market persisted for four to five years after disaster, when we observed a decline in the number of locations and workers at the day labor sites that had become a feature of the post–Katrina landscape.

The turning points in figure 7.1 correspond to the periods defined by disaster scholars: emergency, restoration, and reconstruction (Kates et al. 2006). The first point, the onset of emergency when the disaster began, is the sharp drop in employment in September 2005. The second is the rapid upturn in construction employment lasting from the emergency period until all the floodwater and debris blocking roadways were removed (about December 2005) and into the restoration period in which infrastructure and essential utilities and public services were restored (about June 2006) (Colten, Kates, and Laska 2008). This sharp rise in construction employment contrasts with the more gradual increase in total non-farm employment, illustrating the importance of the construction sector in the recovery. The earliest arrivals in the city, in addition to residents who were allowed back into habitable homes and neighborhoods, were Federal Emergency Management Agency employees, construction contractors, crews as well as workers seeking day labor or

Figure 7.1 Construction employment in New Orleans MSA, 2005–2014. *Note:* Data exclude proprietors, self-employed, unpaid family or volunteer workers, farm workers, and domestic workers. Persons on layoff the entire pay period, on leave without pay, on strike for the entire period or who have not yet reported for work are not counted as employed. Author's calculations from the U.S. Bureau of Labor Statistics (2014).

more permanent employment. Many construction workers were sheltered and employed in and around the French Quarter, which was in the unflooded area of the city and which the city government was eager to revive as the economic engine of the tourist industry. It was here that many early returning New Orleanians experienced the shock of seeing Latin American faces and hearing Spanish and Portuguese spoken in the streets.

The third turning point was in June 2006, when construction employment peaked and then leveled off through the continuing reconstruction period. Reconstruction includes the rebuilding of private residences, businesses, roads, highways, parks, schools, hospitals, and public housing, which has sustained employment in the construction sector. Much of this work involves heavy construction, civil engineering, or specialized construction skills, and attracts large out-of-state construction firms and their crews. These larger, publicly funded projects do not employ as many low-skill workers, who are often Latino immigrants, to the same extent as dangerous, dirty, and demeaning cleanup jobs prevalent in the emergency and restoration periods. Neither do they employ many New Orleans residents who are not connected to the out-of-state firms and who often lack the specialized skills that these projects demand (Donato et al. 2007).

The timeline of the recovery of the built environment corresponds roughly to changes in the size and racial-ethnic composition of the population, as labor demand shifted and housing stock was restored (figure 7.2). During the emergency and restoration periods, many observers noted the sizable foreign-born Latino population, although none could estimate their numbers since there was no firm data on the population as a whole and many of the construction workers were highly mobile and therefore difficult to enumerate (Fussell 2009a; 2009b; Stone et al. 2007). By mid-2006, the city's population was only half its pre-Katrina size and was whiter, older, wealthier, and included more Latinos (Frey, Singer, and Park 2007).

With more continuous data from the U.S. Census Bureau, we can now see that in 2004, the last full year before Hurricane Katrina, the population of the metropolitan area was about 53 percent non-Hispanic white, 38 percent non-Hispanic black, 4 percent non-Hispanic "other," and just under 5 percent Hispanic. After the disaster, the total population decreased dramatically, particularly in severely flooded Orleans, St. Bernard, and Plaquemines Parishes. Between 2004 and 2006, the non-Hispanic white population decreased by about 13 percent and the non-Hispanic black population decreased by about 36 percent. While whites have regained their pre-Katrina size, the number of blacks remains lower. The more severe impact of the disaster on the African American population is attributable in part to the more severe impact of the flooding in the City of New Orleans (Orleans Parish) which had a majority black population. Within the city, low-income and African American neigh-

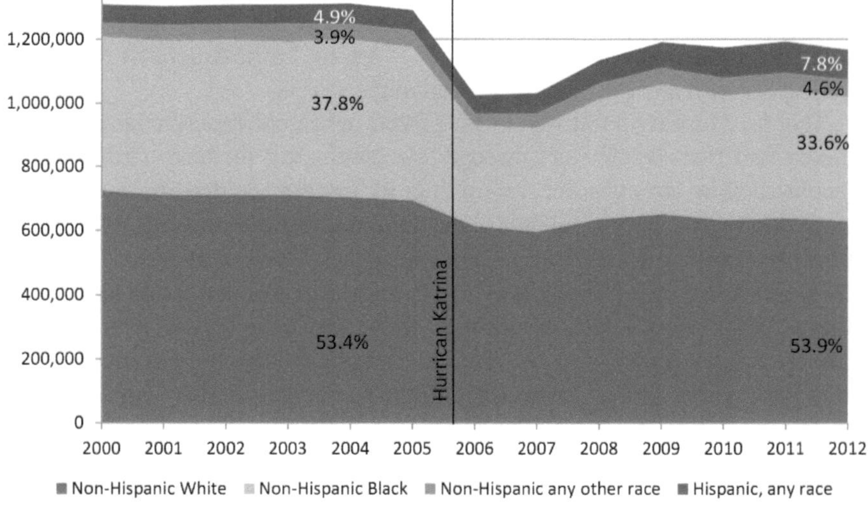

Figure 7.2 Racial and ethnic composition of the New Orleans Metropolitan Area, 2000–2012. *Note*: Percentages before Hurricane Katrina marker are for 2004 and percentages after marker are for 2012. Author's calculations from the U.S. Census Bureau (2014).

borhoods were more severely affected, and residents of these neighborhoods faced greater obstacles to recovering and returning home (Fussell 2013; Fussell, Sastry, and VanLandingham 2010; Logan 2005).

In contrast to the non-Hispanic population, the Hispanic population decreased by only about 9 percent between 2004 and 2006 and their numbers grew beyond their pre-Katrina size, from about 64,000 in 2004 to a peak of 95,000 in 2011. These statistics likely underestimate the size of the Hispanic population, especially in the first several post–Katrina years when many Latino immigrants were moving in and out of the area and living in conditions that may have made it difficult for Census Bureau enumerators to locate them. However, it is clear from figure 7.2 that the arrival of the post–Katrina Latino population is responsible for the growth of this group. In the next section, we describe the political economy that was conducive to the growth and racialization of Latino and Latina newcomers.

CONSTRUCTING A RAPID RESPONSE LABOR FORCE OF LATINO IMMIGRANTS

The federal policy response to Hurricane Katrina was to promote a market-driven recovery. Several policies intended to streamline rebuilding allowed large contractors to enjoy profit windfalls while at the same time incentivizing the use of the cheapest, most exploitable laborers available and ignoring strategies for incorporating displaced, largely minority workers from the region.

First, although lasting only two months due to widespread criticism, in September 2005, President Bush suspended the Davis Bacon Act requiring government contractors to pay prevailing wages (Luckey and Shimabukuro 2005). Since labor often costs as much as materials in construction projects, or more for cleanup projects, this represented an opportunity to alleviate nationally high and rising labor and material costs with lower regional labor costs (Murray 2005).

Second, key federal agencies loosened regulations in Katrina-affected areas. The Department of Labor enacted a forty-five-day suspension of the requirement that employers be able to prove employee eligibility to work (Wasem 2005). Equal opportunity hiring rules for federal contractors were also suspended (Dale 2005). The Occupational Health and Safety Administration suspended inspections, assuming an advisory rather than regulatory role (Delp, Podolsky, and Aguilar 2009). These changes amounted to a labor market that was largely made up of unauthorized Latino immigrants, often working as day laborers, who were subject to dangerous working conditions cleaning up streets strewn with flooded cars, fallen trees, pieces of buildings and household objects that the floodwaters had lifted and left helter skelter.

In short, the employer-regulated labor market offered migrant workers higher wages than they could obtain in other local labor markets in exchange for enduring significant danger, degradation, and dirt.

Third, powerful, non-local groups were well positioned to capture early profits as the federal government awarded millions of dollars in no-bid contracts for cleanup and temporary housing. These went to large construction and cleanup firms, many of which were politically connected government contractors (Trichur 2007; Yukins 2005). Winners of these contracts, as well as subsequent ones awarded through normal competitive bidding procedures, subcontracted to multiple, often maze-like levels of smaller firms. This drove down costs, but also impeded regulation and accountability. Several researchers cite extensive subcontracting as the key mechanism for driving down post–Katrina labor rates (Trujillo-Pagan 2012a; Gorman 2010; Fussell and Valenzuela 2010). Myriad small-scale subcontractors or independent contractors hired work crews, often Latino immigrants, through existing social networks in and out of the region or even outside the United States. These intermediaries not only cultivated migratory paths into New Orleans, but also created cost savings for larger firms by mobilizing, managing, and controlling the cheap, flexible labor larger firms were demanding. The weak regulatory environment enhanced subcontracting profitability by enabling smaller firms and independent contractors to cut costs not only through wages and benefits, but also through immigration, tax, and safety non-compliance (Drever and Blue 2011; Fussell and Valenzuela 2010).

Thus, early policies for addressing New Orleans's devastation structured employment, migratory patterns, and labor relations in a manner prioritizing global, national, and even local elites' interests over local, displaced, poorer residents' (Vinck et al. 2009; Delp, Podalsky, and Aguilar 2009; Fussell and Elliott 2009; Pais and Elliott 2008; Trichur 2007). First, they signaled that speed would be prioritized over workers' rights and safety, leading employers to expect a "culture of non-regulation" (Fussell and Elliott 2009, 388). Second, by encouraging unauthorized and low-wage workers' migration, they established early momentum for using a temporary, low-skill, migrant labor force (Delp, Podalsky, and Aguilar 2009). Third, even though unauthorized immigrants constituted only a portion of the workforce, their status allowed employers to set terms that lowered the wage floor. Competition from local residents was minimized by the high housing costs, lack of schools, and uncertainty about rebuilding plans that deterred many displaced low-wage workers from returning (Holzer and Lerman 2006). In short, the suspension of federal labor and immigration regulations and the weak enforcement of those regulations created an employer-regulated labor market that for years afterward normalized work conditions that only a low-skill, foreign-born, and undocumented labor force would accept.

LABORING IN POST-KATRINA NEW ORLEANS

The labor and living conditions of Latino immigrants after Hurricane Katrina caught the attention of many social scientists simply because the scale and visibility of this localized, time-compressed labor demand made visible the employment conditions of Latino immigrants throughout the United States. During the emergency and restoration periods, when low-skill cleanup and demolition work predominated, several investigations documented the poor working conditions of construction workers in New Orleans, especially the Latino workers (Delp, Podalsky, and Aguilar 2009; Donato et al. 2007; Drever and Blue 2011; Fussell 2009a, 2009b; Vinck et al. 2009; Weil 2009). One 2006 survey found that almost half of construction workers were Latino, about half of whom were unauthorized. The unauthorized Latinos earned significantly less and experienced more employer abuses, such as wage theft and unsafe working conditions (Vinck et al. 2009). Another early study found that workers encountered many workplace hazards and workplace safety inspectors who had little ability or desire to hold employers accountable (Delp, Podalsky, and Aguilar 2009). Workers endured long days in harsh, unsafe conditions in a city with little operational infrastructure, and spent their nights in substandard, overpriced, overcrowded, often makeshift housing (Weil 2009; Drever and Blue 2011). As the emergency and restoration operations ebbed, environmental and housing conditions improved, but not before the employment terms for Latino immigrant construction workers had been set.

The terms of employment for low-skill construction workers were consistent with what sociologists describe as "bad jobs" (Kalleberg, Reskin, and Hudson 2000). These are non-standard jobs that lack an employer who assumes legal responsibility for deducting Social Security taxes or paying unemployment insurance premiums; they are not associated with a single place of employment; employers do not control how workers do their jobs; and workers cannot assume that their employment will continue. In these precarious jobs, wages are typically low. While there are many occupations that share these traits, statistical analyses of national data show that among men, the foreign-born and workers in the construction industry and in businesses providing repair services are especially likely to hold these jobs. Evidently, employment relations among construction workers in New Orleans after Hurricane Katrina were a more visible case of widely accepted U.S. construction industry practices.

These workers were vulnerable to labor abuses on the job and criminal victimization off the job. Most importantly, the legal marginalization of unauthorized immigrants kept them from reporting crimes against them to law enforcement authorities (Fussell 2011; Gorman 2010; Vinck et al. 2009). Employee complaints about not getting paid or being abandoned at the work site, denied breaks, or not having protective equipment were simply met with employer threats to "call immigration." This deportation threat dynamic also heightened Latino construction workers vulnerability to robbery, as it became known that unauthorized immigrants carried their cash wages and that they were unlikely to report their victimization to the police (Fussell 2011). This is a particularly insidious instance of the post–Katrina racialization of Latinos.

Racialization links Latinos' employment in construction labor and their practice of seeking work through day labor corners with their physical appearance and use of Spanish or Portuguese. Prior to Hurricane Katrina, day labor in construction was rare and mainly arranged through informal social networks or temporary work agencies. In the chaotic circumstances that ensued after Hurricane Katrina day labor pick-up sites emerged on high traffic street corners and outside of home improvement stores such as Home Depot and Lowe's. Many workers arrived in New Orleans working for a particular contractor, but as demand for low-skill labor waned after the emergency period, day labor sites swelled with Latino immigrants searching for work (Trujillo-Pagan 2012b; Gorman 2010). The number and size of these day labor sites had reached a peak by 2008, but as demand for low-skill construction labor slackened many of these workers moved on to other cities (Fussell and Valenzuela 2010).

The ebb and flow of day labor sites according to the city's recovery evidences that most post–Katrina Latino migrants were highly mobile "hurricane chasers" (Fussell 2009a). In a study of construction workers in 2006, only 14 percent of Latinos intended to stay permanently in the city compared to half of non-Latinos (Vinck et al. 2009). Fussell (2009b) found that Latin American immigrants who intended to move on were more likely to be recently arrived unauthorized immigrants, who were younger, had fewer social ties, and weak English skills. These highly mobile workers also earned lower than average wages. The Latinos who were more likely to stay were residents of the city before Hurricane Katrina and had stronger social networks and better employment arrangements.

BLACK EXCLUSION, BROWN EXPLOITATION

In New Orleans, African Americans had filled jobs in construction since the city's beginnings (Fussell 2007). Holzer and Lerman (2006) predicted that the rebuilding effort could employ precisely these displaced construction workers and laborers. However, because many displaced workers faced multiple disadvantages as a result of the disaster, without specific employment policies favoring displaced residents, rebuilding would be unlikely to employ them. Pais and Elliott (2008) highlight this struggle between more and less affluent residents during recovery: as poorer residents were pushed out of an inflationary housing market that eradicated public housing, affluent homeowners upgraded their housing using construction contractors who preferred Latinos immigrants over their native-born, black counterparts. Indeed, the New Orleans residents who were the slowest or least likely to return to New Orleans were African Americans, less-educated residents, renters, those outside the labor force, the poor, and the unemployed, who were all more likely to have suffered housing damage (Zissimopoulos and Karoly 2010; Fussell, Sastry, and VanLandingham 2010; Groen and Polivka 2010; Frey, Singer, and Park 2007). These circumstances were an important factor contributing to the exclusion of African American residents of the city from the post–Katrina construction labor market.

Combined, the employment terms that Latino immigrants were forced to accept and the displacement of many African American residents fueled the racialization of Latino workers. They were stereotyped as the only group willing to do the cleanup work (Hetzler, Medina, and Overfelt 2007; Trujillo-Pagan 2007). Mayor Nagin's blanket labeling of Latinos as "Mexicans" epitomized the nativist, homogenization of a heterogeneous population in terms of citizenship, nationality, and length of residency in New Orleans. Latin American immigrants' ethnicity became a marker of their marginality (Fussell and Elliott 2009, 387). This labeling process, reinforced by the Immigration and Customs Enforcement (ICE) raids at high profile day labor sites, led to a public perception of Latinos as "inferior and foreign." Recovery thus became racialized, as various actors used physical and social markers to categorize all Latinos as unauthorized immigrants who could be both exploited and vilified (Trujillo-Pagan 2007; Hetzler, Medina, and Overfelt 2007; Fussell 2011). The social process of labeling immigrant workers as the reconstruction labor force left a strong imprint on the racial and ethnic organization of the local construction labor market, even as demand shifted from unskilled to skilled labor (Vinck et al. 2009). According to Pais and Elliott (2008, 1422), "As functional recovery is achieved and new growth begins, many of these 'reconstruction' jobs disappear, but not before local preference for and experience with immigrant labor becomes (further) institutionalized . . . changing local ethnic systems of stratification and the allocation of resources that flow through them."

In a 2009 study of construction workers, many characterized the construction labor market as fiercely competitive, with pay rates driven down by subcontracting and competition among workers, particularly the low-skilled (Fussell and Valenzuela 2010). Construction workers distinguished between pre-Katrina workers, including blacks, whites, and Latinos, and post–Katrina Latin American immigrants, most of whom were Spanish- or Portuguese-speaking and who were perceived as being uniformly unauthorized. Pre-Katrina construction workers argued that while the unauthorized migrant workers may be exploited, being "local" worked against them when they sought work. Pre-Katrina construction contractors reported difficulty competing for larger, more lucrative jobs, perceiving that out-of-state contractors got a head start over displaced businesses. Almost all the pre-Katrina construction workers reported losing work to Latino immigrants, attributing this to Latino immigrants' willingness to accept lower wages. They argued that out-of-state "fly by night" operators won bids by using lower cost immigrant labor and performing inferior work. Local labor activists characterized the racial dynamic of this competition for employment as black exclusion and brown exploitation.

SOCIAL SCIENCE PERSPECTIVES ON RACIAL AND ETHNIC LABOR MARKET DYNAMICS

Many of the construction workers and other residents of the city felt threatened by the Latino immigrants and the employment practices that attracted them to New Orleans. Indeed, the "immigrant threat hypothesis," that immigrants threaten to take natives' employment and lower their wages, especially those of low-skill and minority workers, has been tested by economists and sociologists. In general, macrolevel analyses find no or only weak evidence that immigrants negatively affect natives' pay and employment (Borjas 1987; Card 2005). When negative effects are detected, they apply to workers with low levels of education (Borjas 1987). Others have found that low-skill immigrant and native labor are complementary, positively impacting natives' earnings, particularly those of more educated workers (Card and DiNardo 2000; Kugler and Yuksel 2011; Ottaviano and Peri 2006). While providing mixed support for the immigrant threat hypothesis, these aggregate studies may average out effects that are evident in local cases.

To better understand how immigrants may impact local labor markets, researchers have studied cases of exogenous shocks which produced rapid inflows of migrants to a labor supply. Card's (1990) study of the arrival of over 60,000 Cubans to Miami during the Mariel Boatlift found no evidence of a negative effect on native and previous immigrant workers' pay and employment. He attributed this to Miami's immigrant-friendly mix of economic activities which easily absorbed these low-skill workers. Similarly, Kugler and Yuksel (2008) found that the arrival of Central American workers in Texas following Hurricane Mitch decreased employment for native workers with low levels of education but increased the earnings of those with higher levels of education. More recently, McIntosh (2008) and Lilliedahl (2009) investigated how an influx of Katrina evacuees affected local labor markets. McIntosh (2008) found a significant but small impact of New Orleans's displaced residents on both employment and wages in Houston. In

Houston and Baton Rouge, Lilliedahl (2009) found a significant but small impact on employment and no impact on wages. These studies all suggest that any discernable impacts are small and depend on the local contexts, national employment trends, and the composition of immigrant and native populations (Kugler and Yuksel 2008; Card 2005; Borjas 1987; Liu 2011). The takeaway for our case is that whatever the impact of the Latino immigrants on the employment and wages of native workers might be, it is likely to be confounded with other influences on both the local labor market and non-local labor demand (such as "competing" disasters or economic booms or downturns).

These aggregate studies of the effect of in-migrants on local labor markets neglect the role of race and ethnicity in shaping employment and wage outcomes. Keys to these outcomes are the relative size of a minority population and their ability to bargain collectively (Tienda and Lii 1987). Some sociologists hypothesize that larger minority groups may benefit because some members overflow into higher paying jobs or gain power which allows them to establish specific employment niches (Wilson and Portes 1980). Others posit that larger minority groups suffer worse outcomes because majority groups perceive them as a threat and construct practices that either exclude them (Waldinger and Bailey 1991; Waldinger 1997) or subordinate them, split the labor market, and drive down wage levels (Bonacich 1972). In New Orleans, the African American population, while large, is also quite impoverished: about a third live at or below the poverty level, around the same proportion are working class hovering just above poverty, and only about a third have "spilled over" into the middle and upper classes (Greater New Orleans Community Data Center 2013c; U.S. Census 2014). In short, most African Americans have been excluded and subordinated in the local labor market. So it is not surprising that African Americans would feel threatened by Latino immigrants' arrival, particularly in construction specialties such as painting, plastering, and brickwork, where they have long held occupational niches.

Sociologists have examined ethnically dominated employment niches to see whether these lead to better or worse labor market outcomes for immigrants (Liu 2011). Owners and managers of firms that employ co-ethnics in niche occupations generally benefit the most, while racial and ethnic minorities in the niche occupation suffer wage penalties, whether they are the same or a different ethnicity than the employer (Catanzarite 2000, 2003; Smith and Elliott 2002). It is difficult to determine whether this is the outcome of social exclusion through preferential hiring of in-group members, or the subordination of immigrants by denying them any but the lowest-paid positions. Whether social exclusion or subordination operate, these practices associate specific ethnic groups with specific jobs. Nationally, construction employment for Latinos has expanded, and by 2006 one in four construction workers was Latino, most being foreign-born (Pew 2007). As we have seen in our case study, this national transformation was duplicated in New Orleans, where Latinos had become the preferred low-skill construction labor force. Thus, the story of black exclusion, brown exploitation resonates with this literature and with the case of post–Katrina New Orleans, where out-of-state construction contractors brought new employment practices, such as subcontracting and non-local network hiring, to fill the construction jobs that were so abundant in the recovering region.

CONCLUSION

When we look back at the past decade, we feel that the phrase black exclusion, brown exploitation most aptly captures what happened in the immediate post–Katrina period. Many of the conditions that attracted the rapid response labor force of Latino immigrants and prevented the return of African American residents have disappeared. Federal regulations apply to all new construction contracts, including policies requiring employment quotas for minorities and local residents. ICE has stepped up their enforcement actions. These policies cannot change the institutionalized practice of subcontracting low-skill labor or the substitution of locally based hiring networks with out-of-state ones. While the dominance of the construction labor market by large non-local general contractors is harmful to the local construction industry, the predominance of tourism, oil and gas related activities, port activities, ship building, and the education and health industries make it simply one important industry rather than the only opportunity for low-skill workers.

So we turn to the question of whether the post–Katrina Latino population will remain since the forces that attracted them to New Orleans are much abated. There is very little systematic data other than the Census data shown in figure 7.2 to help us answer this question, so we also rely on our on-the-ground observations. We suspect that in the initial post–Katrina years the numbers of Latino migrants was greater than the Census data show. But many of these highly mobile workers were likely to have moved on anyway, although it is impossible to quantify how many were here, and of those, how many have left. It is evident, however, that many have stayed. The increase in the Hispanic population registered by the Census is confirmed by our encounters with Latinos and Latinas in workplaces, neighborhoods, schools, stores, parks, and other places where they were rarely seen before Hurricane Katrina. Indeed, every year since the disaster until 2011 the Census has registered an increase in this population. Surprisingly, in 2012 the Latino population declined slightly, but this is consistent with the slight decline in the metropolitan population as a whole, suggesting that perhaps now the Hispanic population is simply responding to the same migratory drivers as everyone else. In short, it is simply too soon to predict whether this population will grow, stabilize, or diminish.

Despite our scientific uncertainties, New Orleans's culture and social institutions bear witness to a decided Latin American imprint on the pre-Katrina black-white dichotomy. For example, a scan of radio stations picks up several Latin music and talk stations where only one existed a decade ago. Slowing at crosswalks for school children reveal significant numbers of Central American children in the mix. Signs and billboards advertise that lawyers, dentists, and clergy "*se habla español.*" Before Hurricane Katrina, Spanish-speakers outside the French Quarter turned heads, but now it is commonly heard during visits to local hospitals, courts, and sports venues. Whereas before Katrina construction and road crews were either all black, all white, or black-white mix, today's crews include various races and ethnicities. Tortilla and condiment selections in local groceries compete with a growing number of Latin American food stores. While none of this suggests that New Orleans is the new Miami or Los Angeles, there is a palpable sense that our city's history of assimilating new cultures (albeit in a highly stratified, segregated manner) is again at work incorporating the workers and families who have settled here since Katrina. Indeed, when New Orleanians discuss the post–Katrina Latino immigrants, most agree that "we wouldn't have recovered as quickly without them."

The gap between empirical research and our anecdotal observations illustrates two difficulties that we encountered as we studied Latino immigrants in New Orleans after Hurricane Katrina. First, data is scarce in a post-disaster context and it is especially challenging to collect representative data from which to make generalizations about the affected population. Rather than using probability sampling methods, empirical research relies on theoretically grounded, convenience samples. The same challenges confront scholars studying international migration, especially when the migration stream includes large numbers of unauthorized immigrants, since there is no reliable sampling frame from which to sample this population. Second, there is epistemological disagreement over whether disasters are simply exceptional cases that have little relevance for social science more broadly or if they can be used as strategic research sights that reveal everyday social processes (Merton 1969). We often found that journal reviewers or session organizers dismissed our manuscripts due to one or another of these complaints, making this type of research a risky proposition. Our research was most often published in special volumes or presented in panels on Hurricane Katrina or disasters. Thus, it is a challenge to draw connections to the sociological literature on the racial and ethnic dynamics of local labor markets that we reviewed here. Perhaps more rigorous discussions of the linkages between firsthand experiences and empirical research, such as those presented in this volume, will close the gap with new research methods and a greater awareness of the epistemological opportunities afforded to social scientists by disasters and other disruptions to normal social processes.

Chapter Eight

Flourishing or Floundering?

Examining the Career Paths of African American Emerging Adults in Post-Katrina New Orleans

Farrah Gafford Cambrice

Over the last ten years, it has been nearly impossible to detach completely from the topic of Hurricane Katrina. Much of my research is informed by my experiences as a Katrina survivor. When Hurricane Katrina devastated the Gulf Coast region, I was a graduate student at Tulane University working on my dissertation. My dissertation was a would-be case study of a black, middle-class community building in a historical neighborhood located in New Orleans, Louisiana. I was able to conduct only two interviews when the threat of Hurricane Katrina forced me and thousands of others to evacuate the city. After seeing the extensive damage to the city and neighborhood, I doubted the feasibility of my original project. However, by January 2006, I observed a steady, albeit slow, return of residents to the neighborhood; therefore, I decided to revise my project to examine community building in the wake of a natural disaster.

I felt conflicted about my research regarding Hurricane Katrina. While I was grateful to have a provocative dissertation topic, it bothered me that I was benefitting from the misery of others. The feeling was usually exacerbated when I interviewed residents in Federal Emergency Management Administration (FEMA) provided trailers, temporary apartments, or partially refurbished homes. To reconcile my personal dilemma, I established close bonds with residents and routinely attended neighborhood events. My ongoing involvement in the community and with residents fostered more research collaborations with scholars who were interested in Hurricane Katrina.

After five years of talking, reading, and writing about Hurricane Katrina, I was drained.

In 2011, I started to consider the topic of emerging adulthood. As an assistant professor at Xavier University of Louisiana, I spent a considerable amount of time advising students on career plans. Many of the students were incredibly bright, ambitious, and had general ideas of their career goals and objectives. For every student who seemed prepared and likely to flourish, two students were floundering or barely meeting course requirements. Colleagues at other institutions say this is the typical trend among college students. However, many of the students that I mentored were Hurricane Katrina survivors. My encounters with emerging adults, who survived Hurricane Katrina, sparked my curiosity about what it is like for a person to come of age in a post-disaster context. The students were familiar with the city's revamped school system and some lived in the most heavily damaged areas in the city. The reflections and experiences of emerging adults suggested that many unanswered questions remain regarding Hurricane Katrina and the subsequent recovery. It is has been ten years since Hurricane Katrina, yet I am still writing about her. I tried to take my research in a different direction, but for me—all roads lead to Katrina.

At the time of Hurricane Katrina, African American youth residing in New Orleans, Louisiana, were an extremely vulnerable population. New Orleans had one of the highest levels of concentrated poverty in the United States and many of the families living in poverty were African American (Hawkins and Maurer 2012, 115). The city's poorer neighborhoods offered few choices for grocery stores, medical services, community centers, and playgrounds. Segregated neighborhoods typically associated with high crime and poverty rates, limited social networks, and poor schools were also commonplace in New Orleans (Berube and Katz 2005, 5–6). Additionally, New Orleans public schools were in shambles. Among New Orleans public schools, the Louisiana Department of Education deemed nearly seventy schools academically unacceptable; several of the city's high schools had double-digit dropout rates (Perry and Reneau 2012). All the aforementioned issues, coupled with the city's reputation for high levels of violence, made coming-of-age experiences for African American youth very difficult.

The unprecedented damage of Hurricane Katrina created additional challenges for African American youth and their families. The initial images of residents stranded at the New Orleans Superdome and the Morial Convention Center were the first and most vivid indicators that African American families bore the brunt of Hurricane Katrina. The destruction of New Orleans's physical structures and services left many families displaced for extended periods. Nearly 125,000 youth from Louisiana were scattered across the

United States—a disproportionate share were African Americans from New Orleans (Peek and Fothergill 2008, 70).

The challenges and obstacles experienced by African American youth and their families are well documented in research literature. This extensive body of research addressed the challenges of adjusting to new schools/cities and the emotional and psychological trauma experienced by youth of color. Researchers including Peek and Fothergill (2008), Weems, Taylor, Cannon, Marino, Romano, Scott, Perry, and Triplett (2010), and Peek, Morrissey and Marlatt (2011) enhanced our understanding of how Hurricane Katrina impacted the lives of youth. Yet most of the studies were conducted during the first few years of the recovery, leaving us with little understanding of the long-term effects of disaster and recovery on the lives of African American youth.

It has been nearly ten years since Hurricane Katrina. Many of the youth who experienced the storm and subsequent recovery are now at a critical juncture in their lives. Scholars refer to this particular phase in the life course as emerging adulthood (Arnett 2000; Hamilton and Hamilton 2006). Emerging adults or individuals between the ages of eighteen and twenty-five are still transitioning into adulthood and have not completely embraced adult roles. Unlike fifty years ago, modern men and women are likely to delay more traditional markers of adulthood (i.e., marriage, children, and leaving home) and use this time for self-exploration and personal growth (Arnett 2000, 470). Emerging adulthood is also an opportunity to explore various jobs or acquire the necessary credentials by means of post-secondary education.

The goal of this chapter is to examine factors that both impede and foster career paths among African American emerging adults in post–Katrina New Orleans. The term *career path* refers to "the sequence and combinations of various occupational and educational experiences" (Hamilton and Hamilton 2006, 259). The term career path is appropriate for emerging adulthood because it takes into account that enrollment in school and employment can overlap in a variety of patterns during this period (e.g., working full time or part time while working on a post-secondary degree or training). Despite having the autonomy and flexibility to explore various interests, individuals establishing career paths are often affected by external factors, such as discrimination, high school curriculum tracking, post-secondary educational experiences, and access to financial resources and social networks. The educational and economic changes associated with Hurricane Katrina and the subsequent period of recovery are likely to influence the career paths and long-term goals of African American emerging adults, especially individuals who endured the intense and lengthy recovery period. Examining the career paths of emerging adults in post–Katrina New Orleans will also provide a more nuanced perspective of the city's recovery efforts.

NAVIGATING A CAREER PATH IN POST-KATRINA NEW ORLEANS

In some ways, New Orleans seems to be a better place for residents than it was before Katrina. The once crumbling school system has undergone a major overhaul. Two months after Hurricane Katrina, the Louisiana State Legislature voted to take into receivership one hundred and seven New Orleans Public Schools that performed at or below the state average in 2004–2005. The schools were placed under the control of the Recovery School District (Cowen 2010, 6). In the revamped educational system, charter schools outnumbered district institute operated schools, attendance zones were lifted, and new teacher talent was recruited from alternative certification programs like Teach for America (Cowen Institute 2010, 11). In the years following the changes, the city's school system experienced a smaller share of schools labeled academically unacceptable and a larger percentage of students demonstrated proficiency in math and English. The post–Katrina school system even received praise from the head of the United States Department of Education, Arne Duncan. Secretary Duncan stated, "The progress that they've made in four years since the hurricane is unbelievable. . . . Those children were being desperately underserved prior, and the amount of progress and the amount of reform we've seen in a short amount of time has been absolutely amazing" (Anderson 2010).

New Orleanians also witnessed small signs of economic growth and progress (Liu and Plyer 2010, 3). Five years after Hurricane Katrina, researchers from the Greater New Orleans Data Center observed a gradual emergence of more knowledge-based jobs, such as those in higher education, legal services, and insurance (Liu and Plyer 2010, 5). By 2009, jobs in higher education surpassed ship building, heavy construction, and engineering to become the fourth largest economic driver in the metropolitan area (ibid.). The city's increase in wages and the increasing number of entrepreneurs also served as positive signs of economic progress and recovery. In 2004, the average annual wage in New Orleans was $39,842. In 2009, the wage average increased to $45,325, which was only $400 less than the national average (ibid.). In the years following Hurricane Katrina, the rate of entrepreneurship increased significantly. Not only are entrepreneurs considered a source of innovation, but entrepreneurship can create jobs and increase income levels for marginalized groups like African Americans. From 2010–2012, about 501 out of every 100,000 adults started up a business annually in the New Orleans area; this rate was nearly 60 percent higher than the national average (Plyer et al. 2013, 18–20).

While the aforementioned changes in the educational system and local economy may seem promising for emerging adults looking to establish a career path, recent research suggests that continuing racial disparities in education and employment exist for African Americans in the aftermath of Hurricane Katrina. The education reforms in post–Katrina New Orleans have received a fair amount of criticism (Tuzzolo and Hewitt 2006; Buras 2011; Perry and Reneau 2012). Ralph Adamo writes that in 2006 and 2007 many Recovery School District (RSD) operated schools lacked books and food services, had overcrowded classrooms, and employed a large number of uncertified teachers, many who were unprepared for the challenges of the classroom (Adamo 2007, 48). Tuzzolo and Hewitt criticized RSD schools for harsh and punitive discipline policies, metal detectors, and a strong police presence (2006, 64–65). McDonogh Senior High School, for example, a public school operated by officials of the RSD, had nearly thirty-two security guards for a student body consisting of 775 students. These issues are particularly prominent for African American students since they represented the majority of seats in public schools before and after Hurricane Katrina. Many community activists, local residents, and scholars have also questioned whether the post-disaster reforms were veiled attempts to further marginalize the black citizens of New Orleans. Kristin Buras's five-year study on New Orleans examined the racial, economic, and spatial dynamics that shaped the city's education reform. According to Buras, the creation and destruction of schools in post–Katrina New Orleans merely served as a way for white, upper-class entrepreneurs to obtain public and private funds to build new schools and manage charter schools around the city (Buras 2011, 298). Buras writes, "In New Orleans, white entrepreneurs have seized control of a key asset in the black communities—public schools—and through state assistance, charter school reform and plans for reconstruction have built a profitable and exclusionary educational system that threatens to reinforce rather than challenge the political economy of New Orleans" (Buras 2011, 304).

There is also evidence to suggest that post–Katrina changes have not had a positive economic impact on all groups. According to Petrice Sams-Abiodun and Gregory Rattler, African American men are underrepresented significantly in some of the better paying and faster growing industries in New Orleans including professional, scientific, and technical services, educational services, healthcare, and social assistance industries (2013, 11). Sams-Abiodun and Rattler report that "over the last decade the median earnings of New Orleans's African American men who work full-time, year-round jobs have fallen 11 percent to $31,018, while New Orleans's white men have seen their wages rise 9 percent to $60,075" (2013, 12). One possible explanation for this trend, according to the researchers, is that the percentage of college-educated African American males has remained stagnant since the 1980s; only 15 percent of the African American men in New Orleans hold an associate's degree or higher (Sams-Abiodun and Rattler 2013, 11). In post–Katrina New Orleans there seems to be a dire need to promote and offer post-secondary training for this marginalized group. The problem of disconnected youth, or individuals neither attending school nor engaged in the formal economy, is another growing concern for New Orleans (Sellers et al. 2012, 10). Between 2008 and 2010 the percentage of disconnected youth in New Orleans was higher than the national average (7.5 percent compared to 10.2 percent). Nearly 68 percent of the city's disconnected youth, during this time period, were African American (Sellers et al. 2012, 11). Residential segregation, which can result in youth having limited exposure to employment networks, and employer discrimination are two common factors that contribute to higher disconnection rates among African Americans (Sellers et al. 2012, 14). The alarmingly high rate of disconnected African American youth in the years following Hurricane Katrina may be an indication that the city has yet to address its long-standing issues with racial segregation and inequality.

In post–Katrina New Orleans education and employment go hand in hand. With many of the more lucrative employment opportunities in post–Katrina New Orleans becoming more dependent upon post-high school education and training, a quality secondary educational experience is imperative. However, persistent educational disparities indicate that there will be significant challenges for African American emerging adults who are attempting to navigate a career path. Without a quality education and the skills needed for viable employment, many African American emerging adults may be prohibited from experiencing the new opportunities that have accompanied the city's revitalization.

METHODS

To examine the career paths of African American emerging adults, I conducted life history interviews. Researchers use life history interviews to understand participants' lives, their roles, expectations placed upon them, and their aspirations (Valke and Brown 2010, 3). The strength of a qualitative research method such as life history involves the ability to explore meanings and sequences of interrelated events, which may not be evident at the aggregate level.

From February 2013 to July 2013, I conducted, recorded, and transcribed thirty-one life history interviews. I recruited participants using convenience and snowball sampling. I developed a snowball sample by contacting several former students who experienced Hurricane Katrina. I also asked several colleagues at a local community college to share a flyer that announced my study to their students and advisees. My research assistants, who represented the desired demographics of the project, also posted flyers describing the study at their places of employment. To be included in the study, participants needed to meet the following requirements: (a) to have lived in the Greater

New Orleans area before Hurricane Katrina, (b) returned to live in the New Orleans area after the devastation of Hurricane Katrina, and (c) be between the ages of eighteen and twenty-five at the time of the study.

The interviews were loosely structured and probes were used, as needed, to obtain more detailed information from the participants. Each interview lasted forty-five minutes to one and a half hours. The interviews took place in my office, local coffee shops, and restaurants. Participants were offered a $25 gift card as an incentive to participate in the interview. Prior to the interviews, I received informed consent from each participant, allowing me to record and transcribe interviews. To protect the confidentiality of the participants, I used pseudonyms for each one.

The final sample consisted of thirty-one emerging adults (twelve men and nineteen women). The participants had varied backgrounds regarding household composition during adolescence, number of siblings, and socioeconomic status. Although data were collected from thirty-one participants, I have chosen to highlight four case studies because the narratives represent some of the general challenges and successes that African American emerging adults are facing in post–Katrina New Orleans.

FLOUNDERING: TAMMY AND ALLEN

Tammy's Story

Tammy Jackson is a twenty-one-year-old fast food employee who attends a local community college part time. She was an eighth grader at the time of Hurricane Katrina. Tammy's family was financially unable to leave the city during Hurricane Katrina so they spent half a week in the Superdome. Tammy cried when she recalled the experience. "We were there for almost a week. It was like living in a sewer. Literally, it was like people would use the bathroom anywhere. I couldn't go to sleep because it was so much was going on" (personal interview, April 8, 2013). After nearly one week, Tammy and her family, like many families trapped at the Superdome and the Ernest Morial Convention Center, were evacuated to unfamiliar cities where they had no friends or family members. Tammy and her family were initially evacuated to Corpus Christi, Texas, before eventually ending up in Dallas, Texas.

After arriving in Dallas, Tammy did not attend school for an entire year. Thus, she missed an entire year of instruction. Eventually, Tammy adjusted to living in a different city and started to enjoy her new school:

> They didn't have as many distractions in the class as I usually got [in New Orleans]. I felt like I was being challenged. I liked school. I had started running track on the cross-country team. I had just signed up for the debate team. I

> took Spanish in Texas and I was learning how to speak in sentences and write paragraphs. I had a real good teacher. I come back to New Orleans and the class could not count to 10 in Spanish. I could've died. I was like I literally just wrote a children's book for an assignment in Texas and now I am here and y'all still doing colors and numbers. (Personal interview, April 8, 2013)

Tammy and her family moved back to New Orleans by her tenth-grade year. She attended and graduated from an RSD school. Although Tammy took advanced placement (AP) courses in high school, she questioned the rigor of the courses:

> Well, they [the classes] sound good, but in reality I didn't honestly feel like it was worth AP status. I took AP calculus and AP English. I know I am terrible with math; I don't know how I passed it, but I did. In the math, she gave it [the grade] to me to be honest. I mean she helped a lot but other than that. And English, I'm fairly okay in English. (Personal interview, April 8, 2013)

With the help of two high school teachers, Tammy applied for admission to a local university. Tammy was excited about attending college, but even with grants and financial assistance, she struggled to pay for her college education. She attempted to pay for school on her own by working as an exotic dancer in the city's French Quarter:

> I was an exotic dancer for a couple of months in the French Quarter. So, I paid for school like that for about three semesters. I was happy because it was good for me to get the money like that instead of all of those loans. I didn't do it that long. It was fun, but I didn't like the fact that I had to be sexual. I didn't do anything [sexual] with anybody, but I had to convey a certain image, you know. It made my grades terrible because I couldn't find a balance. Then, I realized my grades were going down and I kept forgetting to do school work. Then, I was, like, I'm going to have to cut back and focus on school because it defeats the purpose of working for school if I am doing badly in school. (Personal interview, April 8, 2013)

When the financial and academic burdens became too heavy, Tammy decided to withdraw. She has not completely given up on the idea of earning a degree. Recently, Tammy enrolled at a local community college, which she attends part time. She spends the rest of her time working as a cashier at a local fast food chain. I asked Tammy to discuss her long-term goals:

> To be honest, I realized that I wanted to go into education when I went back to visit my high school teachers. Honestly, it sounds like that is where I am headed. I hope to graduate in 2015 after I get my bachelor's degree. I learned about the City Year program. They give you grants for graduate school, they give you loan forgiveness, or I would like to participate in Teach for America.

> They give you money for graduate school and loan forgiveness. (Personal interview, April 8, 2013)

Tammy explained to me that she does not know what she would study in graduate school if she attended, but she realizes the importance of having a mentor or connections. "I just need guidance, to be honest. Once I get guidance, I can figure out what is next. I need someone to help me move from a college student to a career woman" (personal interview, April 8, 2013).

During our interview, Tammy mentioned the possibility of leaving New Orleans for better job opportunities. However, she admitted that she does not have the finances she needs to move to a new city. Although she is currently trying to save money to move, the process is slow. Tammy is only able to put $50 a month in her savings account. Ultimately, Tammy would like to leave New Orleans because she does not believe that the city has many opportunities for someone who does not have the right connections.

Allen's Story

Like Tammy, twenty-one-year-old Allen Smith relocated to Dallas, Texas, after Hurricane Katrina. He was in eighth grade when Hurricane Katrina devastated New Orleans. Before the storm, Allen said he was attending one of the best all boys schools in New Orleans where he excelled academically, but experienced some social and behavioral challenges. Allen said:

> I was so smart. I had to take a test to get into that school. All of my teachers kept saying you have to go. Go there [Jesuit High School]. But, they didn't tell me that the discipline was going to have me in detention every day for doing small stuff. And, that they [school administrators] would think I was setting up gangs in the school. I was cool with everybody. I was a popular person up in there. (Personal interview, April 25, 2013)

The transition to his new school in Dallas was not particularly easy either. Allen said:

> I was chilling with nothing but New Orleans people when I started school in Dallas because they were jumping [fighting] us. They thought we were coming down there to mess it up. In 9th grade, after Katrina, I skipped class because we didn't like some of the teachers. I had a Spanish teacher who didn't like us [students from New Orleans]. He would always pick on us. There would be certain situations where he would say something that he knew would make us mad. It would be something that dealt with the city. "We have a Riverwalk in San Antonio, do y'all have a Riverwalk in New Orleans." Then he said "I'm sorry y'all had a Riverwalk in New Orleans." (Personal interview, April 25, 2013)

After graduating from a high school in Dallas, Allen moved back to New Orleans. Currently, Allen is a server and bartender at a Red Lobster restaurant. Allen stated:

> I like waiting tables. I like the service industry. I like bartending. Serving is like one step under bartending. Serving is like you get paid by the day. I can't ever complain about getting paid by the day. I do a lot of things that keep me happy during the day. I like doing what I do. Ain't nothing wrong with doing what you do and liking it. I want to be the best bartender in the world. I want to bartend in Vegas. I want to do flip bartending [flair bartending]. I want to flip the bottles around. (Personal interview, April 25, 2013)

Allen's career goals are varied and somewhat fragmented. In one part of the interview, Allen mentioned his devotion for bartending. By the end of the interview, Allen discussed his desire to become a video game designer and his slight interest in a music career. Before moving back to New Orleans, Allen briefly attended a local community college in Dallas. During our interview, he talked about returning to college:

> I'm trying to go back [to community college] for the fall. I'm trying to see what is up with that. If everything works out with school, I could be working on game designs. And, I know I really got to want it. Like I told you last time I went to school, I made a video game. I got a good grade in my video game class, but as far as writing an essay for English and doing my math classes, I didn't do that. I was also missing my money and I wanted to start bartending again. (Personal interview, April 25, 2013)

When I asked Allen about mentors who could help him, he provided the following response:

> I have a lot of mentors. Everybody I hang around. I hang around older people and I see the lives they have and how they are trying to make a family. I mean I look up to a couple of people because I have to get their advice on things. I look up to my big cousin who is like a big brother and my cousin, Dave, who is showing me how to take care of a family and my co-worker's cousin who first showed me rapping. And, my Dad is like the wisest man I know and my mom was like on the Dean's list at her college. (Personal interview, April 25, 2013)

Despite not having solid career plans, Allen seemed committed to staying in the city of New Orleans. He loves the city that he grew up in and wants to be a part of the city's recovery. Allen said:

> I want to be one of the people who come and help fix things [in the city]. I want to be the one that fix these streets and make these moves to fix these neighborhoods up. Yeah, we need tourism, but we can have other businesses in the city, too. (Personal interview, April 25, 2013)

However, Allen's devotion to New Orleans does not keep him from being critical of the city. During our interview, he told me that he questions if there are any real opportunities for African Americans in New Orleans. Sometimes, he believes that the city officials of New Orleans care more about tourism than they do about the residents.

FLOURISHING: REGINA AND DARNELL

Regina's Story

Regina Taylor was twelve years old when Hurricane Katrina struck the city of New Orleans. Her parents had recently purchased a new home in the Lakeview area of the city. Regina and her mother evacuated the city with other family members to Mississippi. After learning about the severity of the storm and the damage to their home, Regina's mother thought it would be in her best interests to move to North Carolina temporarily so Regina could enroll in school immediately and have a sense of normalcy. In North Carolina, Regina lived with a close relative and attended Bradley Junior High School. "I had never been to a school this big. It had a big gym and an Olympic sized pool and a cafeteria with five lines and all these types of things. That really amazed me" (personal interview, June 21, 2013). Although Regina was impressed with her school during the evacuation, she admitted that she did not make any new friends or really get involved in her new school's extra-curricular activities. "I went to class and went through the motions. I didn't try to get involved. At my school in New Orleans, I was in everything" (personal interview, June 21, 2013).

After six months in North Carolina, Regina returned to New Orleans. She and her parents lived in an apartment made available by another family member. Eventually, her family moved back into their Lakeview home. Regina attended and graduated from Benjamin Franklin High School. Benjamin Franklin has a selective admissions process (Calefati 2008). It has been named a Blue Ribbon School three times by leaders of the U.S. Department of Education and has appeared on *U.S. News & World Report*'s list of America's Best High Schools (Calefati 2008). As a student at Benjamin Franklin, Regina took AP courses and participated in various extracurricular activities. Regina believed that the experiences in AP courses and extracurricular activities taught her leadership skills and the importance of teamwork. Regina stated:

> I was a B student. Being a student at Franklin was the first time I had ever gone to a school and didn't have an A average. I think that was a good experience because I began to not weigh myself on a numerical scale, but I tried to see how much I learned in a class instead of focusing on just the letter

> grade. It was very rigorous to me; it was also very stressful being in that environment. Not only was it rigorous it was also competitive. A lot of people would compare scores at the school. (Personal interview, June 21, 2013)

After graduating from Franklin, Regina moved to Atlanta, Georgia, to attend Spelman College. Regina explained that most of her family had not left the state of Louisiana to attend college, so her decision to attend school in Atlanta was met with some trepidation. Regina stated, "They were worried and said that it would be a lot of responsibility and that I wouldn't have much family. I think at first they were apprehensive but they think it is for the better" (personal interview, June 21, 2013).

As a college student, Regina takes advantage of opportunities inside and outside of the classroom. She is a very active member in her sorority. Last summer, she participated in a teaching fellows program in Ecuador. Regina is a year away from completing her bachelor's degree, but she has already started thinking about her next steps. On the day we met to talk about her post–Katrina experiences, she had just participated in a tour of Loyola University's law school. In the future, Regina would like to return to New Orleans to study and practice law. Regina stated:

> I do want to eventually settle here [New Orleans]. I really like it and I want to come back home. Not just because of my family, but I really just like the vibe. I like the people. I like the culture. A lot of people don't see the potential that is here. I see a lot of people my age who go to school and don't want to come back. They believe in order to be successful you have to go somewhere else. I am happy that I see a lot of potential here. The city is already a great place, but I think it could be so much better. I just wish other people could see that. (Personal interview, June 21, 2013)

Although her family includes several professionals, Regina has developed mentor/mentee relationships outside of her family. Her mentors include a juvenile court judge who is a Spelman alumna and a former high school classmate who Regina has emulated by attending Spelman and joining the same sorority. In addition to having mentors, Regina explained that attending Spelman with young women who share a similar ambition has been beneficial to her personal growth. Regina stated:

> When I went to Spelman for a visit, I felt at home and meeting people who had gone to the school already, I just felt like I just wanted to be like them. I knew that I wanted to excel academically, which is why I chose that high school [Benjamin Franklin High School] and why I chose Spelman. (Personal interview, June 21, 2013)

Darnell's Story

In August 2005, Darnell Martin was entering the tenth grade. In many ways, Darnell and his family personified what it meant to be black middle class in New Orleans. Pre-Katrina, Darnell lived in New Orleans East. New Orleans East was home to many of the city's African American professionals, educators, businesspersons, and politicians (Pastor et al. 2006, 26). Darnell's mother is a principal and received her education from one of the area's historically black colleges. Darnell attended and graduated from St. Augustine High School, which is a historically black, Catholic school. St. Augustine has a reputation in the African American community for producing some of the city's better known politicians, judges, and musicians. For middle-class African American families living in New Orleans, Catholic schools, like St. Augustine, offer parents an alternative to local public schools (Dequine 2011). Catholic high schools, like St. Augustine, also serve as a deterrent or antidote to the perils of street life by offering stern discipline.

In the initial aftermath of the storm, Darnell and his family temporarily relocated to Texas where he attended public school for one semester. It did not take very long for Darnell's family to enroll him into a local school. Darnell explained that his school in Dallas was a really good school and the people were nice, but he longed to return to New Orleans. While Darnell did not encounter explicit negative racial attitudes in his new school, he believed some of the people he encountered had a very limited view of New Orleanians. Darnell stated:

> Even though people in Dallas treated us nice, it wasn't home. And, that's one thing people in Dallas didn't understand; that we were good people. We had nice cars and everything. We were not the people in the convention center. We were not poor people. We were not uneducated people, you know. (Personal interview, July 14, 2013)

In less than a year after Hurricane Katrina, Darnell and his family moved back to New Orleans and back into their family home in New Orleans East. Darnell went on to graduate from St. Augustine and attended one of the city's historically black universities. Initially, Darnell decided to major in business until he noticed that several of his peers were majoring in pre-pharmacy. After a brief stint as a pre-pharmacy major, Darnell acknowledged that he hated it and changed his major back to business.

In addition to the formal curriculum, Darnell explains that he picked up soft skills that have contributed to his current success as an entrepreneur:

> My department and professors gave me business etiquette, you know, as far as knowing what I need to wear to business meetings, the language I need to speak. Practical knowledge: that even though I may not be working in a finan-

> cial setting, like a bank, I can still use those skills in everyday life and in my own business. (Personal interview, July 14, 2013)

Nearly ten years after Hurricane Katrina, Darnell earned his bachelor's degree. Darnell worked briefly for an Atlanta-based company before starting his own business in New Orleans. His company provides website design, social media marketing, and search engine optimization (SEO). Darnell's passion comes out when he speaks about his career. He stated:

> The best part of my job is turning people's vision into reality. My business is one thing I can do for free. It's amazing how successful I am at it because I love it. I go to blogs like Inc.com, which is for entrepreneurs, researching people like Russell Simmons, Richard Branson, um, you know, the CEOs. I am just always trying to learn—trying to evolve. I have a lot of clients. I do the IT work for Xavier Preparatory school. I do the IT work and stuff for the school district where my grandmother is an administrator. I am just about finished with a website for Beyonce's publicist in New York City. So, it's constantly expanding and I've learned all these lessons and I'm just 22. It's only up from here. (Personal interview, July 14, 2013)

Darnell believes that he has been successful because he is not afraid to take risks. He does not worry about failure because he has a strong support system and he knows how to learn from mistakes.

CONCLUSION

Having endured Hurricane Katrina and several years of the city's revitalization efforts, emerging African American adults like Tammy, Allen, Regina, and Darnell are now making decisions regarding their future career plans. The current research presents the narratives of four participants from a larger study on African American emerging adults who are Hurricane Katrina survivors. Tammy, Allen, Regina, and Darnell's experiences reflect factors that impede and foster career path development of African American emerging adults in post–Katrina New Orleans.

Several of the emerging adults I interviewed are encountering difficulties developing a career path or floundering. Tammy's and Allen's stories provided glimpses into some of the challenges that African American emerging adults are facing in post–Katrina New Orleans, where it remains seemingly difficult for low-income and working-class African Americans to move up the socioeconomic ladder. The most obvious challenge for those who are floundering is the inability to acquire post-secondary education and credentials. In order to participate in some of the growing job sectors in the "new" New Orleans economy, post-secondary training and credentials will be necessary. Several of the participants in my research were struggling (academically and/or financially) to complete college or lacked some form of post-high school training. Similar to Tammy, many participants were also very critical of their post–Katrina educational experience. Even after what many have considered a successful overhaul of the public education system in New Orleans, the narratives from emerging adults in this study indicate that some students might still be underserved by public schools. Understanding the experiences of emerging adults will be necessary if city officials and educators want to continue the important strides in post–Katrina education reform. Hurricane Katrina survivors, in particular, possess a comparative understanding of various school programs and curriculums after attending different schools during the evacuation period. In other words, the dispersal to non-New Orleans public schools in the initial aftermath of the storm can provide a more nuanced perspective of the limitations and strengths of the city's new school system.

Regina and Darnell are blazing the trail on the path to full adulthood. They represent the emerging adults in my research who are flourishing, or successfully moving toward career goals. Regina's and Darnell's resumes include a wealth of experiences that compliment long-term career goals. They have taken advantage of the career socialization and extracurricular activities made available in high school and college. To be clear, both Regina and Darnell experienced bumps in their college careers. However, they were able to navigate the bumps and neither one discussed feeling academically underprepared for the college experience. Darnell has a degree and Regina will likely have a degree by the time this research is published.

Regina and Darnell, like other successful emerging adults in the study, attended some of the better schools in New Orleans after Hurricane Katrina. Regina graduated from what many New Orleanians agree is the best public school in the city, Benjamin Franklin. Along with several other adults in the study, Darnell attended private or parochial schools like St. Mary's Dominican High School, Isidore Newman School, and St. Augustine High School. Before Hurricane Katrina, the troubled public school system in New Orleans was responsible for one of the city's most unique features—a robust network of private schools. Nearly one-third of the city's population of school-aged children attended private schools (Newmark and De Rugy 2006, 15). The narratives from this research indicate that there continues to be a hierarchy in the city's education system and private schools are at the top of the hierarchy. One of the participants in the research put it like this, "In New Orleans if you are black middle class you go to Catholic school if your parents can pay the tuition" (personal interview, May 29, 2013). Education and training of African American youth will be imperative if New Orleans plans on developing and maintaining a robust economy. In the next fifteen years, demographers predict that nearly 52 percent of working adults in the city will be people of color (Sellers et al. 2012, 13). The importance of receiving a college education extends beyond New Orleans. Increasingly, people in the modern world are influenced by technological advancements; therefore, it is likely that occupations worldwide will require some post-high school education or training. By 2018, the U.S. economy will create 46.8 million openings and nearly two-thirds of these jobs will require workers with at least some college education (Sellers et al. 2012, 15).

The narratives also indicate that emerging adults who are flourishing also had more social support and access to networks than those who were floundering. Regina tapped into Spelman's alumnae for career guidance and Darnell's first business client was the school where his grandmother had connections. Emerging adults like Tammy and Allen expressed the importance of networks and connections, but their current networks do not appear to be useful to them in developing a career path. Allen cites family members as mentors and positive influences on his life but previous research on emerging adults indicates that "small, tight, and exclusively family based networks" can impede life chances and cement disadvantages for emerging adults (Settersten and Ray 2010, 33). While Tammy realized the importance of a mentor and having the right connections, she spends very little on campus and has not looked into internship opportunities. It is quite unlikely that she will receive the support or mentoring she needs at her fast-food job.

Disasters like Hurricane Katrina can shape the career paths of emerging adults. In post–Katrina New Orleans, the career paths of emerging adults are greatly influenced by external factors such as access to post-secondary education/training and productive social support systems. After nearly ten years of recovery and revitalization, some would argue that New Orleans is headed in a better direction. Unfortunately, racial disparities in education and employment persist leaving some to question if there is anything really *new* about the *new* New Orleans. While some African American emerging adults are on a clear and direct path to adulthood (i.e., financial independence coinciding with an established career trajectory), others have remained quite vulnerable to instability in the aftermath of the disaster. The narratives in this research indicate that the recovery of New Orleans has not entirely alleviated challenges for African American youth as they transition into adulthood. The early career plans and experiences featured in this chapter are particularly insightful to politicians, community activists, policy makers, and business leaders who aim to make post–Katrina New Orleans more inclusive.

Chapter Nine

New Orleans's Katrina Recovery for Whom and What?

A Race, Gender, and Class Approach

Jean Ait Belkhir

This chapter is written from a race, gender, and class (RGC) approach and begins with the Katrina experience of the author and his spouse,[1] as victims, evacuees and also privileged by their white skin color. The author begins with some thoughts on the root causes of the catastrophe-words written in the weeks after Katrina, while much of New Orleans remained under water. The next part of the chapter focuses on post–Katrina New Orleans and combines personal observations with the post–Katrina literature to explore how race, gender, and class frame New Orleans today in 2014.

For a week or so in late August, we checked daily on the progress of Hurricane Katrina as it formed near the Bahamas, crossed Florida into the Gulf of Mexico, and began to move in the general direction of New Orleans.

[Saturday, August 27]—Plaquemines, a coastal city, was the first to be evacuated. On Saturday afternoon, Mark, our landlord living next door on Painters Street, left with his father for Lafayette, saying that "the cyclone which is coming is very strong and very dangerous and you should better leave. If you stay, go to my house, which is more solid."

The next day [Sunday, August 28—the night of the hurricane] before the hurricane struck, we started taking precautions to secure our home and prepare for a possible evacuation but good news was not coming and we left for Baton Rouge. It was bumper to bumper, miles and miles of traffic, cars broken down abandoned on the side, even a bus overturned in a ditch. Twenty miles later we decided to go back home. Having nowhere to go we thought we would be safer in our landlord's house. By 9:00 pm the city was under curfew.

[Monday, August 29—after the storm struck the city in the early hours] What a night! We won't forget that. The hurricane was scary. Our place had suffered heavy winds but not much damage. We didn't get flooded into the house. The eye passed over. We thought the city was doing well. Then, around noon, without understanding what was going on, we heard on the radio, "If you have a car with gas, you have one hour to leave, after that it will be too late." We realized we still had a chance, but slowly over the next thirty-six hours the water rose.

By Tuesday evening [August 30] there was eight feet of water in our streets and four feet on our floor despite the clearing skies. In fact, we missed hearing on the radio that the levees had broken. We were good until the breach sent a churning sea of water from Lake Pontchartrain coursing across Lakeview and into Gentilly (our district) and the other parts of the city farther south and east. By the end of the day we were trapped like rats. We swam with a bucket with some dry clothing and important papers through the smelly and ugly water—full of oil and everything else—that had flooded our entire neighborhood. I disappeared for a few seconds deep in the water until we reached and climbed up to the second floor of our hosts (Latisha and Shawn—both African American), as night fell. Their house was unstable with huge holes in the roof. Jean reached the roof and stayed night and day to flag down helicopters using a light and a cloth, which were already plucking people off roofs. But they never picked us up. Finally, Jean saw a private citizen motorboat and the four of us began screaming, "Help, please help." As the boat made a turn, one of the two men said, "We will come back before dawn."

Fifteen survivors piled onboard the motorboat and we began an unbelievable journey into our neighborhood. With a broken heart, we discovered the extent of the terrific and stupefying disaster. The scene was unreal. We were heading toward Elysian Fields and the boat stopped at about 200 meters before the Gentilly crossroad. After leaving the boat, we were told that the American Red Cross would take care of us at the Saint Martin School. With the water up to our knees, we walked to the school, in almost total darkness. Slowly but surely our group became smaller and smaller until we found ourselves alone, with the water rising from our knees to the top of our thighs. The sun was gone and things got more and more scary. So, we went back where the boat dropped us off as fast as we could. Luckily, we saw a lighted spot with a group of about thirty people—two dialysis patients, a woman with Alzheimer's, and a young mother with her newborn baby girl—sitting on the dry ground along the wall of a hardware shop. Latisha, as a twenty-year-old nurse, took care of the people in need with an amazing commitment and professionalism. It was our first night on the dry cement where we were all side by side along the wall. No way to sleep! In a mixed group with black and white, somehow, Mike established a solid and united community with some rules: no smoking, keep cleaning the space, respect each other, take care of each other, and share what we had (which was not much—one gallon of water for all of us).

On Wednesday [August 31], we heard that a helicopter would come to pick up the sick and elderly people and the mother and baby. We spent hours clearing a spot for the helicopter to land, but it never came.

On Thursday [September 1], early in the morning, a National Guard boat stopped at our spot and we were told that they hadn't received any orders to evacuate anybody, even the sick people. After a "combo party" organized by a black pastor from the Gentilly neighborhood, a boat came to bring people to the University of New Orleans (UNO) to be lifted out at the New Orleans airport. But that was too good to be true.

When we got to UNO, there were not enough helicopters to bring all of us to the Lakefront airport, two miles farther. We were told, "If you want to leave New Orleans tonight you have to reach the airport on your own." Dark and rain were coming, so under those fantastic conditions, we decided to move on. Finally, after walking in the dark, under the rain, falling in the mud, and being lost because of the flooded road, we reached the Lakefront airport two or three hours later. At the airport we became part of a group of over eight hundred people—most of them women of color with kids—sharing only one mobile bathroom and a huge sleeping room: the landing runway. Side by side, lined up on the runway with helicopters landing and taking off all night long we tried to sleep. The most shameful side of the story was that all the law enforcement agencies were heavily armed and treated us like we were "prisoners or refugees"! Helicopters landed continually and the wind from their blades blew trash over our bodies! Of course, being able to leave New Orleans tonight was one more lie.

On Friday morning (September 2), military helicopters airlifted more than 800 people to Louis Armstrong International Airport where we boarded a military jumbo airplane to San Antonio, Texas, within several hours. We sat beside a young African American single mother and her three children. She told us how she rescued each of her three kids from her flooded home one by one; she was exhausted. On Saturday morning [September 3] she was found dead on her cot in the middle of her children.

"Welcome to San Antonio." After lining up several hours we were then transported by buses to the closed Levi Strauss manufacturing plant. The building we were in had about 1,000 people, mostly black, and again single women with families outnumbered the men. We received a wristband for a cot within a specified sleeping zone, where the lighting never quite faded to dark. Our feelings about being in the shelter were two sided. We had food, a roof, and the people were pretty welcoming. However, we felt that, as whites,

we were treated a little differently and given privileges because of our skin color: being invited for dinner several times, receiving several job proposals, and volunteers telling us, "It isn't safe for you to be here, feel free to come to our home." Indeed, Katrina showed that skin color does matter in the United States.

We lived in the shelter for about three weeks. Then we moved to a guest house in Baton Rouge for three months where we probably felt the most lonely and depressed. Our comfort zone has been totally taken away. By September 29, 2005, the administration of the Southern University at New Orleans asked each of the faculty members to come back to Baton Rouge to sign an attendance roll. Jean was to sign the role and also to be prepared to teach online courses or else risk losing his job. Fortunately, while we were displaced we had the chance to fly to Paris, France, to rest one week with our family who were scared to death about us.

Six weeks later [in October], we were finally allowed to visit our home in New Orleans, to assess the damage and pick up essentials, and then leave again. We were certain the house was badly damaged, but we could not imagine what we saw driving into New Orleans and in our neighborhood! As we approached our block, we began to feel the pain in our chest. Everything in our rented house was totally ruined. No, that is not a strong enough word. Soaking for weeks in fetid water then left for months to sit unprotected in the humid air of southern Louisiana. Everything was gone—home, books, car and bicycles, but we were ALIVE and full of hope!

On January 17, 2006, we were on the move again when we came back to New Orleans to begin work. Jean started the spring semester in a high school on Napoleon Street and we were lodged at the Marriot Hotel until April 1, 2006, when we got a FEMA trailer. Even today at Southern University of New Orleans (SUNO), a historically black university, they have replaced the trailers by using mobile classrooms. SUNO rejected the idea of combining with the UNO. When SUNO did reopen it became the first college in trailers; the last trailer left during spring 2013 to be replaced by a huge modular building, hosting classrooms and offices.

Hurricane Katrina revealed the true nature of the extreme RGC inequality and Third World poverty in the so-called richest world and democratic country. After Hurricane Katrina hit on August 29, 2005, the policy of all three levels of government has been open war to privatize public healthcare, public housing, and public schools. System change is long overdue. It's time to fight for a new form of society based on RGC equality and democracy.

RACE, GENDER, AND CLASS INTERSECTIONAL ANALYSIS

The catastrophe that visited the Gulf region in the wake of Hurricane Katrina demonstrated that exposure to the hurricane's devastation was a function of not only place, but also RGC. Katrina has stoked deep national divisions and widespread international derision. Disasters, whether natural or human-made (and Katrina is both), are revelatory mirrors that expose a society's subterranean fissures, the existing socioeconomic inequalities and political pathologies. Katrina has provided a giant and agonizing mirror for America, in the full view of the world it normally despises, forcing it to look squarely in the face, to its profound shock and shame, all those marginalized people it silences with its strange but seductive myths of equal opportunity and the American dream. Race and class, the enduring systemic and symbolic deformities that mark and mock the fantasies of American exceptionalism, have revealed their simmering presence in the teeming masses that were huddled in the biotoxic sports arenas, waiting in the sweltering patches of broken bridges, or waving desperately from the rooftops of submerged buildings.

New Orleans is a city "underdeveloped" by capitalism. Social services are chronically underfunded and many New Orleanians are locked in a cycle of poverty spurred by inadequate schools and lack of living wage jobs. Despite its once massive port, a seventy mile petro-chemical (and cancer) corridor, and New Orleans's rich historical significance, the city has—like Third World Caribbean islands—depended upon a tourism industry for sustenance (Caldwell 2006).

The poverty and blackness of those most affected by the disaster—particularly the poorest of the poor, socially marginalized women of color (Enarson 2006)—was obvious to anyone watching the media in the days following the levee break. The plight of these victims underscores the existing RGC inequalities in New Orleans, but also provides a lens to examine racism, sexism, capitalism, and poverty in the United States as a whole (Caldwell and Dubinsky 2005, 2006; Enarson 2006).

In 2003, the New Orleans *Times-Picayune* produced a five-part series that predicted that upwards of 100,000 people would likely face death in the event of direct hit of a Category 5 hurricane. Despite this well-known fact, city and public school buses flooded while residents were stuck in the city and the Superdome—the "shelter of last resort"—with no way out. The *Times-Picayune*'s series, written by John McQuaid and Mark Schleifstein, was uncanny in its prescience. "It's only a matter of time," they predicted, outlining a scenario that has gone according to script. "Evacuation is the most certain route to safety but it may be a nightmare," they wrote. "People left behind in an evacuation will be struggling to survive. Some will be housed at the Superdome, the designated shelter in New Orleans for people too sick or infirm to leave the city. Thousands will drown while trapped in homes or cars by rising waters."

Institutional policies favor ruling class interests, but the flip side of these policies is for purveyors of ruling class ideology—including many working-class whites—to blame the victims hit hardest: poor African Americans. This interclass antagonism only sharpens race and class inequalities (Caldwell and Dubinsky 2005, 2006). Eugene Robinson writes in the *Washington Post* that:

> After seeing who escaped the flood and who remained behind, it's impossible to ignore the shocking breadth of the gap between rich and poor. It's as if we don't even see poor people in this country anymore, as if we don't even try to imagine what their lives are like. . . . To be poor in America was to be invisible, but not after this week. (Robinson 2005)

The poor in New Orleans, and throughout the United States, are disproportionately African American. Many people were shocked by the images they have seen on television and that the thousands of poor people living in New Orleans were African American. It was the face of exhausted low-income African American women, many single mothers among them, whose pleas for food and water were broadcast around the world from the Superdome, women more than men who were evacuated from nursing homes, and women more than men whose escape of sorts was made with infants, children, and elders in tow. Many residents of the city's most impoverished areas suffered for days without supplies of food, water, or basic provisions for health and public safety (Gault et al. 2005; Enarson 2006).

The hurricane and the subsequent flooding exposed the special vulnerability of women, children, the elderly, and the disabled by revealing the harsh intersection of race, gender, class, ability and life expectancy. Many people were unable to escape not only because of poverty, but because they were not physically able to punch through rooftops, perch on top of buildings, or climb trees to survive. Horror stories of people abandoned to drown in nursing homes and hospitals emphasize that any disaster preparedness planning must take into account those unable to evacuate themselves.

The horrific images that emerged from New Orleans and the Gulf Coast in the wake of Hurricane Katrina have brought issues of RGC in America to the forefront of public consciousness. Television and newspaper reports repeatedly highlighted the extent to which those with resources largely managed to escape the terror of the storm and its immediate aftermath, while poor, mostly black residents suffered unspeakable distress and suffering. Economic status across race and gender did play a central role in the ability of residents to recover from the devastation in the months, and certainly years ahead. Katrina's devastation is of course linked to specific environmental, economic, social, and political circumstances in the region—for New

Orleans, its position below sea level, its high poverty rate, the racial dimensions of that poverty, and funding cuts for levee maintenance, among other factors, have all helped shape the effects of the storm (Mulcahy 2006). But in a larger context, the relationship between poverty and disaster that has been emphasized after the storm is not unique to New Orleans and Hurricane Katrina. The history of hurricanes in what can be called the Greater Caribbean—the islands of the West Indies and the states along southern Atlantic and Gulf coasts—offers repeated evidence that the RGC marginalized people have often felt the effects of hurricanes most severely.

RACE, GENDER, AND CLASS MATTER IN POST–KATRINA

As we know by now it is impossible to begin to understand the continued impact of Katrina without viewing through the lenses of RGC. Katrina exposed the region's deep-rooted inequalities of RGC. Katrina did not create the inequalities; it provides a window to see them more clearly. But the aftermath of Katrina has aggravated these inequalities. Over three thousand public housing apartments occupied before Katrina, plus another thousand under renovation, were bulldozed after Katrina (Reckdahl 2011). New Orleans is now the charter school capital of the United States (Quigley 2013). The main public healthcare provider, Charity Hospital, which saw 350,000 patient visits a year, remains closed. We can observe that New Orleans is now whiter, more male, and more prosperous (Quigley 2013). Although jarring, the facts can only be shocking to those who have willingly ignored systematic evidence of what Michael Harrington fifty years ago called the "The Other America."[2] Michael Harrington may not have specifically mentioned RGC in his popular book, but RGC social scientists and political activists have long tried to draw the nation's attention to the scope of racialized, gendered, and classed poverty in the United States.

Ten years later after Katrina, we are forced to look at New Orleans, to really begin understanding that New Orleans has changed (and is changing) but for whom and how? The post–Katrina recovery kept New Orleans's structural inequalities intact and laid bare the consequences of ignoring.[3] The changes in the public sector have been widespread. Indeed, the recovery policy has opened the door to the principles of the free market into healthcare, education, and housing with the support of all three levels of government and the private sector. The recovery process made clear, however, that New Orleans rebuilding is not going to resolve the current RGC disparities.

NEW ORLEANS POPULATION

The official population of New Orleans now is 369,250 residents, compared to 455,000 when Katrina hit New Orleans. The African American population of New Orleans shrank by 61 percent or 213,000 people, from a pre-Katrina number of 302,000 down to 89,000 (Quigley 2013), but there are also fewer whites than before. Though the population of the city is smaller overall, the share of whites and Hispanics living in the area grew while the share of African Americans decreased (Mack and Ortiz 2013).

NEW ORLEANS PUBLIC HOUSING

The topic of public housing in New Orleans is much too broad and multifaceted to address here, so I will focus upon a few facts exposing the so-called recovery process in New Orleans after Katrina. The city's six most renown housing projects were racially segregated—two for whites, four for blacks—as was the case throughout much of the South. About one-third of the 5,000-plus displaced residents have found other public housing according to National Public Radio (Quigley 2013). The Louisiana Republican Congressman Richard H. Baker was nefariously jubilant at the bulldozing of the New Orleans housing projects. Baker thanked Katrina for doing the urban landscape a favor, remarking, "We finally cleaned up public housing in New Orleans. We couldn't do it, but God did." While some see the hand of providence in Katrina's collateral damage, historically speaking, the spirit of ruthless capitalism has had a lot more to do with bulldozing the public housing in New Orleans (Long 2007). The truth is that the city's recovery left the free market wide open to install its principles of privatizing the major public institutions in New Orleans. In reforming public housing specifically, politicians and bureaucrats in New Orleans are no longer expected to enact the same kind of good-sense policies, such as equivalent elimination,[4] that were part of the 1937 Housing Act (Long 2007). This made it possible for them to demolish thousands of units of public housing in the midst of a staggering post-disaster housing crisis. Paralleling 2007 housing policy, a quotation from an 1898 New Orleans *Times-Picayune* article reads, "the city government is trying to drive [poverty] out of the most prominent localities and into obscure neighborhoods where decent people will not be constantly offended by [the] open and shameless flaunting of the poor" (Long 2007). With the "cleaning out" of the public housing we observe a push to make New Orleans more gentrified than before Katrina.

NEW ORLEANS GENTRIFICATION

Now, after Katrina, the city finds itself at a delicate moment in its rebuilding. Private and government investment is fueling the push to overhaul some of the city's troubled but culturally rich neighborhoods near the French Quarter, where poor families are being replaced as wealthier ones move in. While the city is in a boom and even gentrifying, some questions remain as to whether gentrification will wither the roots that grew the city's distinctive identity. As Gary Clark, a politics professor at Dillard University noted, "New Orleans is becoming a boutique city like San Francisco. . . . You may see black middle class moving in, but with gentrification there are overwhelmingly white individuals of means who become the new urban pioneers" (*Gazette* 2012). The number of whites, although smaller than before Katrina, has grown as an overall percentage from 28 percent to 33 percent of the city's population. The city has its first white mayor since the 1970s, while the City Council now has a majority of white members (*Gazette* 2012).

However, gentrification is not new in New Orleans. In fact writers and artists settled in the French Quarter in the 1920s and 1930s, and by the 1970s the French Quarter was largely gentrified as the process continued downriver into the adjacent Faubourg Marigny and upriver into the Lower Garden District.[5] It progressed through the 1980s to the 2000s but only modestly, slowed by the city's abundant social problems and limited economic opportunity. New Orleans in this era ranked as the Sun Belt's premier shrinking city, losing 170,000 residents between 1960 and 2005 (Campanella 2013; *Gazette* 2012). The relatively few newcomers tended to be gentrifiers, and gentrifiers today are overwhelmingly transplants.

Campanella (2013) shows that gentrification hot-spots today may be found along the fringes of what is somewhat jokingly dubbed the "white teapot," a relatively wealthy and well-educated majority-white area shaped like a kettle in uptown New Orleans, around Audubon Park near Tulane and Loyola universities, with a curving spout along the St. Charles Avenue/Magazine Street corridor through the French Quarter and into the Faubourg Marigny and Bywater. Comparing 2000 to 2010 census data, Campanella shows that the teapot has broadened and internally whitened, and the changes mostly involve gentrification. The process has also progressed into the Faubourg Tremé (not coincidentally the subject of the HBO drama *Tremé*) and up Esplanade Avenue into Mid-City, which ranks just behind Bywater as a favored spot for post–Katrina transplants (Campanella 2013). Without a doubt, the current gentrification in New Orleans and the elimination of the public schools will exacerbate the problem associated with New Orleans segregated educational system.

NEW ORLEANS PUBLIC SCHOOLS

Gabor (2013) examines the rise of charter schools in post Katrina New Orleans, raising an important question, "Are New Orleans's schools a model for the nation or a cautionary tale?" New Orleans public schools have a long history of failure connected to the city's high poverty rates and racial diversity, but post–Katrina New Orleans has experienced a second flood, a school reform surge characterized by charter schools, Teach for America (TFA), and education reformers from outside the city and the South. Charter schools represent reform policies supported both by Democrats and Republicans that view public school traditions, teacher certification and teachers unions, as root causes of poor academic outcomes. To eradicate those in-school problems, choice and competition are embraced as the primary tools for reform (Gabor 2013; Layton 2014).

The Louisiana state government of Democratic Governor Kathleen Blanco used the disarray after Hurricane Katrina to fire or push into early retirement all the public school teachers and workers in Orleans Parish (New Orleans). A class action suit by eight fired employees revealed the number of workers terminated was over 8,500 (*Times-Picayune* 2008). The state school board took over most of the schools and proceeded to "charterize" them—that is, hand them over to private organizations, both non-profit and for-profit. Charter schools are publicly owned and government-funded, but privately managed. The state school board has thirty-eight schools privately run and thirty publicly run. The Parish school board runs four schools directly and oversees twelve charter schools (*Times-Picayune* 2009).

According to Cohen (2014), it is hard to believe, but the New Orleans public school system—nominally the New Orleans Recovery School District—is entirely comprised of charter schools. After Katrina had devastated the entire New Orleans public school system, the state created the Recovery School District to run the system, and in doing so placed its bets on charter schools. The changes in the public sector have been widespread (Jordan 2011).

New Orleans is a unique place to start. New Orleans is the nation's first all-charter school district. Indeed, Mullins (2014) reports, "the Big Easy is taking a unique approach—New Orleans will begin the next school year with America's first all-charter school district. In September 2014, Louisiana's Recovery School District will close the last of its public schools that have not been turned into charters, leaving it a 100 percent charter school district." There are now more than thirty different charter school operators in New Orleans alone (Quigley 2011). As reported by the Institute on Race and Poverty of the University of Minnesota Law School, "The reorganization of the city's schools has created a separate but unequal tiered system of schools that steers a minority of students, including virtually all of the city's white students, into a set of selective, higher-performing schools and another group, including most of the city's students of color, into a group of lower-performing schools."[6]

In addition to the segregated and lower performing schools, economically marginalized students of color in New Orleans may also be challenged academically by their lack of access to adequate public healthcare.

PUBLIC HEALTHCARE IN NEW ORLEANS

At a post–Katrina relief clinic in 2005, local residents lined up at a health fair and doctors treated them for everything from diabetes to heart disease. But also among the stressed health conditions, doctors found a lot of people who had lost their jobs, lost their health insurance, lost their physician and their hospital (PBS 2006). Despite this obvious healthcare crisis, Charity Hospital—New Orleans's largest public hospital—remains closed, as do half the hospitals in the city. It is not clear whether it will reopen. Instead, local elites decided to shift indigent care and its state and federal compensation to private hospitals with people traveling as far as eighty-five miles to the Earl K. Long Hospital in Baton Rouge which reports a 50 percent increase in uncompensated care (Quigley 2007). Closing Charity is just a political myopia. In addition, the existence of a public hospital is deeply ingrained in the Louisiana psyche (Long 2007).

Charity in New Orleans was founded in 1736.[7] Under the impact of Huey P. Long—who some consider a most eloquent populist and the greatest ever Louisiana governor—a statewide system of Charity hospitals was developed in the late 1930s and early 1940s. The present New Orleans Charity Hospital was built in 1938, with federal funds from the New Deal (Morrison 2010).

Lovell (2011) juxtaposes the hallmark of Charity's iconic safety net network with the new challenge arising from the federal government's creation of the Medicaid program, which concentrated the poor and uninsured exclusively to Charity system hospitals. The uniqueness of Louisiana's Charity Hospital system was rooted in the principle that everyone has a right to medical care—certainly anathema to American neoliberalism and hardy individualism, but founded in the 1930s populist doctrine of the Long dynasty that governed Louisiana for decades. However, the arrival in the 1960s of Medicaid, the major program to assist low-income individuals with obtaining health services, intensified a two-tiered system of healthcare (Lovell 2011). Roberts and Durant (2010) acknowledged that since the Civil Rights Movement, Charity system patients have been predominantly African American. Amnesty International's report echoed the ACLU and ISS reports on the loss of mental healthcare, but also emphasized Charity's closure as a disproportionate loss for the working poor and the uninsured; Charity served a largely poor, predominately minority population through inpatient care, a network of outpatient clinics and the busiest emergency department in the city. Nearly three-quarters of its patients were African American, and 85 percent had annual incomes of less than $20,000. Over half of the indigent care provided by Charity and University hospitals was for patients without insurance, representing two-thirds of the care to the uninsured in the city (Ott 2012).

CONCLUSION

New Orleans has a lot to tell us about RGC; the continued desperate poverty of the city's African American population is, of course, a part of it, but so is the poverty of political debate in New Orleans today. The crisis everlasting—poverty, schooling, health—provides questions about what's wrong in this country.

Katrina forced us to pay attention. We're forced to look at New Orleans and to really see it—one of the nation's great party cities and also one of its poorest. If you go for Mardi Gras or the annual Jazz Heritage Festival, or really if you go any old time, you know its majority black population is mostly hidden from white tourists. Beyond the gorgeous French Quarter and Garden District, it's long been a crime-plagued, gang-ridden, corruption-befouled city. But as long as you stick to the French Quarter, you don't have to care (J. Walsh 2005; L. Walsh 2005). Although jarring, these truths can only be shocking to those who have willingly ignored systematic evidence of what former senator and vice-presidential candidate, John Edwards, topically called the "two Americas" (Strolovitch, Warren, and Frymer 2006). Edwards may not have specifically mentioned RGC during his popular campaign stump speech, but social scientists and political activists have long tried to draw the nation's attention to the scope of racialized, gendered, and classed poverty in the United States, particularly in the South. It is no accident that African Americans in New Orleans are disproportionately poor, or that a disproportionate number of the poor in New Orleans are African American. It is the result of centuries of concerted decision-making by political actors at the local, state, and national levels, going back to the days of slavery and continuing up to our current political moment. While these decisions have had disproportionate effects on African Americans in the southern states, the exploitation of racial animosity also undermined the possibility of a comprehensive safety net that would have benefited white poor and working-class southerners as well. Though many in the media focused on the failed political response in the immediate aftermath of Katrina, little attention was given to the long-term effects of weakened government capacity and its core functions in providing aid, services, and jobs to impoverished urban communities, as well as the historical role of race as a causal factor that has shaped these intergovernmental relations. The story of Katrina is one of a human-made disaster that was predictable, preventable, and reflected decades of public officials working with private industry to place profits over people.

The true tale of the current post–Katrina New Orleans's recovery is one of the privatization of public education and healthcare in ways that will maintain social inequalities. Instead, what New Orleans and the Gulf Coast needed was a massive public works program: a New Deal.

It is a tale of public officials leaving the most vulnerable residents behind, branding them "criminals" after days of inexcusable delay, gunning them down in the streets, treating them like rubbish in evacuation facilities, and shipping them all over the country with no way to return home. The days after the storm saw racially motivated crimes akin to the violence during the Civil Rights Movement that went uninvestigated for years, regardless of numerous eyewitnesses and bodies with bullet holes. The tale of post–Katrina New Orleans is one of dismal social services, skyrocketing housing costs and rates of homelessness, mass closure of public housing, racist housing policies, disaster profiteering, and privatization of the educational system in ways that promote racial and socioeconomic segregation.

Unquestionably, the link between RGC left us trying to figure out why Katrina's destructive force disproportionally impacted the lower social class across racial and gender lines. Then intellectually and theoretically we are pressed by the rebuilding of New Orleans to rethink the concept of RGC in bringing back the concept of class at the center of the triad. We must also "revitalize" the idea that we need a different alternative to the ruthless free market principles imposed upon New Orleans rebuilding process, something very few have considered.

As Freire and Araujo Freire (2004) said, "Without hope there is little we can do. It will be hard to struggle on, and when we fight as hopeless or despairing persons, our struggle will be suicidal." As a result I am aware that I run the risk of being accused of privileging class over race/gender as a category of oppression, an issue that is sharply dividing social activists and theorists on the left and specifically among RGC. We should not be shocked that the rebuilding of New Orleans eliminated all the main public institutions such as public education, housing, and healthcare since we are living in a system which privileges the free market principles, the interest of a class-based economic and political system hierarchical and unequal by its nature. In fact, too few Katrina researchers have stressed the central role of class in the recovery.

Klein (2007) suggests neoliberal capitalism has transformed the provision of crisis relief and social reconstruction to reflect neoliberal values—that is to instill classic private free market economic attributes through the marshalling and reallocation of once public resources. Neoliberal capitalists have no interest in repairing what was. In Iraq, Sri Lanka, and New Orleans, the process deceptively called "reconstruction" began with finishing the job of the original disaster by erasing what was left of the public sphere and rooted communities, then quickly moving to replace them with a kind of neoliberal reconstruction—all before the victims of war or natural disaster were able to regroup and stake their claims to what was theirs.

Regrettably, it seems correct having fears and beliefs that decisions about the future of the city are being made without the most impacted storm victims (Rose and Tuggle 2010; Perry and Schwam-Baird 2010).

Although other cities are reconstructed under neoliberalist policies, New Orleans is a unique case study showing how the recovery process challenges our political beliefs and keeps us asking: recovery for whom and what? Ten years after Katrina, New Orleans has destroyed the most important social institutions which are vital for the poor who are disproportionately racial, ethnic minorities and women. From a sociological and political standpoint I believe that class, not separated from race and gender, is the winner in American politics.

Finally, on the front page of the *Times-Picayune* (August 2014) entitled "Clear Out Now," writer Richard A. Webster reports that "the city gives homeless people a three-day eviction notice to leave the Pontchartrain Expressway overpass. The timing seems to have something to do with the Saint's Friday season opener at the nearby Superdome." Three days later on the front page article titled "Time to Move On!" writer Webster said, "There are about 2,000 people in any given night in New Orleans and Jefferson Parishes living on the streets, in abandoned homes or in temporary shelters, according to Unity" (*Times-Picayune* 2014). April and George are two of the homeless individuals highlighted in the *Times-Picayune* article. April is pregnant with twins and she and George could no longer afford their apartment due to rising rent and the lack of affordable housing in the city. It might be for April and George that the New Orleans recovery is a failure.

NOTES

1. This is our lived Katrina experience as expressed by Christiane Charlemaine, my spouse who experienced Katrina with me.

2. Michael Harrington was an American political activist and educator (1928–1989). He was a tireless advocate of democratic socialism. He helped develop the War on Poverty conducted by presidents Kennedy and Johnson. Harrington did the well-known book titled, *The Other America: Poverty in the United States* (1962). *The Other America* had tremendous impact. In it he spoke up for what he called the "invisible poor": industrial rejects, migrant workers, minorities, and the aged. Harrington's book came to the attention of President John F. Kennedy. As Kennedy biographer Arthur M. Schlesinger Jr. explained it, the book "helped crystallize his determination in 1963 to accompany the tax cut (with) a poverty program." Kennedy died before his plan could be realized, but it was put into effect with impressive results by President Lyndon Johnson. If Harrington had done nothing else his place in history would be assured.

3. See http://www.informationclearinghouse.info/article17181.htm.

4. The Housing Act of 1937 linked all new low-rent housing to slum clearance by mandating an "equivalent elimination agreement": public housing construction must be accompanied by the "elimination by demolition, condemnation, and effective closing, or the compulsory repair and improvement of unsafe or insanitary dwellings situated in the locality or metropolitan area, substantially equal in number to the number of newly constructed dwellings provided by the project." This provision effectively ensured that public housing would not contribute to any significant gains in the low-rent housing stock, since even if "elimination" was accomplished through rehabilitation rather than demolition, the resultant improved properties would probably demand substantially higher monthly rentals. The required link to slum clearance efforts also encouraged public housing construction in inner-city neighborhoods, rather than in more affluent peripheral areas. In this way, public housing itself constituted a form of neighborhood renewal in the form of replacement housing, even as many other neighborhoods were cleared for other purposes, many of which served private purposes much more than public ones. Sources: http://www.hks.harvard.edu/inequality/Seminar/Papers/Vale11.pdf.

5. Also a new toponym: gentrification has a vocabulary as well as a geography.

6. Institute of Race and Poverty. The State of Public Schools in Post–Katrina New Orleans: The Challenge of Creating Equal Opportunity. A report by the Institute on Race and Poverty, at the University of Minnesota Law School May 15, 2010.

7. Charity Hospital was the primary provider for the large poor and uninsured population in New Orleans pre-Katrina. In New Orleans, Charity Hospital was the hub of the LSU system, serving a largely poor, predominantly minority population through inpatient care, a network of outpatient clinics, and one of the busiest emergency departments (EDs) in the country. Nearly three-quarters of its patients were African American, and 85 percent had annual incomes of less than $20,000. In 2003 more than half of the inpatient care provided by Charity Hospital was for patients without insurance, compared with only 4 percent of inpatient care at other New Orleans hospitals. Charity Hospital accounted for 83 percent of all inpatient and 88 percent of all outpatient uncompensated care costs in the New Orleans area. It was also the dominant provider of substance abuse, psychiatric, and HIV/AIDS care in the New Orleans area and the only Level 1 trauma center on the Gulf Coast; the only other center in the state is more than 300 miles away in Shreveport (Rudowitz, Rowland, and Shartzer 2006).

III

Doing Academia through Disaster Recovery

Chapter Ten

Trauma Survivor as Author; Method as Recovery

Jessica W. Pardee

I am who I study. For nine years I have studied Hurricane Katrina, as a survivor and former resident of New Orleans. A trained urban sociologist, after the storm I respecialized in disaster, interviewing public housing women about their new lives. If they could survive, so could I. Yet, how did they do it? In the process of "conducting research," I was forced to deal with their trauma, and my own. This chapter examines what it means to study a traumatic subject of which you are also the subject of study. While personal experiences affect research interests, the experience of researching one's own trauma is intensely different, complicated, and rarely addressed (see Layne 1996; Swain 2013 for exceptions). Reflexivity is one aspect of research which has been well examined, though it barely scratches the surface of the emotional work (Hochschild 1979, 1983) that trauma research, especially research of which you are also a subject, demands.[1]

Yet, the methods books remain silent on how to work through trauma as a scholar-survivor. Instead, they focus on managing sexual harassment or arrest in the field—reasonable issues, but inapplicable to my case. Retraumatization, the deep emotional distress and depression that emerges during the research, analysis, and dissemination processes, is a challenge largely absent in the conversation of "preparing for the field." In fact, the absence of any type of discussion on trauma methodology in several standard research texts, such as Schutt (2009), Babbie (2001), Singleton and Straits (1999), Berg (2009), Denzin and Lincoln (2011), and the Sage QASS research methods book series, is remarkable. In response, this chapter presents an honest reflection on the unanticipated consequences of being intimately connected to your subject. How *do* you handle the trauma of your respondents as you, too, are facing the same trauma and pain?[2] How do you reconcile the benefits afforded to you by your positionality in race, class, and gender hierarchies (Hesse-Biber, 2011; DeVault 1999; Taylor 1998; Weber 2010; Reinharz 1992) when connecting with other survivors through a sense of survivor solidarity? What does it mean for you, your soul, and your work when the trauma and pain you study is also a trauma you acutely feel? Can the benefit of your work help heal the wounds of trauma you experienced as a victim, and later again as a researcher? Can method actually become recovery?

On August 29, 2005, Hurricane Katrina made landfall in Louisiana. Almost a decade has passed, yet the disaster landscape in which I lived after the storm remains fresh as ever in my memory. In this Katrina disaster landscape, "the collapse of the social institutions (i.e., public safety, hospitals, transportation, and so on) led to a setting in which one's life and one's outlook on life were fostered by individual stress and collective trauma, creating feelings of uncertainty and distrust—and a loss of social capital" (Miller and Rivera 2007, 145). That landscape began when I was safely evacuated at a friend's house in Houston, Texas, watching television for any new bits of information about the storm I could glean. Throughout that Monday, I saw the white outer shell of the Louisiana Superdome rip off, the ceiling caving in at its centermost point. In the adjacent high-rise hotel buildings, windows were blown out and their blinds flapping in the wind. I watched further as news reporters hid behind postal boxes to prove they were "true" weathermen, all the while their stupidity seemed to downplay the severity of the storm. It was stressful, yet exciting to watch, and expected for a storm of this size—a strong Category 3.

What was unexpected was the aerial photo of a broken levee that greeted me on Tuesday morning. Turning on the television, I expected to see clear skies so I could return home that afternoon, with the worst of the wind long past. Instead, that image and those that followed—SWAT teams roaming the city at night, "looters" being held at gunpoint, thousands of people waiting for help at the Superdome and Convention Center, snipers shooting at the hospitals, and families stranded on rooftops and public housing balconies—came to frame my understanding of the catastrophe before my eyes. I had escaped the immediate crisis, but why was this happening in my city? And looking back, how did we ever allow the subsequent social response to fail as it did? How did rescue and remediation efforts become manipulated into publicly sanctioned displays of racism, classism, and sexism (Pardee 2014; Idakula [2007] 2011; Tierney, Bevc, and Kuligowski 2006; Drier 2006)?

As the story of the broken levees began to unfold, I was embraced with a sense of helplessness. What do I do? Are my friends safe? Do I have a home to return to? What happened to the women I had planned to study? The very weekend of Hurricane Katrina, I was supposed to complete final revisions on my dissertation prospectus. I was supposed to evacuate on a writing holiday and return with a final draft in hand. I was supposed to study how low-income women were adjusting to their newly constructed, privately managed, publicly subsidized HOPE VI housing units. Now, as the flood maps of the city emerged, as water levels rose, as more levees ruptured from pressure bursts and overtopping (NOVA 2005), I realized that one of my two research neighborhoods was flooded with over eight feet of standing water. All the new hopes and dreams, new chances, and new housing were uninhabitable, devastated like the methodological validity of my comparative case analysis.

I took action where I could. Within weeks, I changed my study completely to find these same women, to learn how they would survive the transition into a new life, one undefined due to the chaos that Katrina created. How do women with few, if any, resources recover from a storm like Hurricane Katrina (Pardee 2014)? The literature on disaster recovery describes a return to normal (Couch 1996, 68) that was simply unavailable after the storm for low-income families, especially those families whose public housing units were systematically demolished at site after site across the city (see Arena [2012] for a detailed account of this mass public housing retrenchment, and Belkhir's work in this volume for an examination of post–Katrina gentrification). Likewise, when the concept of failed recovery is described with the same characteristics as living in daily urban poverty (see Erikson 1994; Freudenberg 1997, 1993; Edelstein 2004; Picou, Marshall, and Gill 2004; Adams et al. 2002; Roberts and Toffolon-Weiss 2001 for discussions of disaster recovery; corresponding poverty research: Wilson 1987, 1996, 2010; Massey and Denton 1993; Murray [1984] 1994; Dreier, Mollenkopf, and Swanstrom 2001; Edin and Lein 1997; Rainwater and Yancey 1967), what does recovery even mean for people who are low-income? (See Pardee (2014) for an extended discussion of this question.)

I barely knew how I would get by, which led me to be even more deeply obsessed with learning the fates of the low-income, Black and African American women within these two communities.[3] Somehow, I felt both a sense of duty and of desperation to locate and interview these women—not to abandon them after the storm—as if maybe in hearing their stories, I might find a way to reconcile the deep feelings of loss and trauma that accompanied my own, giving meaning to this catastrophe. Implicitly, albeit unknowingly, I was engaging in feminist praxis, by redesigning the study as I did. According to Taylor, "the core of a distinctive feminist methodology [is]: a focus on gender and gender inequality, a spotlight on the everyday experiences of women, reflexivity as a source of insight, an emphasis on participatory methods, and a policy or action component" (1998, 360). My compulsion to honor these women by making their stories heard and part of the written Katrina record harkens back to the goal of feminist research—"to make women's experiences visible, render them important, and use them to correct distortions from previous empirical research and theoretical assumptions that fail to recognize the centrality of gender to social life" (Taylor 1998, 360). In this way, my work documents and theorizes the lived experiences of low-income, African American women in a disaster, where existing literature on women's disaster experiences are limited overall (Enarson 2012; Enarson and Morrow 1998; Fothergill 1998, 1999b), especially their intersectional disaster experiences (see Weber and Peek's [2012] volume for an exception).

Returning to New Orleans in late September 2005 to assess my apartment, loss was everywhere I turned. While I have never regretted studying Hurricane Katrina as a survivor, it has caused me to grieve the experience on a deeper level than I ever expected, one which still leaves me raw in select moments after nearly a decade. It is this grief, this trauma, and its significance in shaping my scholarly work that is the focus of this chapter. For how do you study a topic of which you, yourself are the subject? How do you survive a terrible trauma, and then manage the inevitable feelings that emerge as you study that same event? How do you balance academic protocol and discourse against your own humanity and personal needs? For me, it was a complicated, extended process.

SCHOLAR-SURVIVOR REFLEXIVITY

At the time of data collection, I would categorize myself as a post-positivist methodologist (Guba and Lincoln 1994), who was doing mixed-method research under the supervision of largely quantitative and positivist-oriented scholars. I was silently a political feminist, but not a feminist scholar, as I struggled to situate the narrow gender-only focus of feminism (as I understood it at the time) against the intersectional experiences of my own life, and the lives of the women who I studied. For me, race and class mattered more than gender. While I appreciated the feminist critique of positivist research methodology and took efforts to treat respondents as equals, I still viewed them as "respondents" telling "stories" that I would "study" (Singleton and Straits 1999; Schutt 2009; Pardee [2007] 2011). Now, almost a decade later, I consciously work to identify them as women who shared their lived experiences with me (Pardee 2014) in an effort to give well-deserved respect to those who opened up broken, exhausted hearts in the hope of preventing a social disaster such as the Katrina response from ever happening again. This professional resocialization is difficult, recent work. In the last few years I have increasingly become aware of the reality that my performance of data collection, as well as the action-oriented goals which were privately explicit for me as I conducted my analysis and painstakingly selected the language within my book, were inherently feminist (Taylor 1998). My reluctance in accepting this academic positionality reflects an ongoing academic tension over the researcher role and objectivity in the discipline, as perceived by myself and as I expected it of the various compositions of my dissertation committee.[4]

Trained in a positivist perspective, I was taught to ask set questions, using identical wordings without veering from the script, and not to share personal information, while emphasizing reliability, validity, and objectivity in the process (Schutt 2009; Singleton and Straits 1999; Converse and Presser 1986). The goal was to collect data in such a way that the interviewer becomes interchangeable, while the responses would be identical. Personal information, friendly banter, or explaining a question's meaning were all potential sources of bias. Yet, as a scholar-survivor (my standpoint a la Harding), behaving objectively as a woman shares the intimate details of her trauma is simply unethical. To remain impersonal while asking questions about a woman's time spent stranded at the Louisiana Superdome, the death of friends or family, material losses of her home or belongings, as well as financial losses of jobs, social assistance, or other limited resources, was offensively exploitive if I wasn't willing to provide, at minimum, the nurturing support of a feminine listener during the interview. In this way, my own gendered self-expectations positioned me to reject masculine forms of absolute objectivity and perform the researcher role as a feminist methodologist once the open-ended questions began (Taylor 1998; DeVault 1999; Harding 2004; Blizzard 2007). Not inconsequentially, I increasingly questioned the logic of the assumptions surrounding interviewer bias at this time—for example, if rapport is important for data gathering in qualitative studies (Berg 2009), wouldn't it also yield more accurate responses to quantitative questions?

I was also aware that a feminist methodological approach which values human connection, respect, and women's empowerment (Taylor 1998; DeVault 1999; Blizzard 2007) was important to me as an emerging independent scholar. In practice, I split the difference by behaving like a positivist during the quantitative section of the survey, while reserving my feminist openness to full disclosure and sharing of experiences until the open-ended questions at the interview's end. I maneuvered this balance gingerly, in an effort to meet the goals of researcher objectivity, while sustaining the respect and empowerment afforded by feminism. Admittedly, I also willingly used that positivist researcher role as a mechanism to manage my immediate emotional reactivity when faced with detailed traumatic descriptions during the interviews. With concrete questions to ask, a "professional" (masculine) role of sticking to the script provided a mask of objectivity to hide behind in those moments when my heart was breaking. The mask was not impervious. There were interviews, especially in the open-ended question section, when the interview and note taking stopped so the woman and I could just connect about her pain, and our shared experiences as Katrina survivors. Through this survivor solidarity, I found using a blended performance of positivist and feminist researcher roles in alternation allowed me the fortitude necessary to record the devastating accounts women chose to share (to be discussed below). In this way, my positivist performance overtones were tampered down by my feminist undertones. Research bias arguments were rejected in practice as I embraced my standpoints as a fellow storm survivor, as well as through the other identities I shared during the interview (Harding 2004).

PERFORMING METHODOLOGY THROUGH A SURVIVOR–SOLIDARITY STANDPOINT

Being a Hurricane Katrina survivor put me in a unique place as I began locating women to interview. I returned to live in New Orleans in early October 2005, and began data collection soon thereafter. Like the women who spoke with me, the rawness of the storm was still fresh. In retrospect, my success has largely to do not with my personal ability to establish rapport, so much as my respondent-granted legitimacy to research the topic from a survivor–solidarity standpoint. This standpoint was supported by, and blended with, other statuses we shared, particularly social class and gender (Harding 2004).

As a child born at the bottom of the working class, I received WIC and free lunches from elementary school through high school. Both my parents worked; my family is large. In college, we received anonymous gifts from generous townsfolk who blindly donated clothing and other goods to my family. I was embarrassed of my family's status growing up, which fueled my efforts to go to college. Now, I respect my parents' work ethic—hard work in an economic system with unequal rewards. This standpoint translates to my research because I do not blame or judge the poor; I recognize the challenges to being "successful" in a competition-based political economic system, where by design some groups are denied access to social mobility. Through sharing my identities, of being the oldest of five children and the first to complete college, I built a rapport that went beyond survivor solidarity.

As I approached each interview, I had specific manners in which I presented my identities in an effort to minimize barriers based on race, class, and education. First, I was vetted by a Black reverend in the city who provided a list of women he thought would speak with me. With his endorsement, I was able to introduce myself and explain why I was calling for an interview. In the first fifteen seconds, I'd say "Father Sam [pseudonym] said you might like to talk to me." Because he had provided their names, the trust in him was transferred in part unto me.

The second tactic I used was honesty about my own history, which was essential when making cold call contacts. Within the first minute, I would share my identity as the oldest of five children, explaining that the research was for my dissertation. I would slip in that I was the first to go to college and finish. These standpoints would be interspersed amid the dry positivist disclaimers of research risks and contact information required by the institutional review board (IRB). I used my big family identity to symbolically represent my lower-class origin, which helped to offset my status as a student at "Tulane," an expensive private institution.

The third tactic was open disclosure about my Katrina experiences, which framed my interests as genuine, especially because I am a woman. Discussing emotions is a feminine gender expectation, which reinforced the notion that I understood the depth of trauma and loss I was asking women to recount because I was from New Orleans and we were both women (Taylor 1998; DeVault 1999; Harding 2004). I, too, evacuated and returned to live in the post–Katrina disaster landscape. I felt a shared loss, expressed through post-interview conversations about NOLA's slow recovery. I was open about how I was graced with no deaths in my close social circles, yet how many people I knew lost so very much. I saw the destruction within these women's neighborhoods firsthand and shared the recovery status with them. As their temporary in-town informant, when I told women their story was important to me and that I didn't want their experiences to be forgotten, it was true and they knew it.

This is not to suggest that outsiders cannot study Hurricane Katrina with deep sensitivity and investment, as many have (see the work of Lori Peek, Alice Fothergill, and Jacqueline Litt for exemplars). Rather, I argue my own humanity and loss became an asset to data collection, not a deficit to it through reduced objectivity as positivist paradigms suggest (Haney and Barber 2013; Taylor 1998; Warren 2000; Harding 2004; Madison 2005; Goodall 2000). When I assess the quality of the data I received, the trust which women placed in me as they shared their experiences, and the seriousness of the losses they sustained, I cannot accept the masculine framework of positivist objectivity as a responsible form of trauma-focused research. Instead, it was my humanity informed by feminist sensibilities which created a safe space for the narratives of survival and loss to be expressed in the first place.

CONDUCTING RESEARCH IN THE KATRINA DISASTER LANDSCAPE

Living in New Orleans during the early recovery was filled with unexpected personal challenges, even surrounding the mundane. Unlike the "living in two worlds" experience following Hurricane Andrew, where people went to work in intact offices and jobsites in Miami, while returning to devastated homes afterward (Smith and Belgrave 1995), in the Katrina disaster landscape visual reminders of devastation were omnipresent. Even as I walked from my house to the coffee shop on the next block, there were piles of tree limbs along the path. Two houses down from the coffee house was a home that had collapsed. Possessions still inside, the walls had folded under and a roof sat on top the pile of rubble. Four blocks in the opposite direction was another house where the end wall fell off. As you walked by, you could see all the contents inside, like a life-sized dollhouse. Here was someone's whole life, open for the world to see. I uncomfortably shot one roll of traditional camera film to capture these images at that time, at my grandfather's request. Creating visual documentation seemed to exploit people's pain, and I, too, wanted to forge ahead toward recovery—whatever that meant.

In those early days, perhaps the most neglected sensory experience surrounding us all was the smell. With power outages across the city, refrigerators held shelves full of rotting food, as mold came to invade the insulated linings of the units. To this day I cannot smell some types of mold, particularly those which came to live in my own fridge. For me, cleanup meant removing the contents of a forty-gallon fish tank covered in maggots, where the three fish I had left were indistinguishable from the murky water within. Next, I cleaned the fridge in a failed effort to salvage it. Ultimately, I found help to drag it to the curb, adding it to its kin. In New Orleans at that time, you could look down the street and see "refrigerator families," sets of multiple refrigerators huddled together in front of empty homes. Many had political graffiti statements, such as "Deliver to 1600 Penn Ave." The clustered refrigerator family pattern was a courtesy between neighbors who had to live within the constant, moldy, rotten stench of the debris-laden city. The refrigerator families stood in locations where their noxious, nauseating odors would only affect you when captured on the wind. These were small but gracious acts of post-storm humanity.

Living within the disaster landscape, I found the idea of absolute objectivity in data collection impossible to implement. While researchers from other places were living between two worlds—the disaster landscape they would temporarily visit and the intact landscape of their everyday lives located elsewhere—I was faced with living in the landscape of loss and it constantly hurt (Smith and Belgrave 1995; Miller and Rivera 2007; Rose 2005). For me, there was only the Katrina landscape with depression, bulldozers, National Guardsmen pointing guns at residents, sexual harassment, suicides, toxic mold, and rejected insurance claims (Pardee [2007] 2011; Rose 2005), all of which drove my choice for compassion and emotional accessibility during each phone call. For, while my survey instrument was a telephone survey, in many ways, I was also unknowingly engaging in a "new ethnography" of the Katrina disaster landscape (Goodall 2000).

From this vantage point of absolute devastation within the disaster landscape of Hurricane Katrina, I began making phone calls. With just one neighborhood allowed to return to live (mine), I relied on telephone interviewing to make contact with survivors. It would be months before other neighborhoods were reopened, especially those with high minority populations. The telephone was the only possible way to find women who were scattered to the winds. To locate women, I worked in multiple directions at once, using a list of resident names from my prior research project on public housing gentrification, while also pursuing other avenues.

For example, I made contact with churches and social service agencies within the city and outside of it, I mailed letters to the addresses from the roster, as well as calling old phone numbers on the chance they might still be connected. I also hung posters in corner stores and on telephone poles in adjacent communities or in places where a friend or family member might see. I left homemade pamphlets in mailboxes of undamaged units, and continued to work every lead I could. I also had a bit of luck when Father Sam gave me a list of contacts, based on the trust we built prior to the storm through conversations about the changes in his neighborhood. Finally, I asked each woman for referrals as well. Out of a starting list of nearly seven hundred names, I secured fifty-one interviews over fifteen months. For the others, the phones were disconnected, and the letters returned to sender. This massive displacement, one which lingers into the present, affected my ability to locate women. It also demonstrated the uneven redevelopment of New Orleans, as evidenced by the 2010 Census data in which over 100,000 fewer African Americans lived in the city when compared to before the storm (U.S. Bureau of the Census 2010).

For me, it was only by leaving the city's disaster landscape in July of 2006, an act of personal survival, when I resumed access to intact societal structures, typical university resources, and stable social relationships (in the sense that large clusters within my social and professional networks were no longer moving away). It also provided me with access to mundane necessities: clean water, open grocery stores, a regular paycheck, and family, coworkers, and new friends who weren't all living in a constant state of pain and loss as they managed the realities of their own recovery experiences and the hundreds of thousands around them.

In many ways, leaving the city by choice, not force, was a key step in my own recovery. When I moved, I disconnected myself emotionally as well as geographically. I chose not to follow the local news through NOLA.com, especially the weather reports or reports on public housing reform. I shifted my research to disaster more generally, and have been inching away from an exclusive focus on Hurricane Katrina. I return to the city selectively and have avoided visiting unless I am attending a professional conference. Other important steps were completing data collection, and disseminating the findings through my dissertation and published book, entitled *Surviving Katrina* (Pardee 2014). Yet, the book took years to write, because examining the data at the level of contextualization needed to do justice to women's trauma meant painstakingly re-reading the interviews again and again, rather than reviewing fragments of them culled by the qualitative coding software. The relief I now feel is largely new, emerging from an unexpected sense of fulfillment and emotional release when the book arrived to me in print. My personal recovery has been defined in part by fulfilling the promise I made to women to make their experiences known, and to empower their losses to become a form of feminist resistance against the repetition of such atrocious response behaviors in the future (Taylor 1998). My personal recovery had to be defined thusly because given the plethora of change among the social structures which framed my pre-storm New Orleans life, there was no pathway back to normal for me.

MANAGING TRAUMATIC DATA

As a New Orleanian, collecting data on the severity of incivility women experienced following Hurricane Katrina was emotionally devastating on a personal level. More women shared their intimate anguish, loss, fear, pain and anger than I ever expected. I felt helpless often, with a counseling hotline number as my only tool to aid them with their emotional recovery. Throughout the interviews, it was clear that there was no censoring of the atrocities women experienced, observed, and chose to share. I documented many accounts of threatened and actual violence, the observed rape of children, as well as the fear and panic of women stranded during the storm itself, as levees broke, water rose, or trees fell through flimsy wooden homes with women and their kin huddled inside (Pardee 2014).

As examples of the type of trauma accounts I was exposed to repeatedly, I provide two decontextualized quotes below. My decision to decontextualize the quotes in this chapter is a result of my own need to be emotionally withdrawn as I engage with the data at this time. In fact, recognizing the emotional work required and respecting my limits is a mechanism of self-care that allows me to do sustained research in disaster given my personal standpoint as a survivor. I have often taken an approach of complete emersion and complete disconnections for periods of about two to three weeks each throughout my time working on this research. As best I can understand it, this approach creates a balancing point between accepting the horrific events that transpired, and recovering from the emotional toll that the content creates. I have learned to know when I cannot push ahead, and when I can. Within the survivor–solidarity standpoint, I have no option for a true psychological retreat—the pain embedded within the fully contextualized experience of Katrina for women who shared their accounts with me is my pain, too. In this way, my standpoint may bias my work, but not in the manner positivist methodologists are concerned with; instead bias emerges in the way in which feminist methodologists critique positivism for its limited contextualization (DeVault 1999).

How do you process traumatic information, and keep composure? How do you stay open to listen, while keeping your emotions under control? For me, I used both positivist objectivity and feminist subjectivity selectively at different points in time to keep the interview going despite my own distress. As I write today, I now embrace a feminist attentiveness to assure I am not being voyeuristic with my data selections below. I share them *only* to make the notable point that more attention needs to be paid in training graduate students in sensitive, ethical ways of engaging in the complexities of traumatic data collection before we send our students out into the field.

> Joanne: Between seventh grade and age thirty, I seen like 150 people shot—one execution style, and shot right there at my feet. But I block that out of my mind. I feared that storm more than I felt fear ever living in the projects. . . . It's like a nightmare I'm not getting over. It's the same way I look at it, ma'am. How can you be in a project and see killing and not be disturbed, but you more disturbed in a hurricane? I seen shooting since the seventh grade, it's like it was normal to you. I didn't have no fear of that, I seen it, but I didn't feel it, I blocked it. But the hurricane, it's 24/7. It is always pitch-dark. It was like, like a nightmare.

> Faith: I bury my son with "ifs, ands, and buts." The police can't even say why he was shot—I can't close the case. I can't say they did a good job. This detective on my son's case is on 50, 60, or more cases. How can he find a killer? I try not to let my kids see me break down. If they see me crying, then they crying all over and they go through the same trauma. I can't say some nights I'm not in my bed crying. I can't let them see it. I have two girls and a boy. If they see you crying, they depressed for the rest of the day.

These quotes are by no means atypical to the collection of accounts women shared. A single woman may have three, four, or more points in the interview where the account of her actual, lived experience was simply stunning, in the worst possible way. Joanne's pain and trauma seep out through her words even now in the written text—contrast that to the lived experience as a scholar-survivor hearing the intonation, cadence, and quivering of voices as tears spill over a phone line. Faith's loss is accentuated by the fact her son was only murdered because she chose to return to New Orleans to care for her aging parents. To hear the guilt and self-blame was difficult, yet to block out absolute empathy as a fellow survivor was impossible. Nearly a decade later, I am still emotionally connected and invested in the content of the "data"—the experience of shared pain between two survivors performing an "interview" in the context of an aspatial disaster landscape. And it is because of this deep personal pain I chose not to maintain contact after I completed the interviews. Disconnection was one of my recovery strategies. Simply stated, it hurt too damn much.

EMPOWERMENT THROUGH SURVIVOR–SOLIDARITY

How do you study a topic of which you are a subject? Can method be recovery? Over time and with reflection, my research has functioned to convert my pain into power, making my pain productive and a form of feminist activism as part of my personal recovery. My survivor–solidarity standpoint created a starting point for my research at which most ethnographers end their work (Goodall 2000). I knew the New Orleans landscape intimately, and the disaster landscape personally. This rich embeddedness positioned me to produce scholarship that subverts stereotypical narratives of Black looters (Tierney, Bevc, and Kuligowski 2006; Taylor 1998; Madison 2005), and replaces such narratives with meaningful accounts of African American families who helped each other when first responders passed them by (Pardee 2014).

Doing disaster research from a scholar-survivor standpoint means embracing the power of your own positionality. As insider, your loss empowers you to know what questions to ask, yet how to ask them with sensitivity. In my work, the probes were gentle and conditional. I prefaced sensitive questions with "if you are comfortable." The goal was a practice of care work, of emotional work—to provide an interview experience which allowed women the choice to decline not only the interview, but individual questions within it. This standpoint also means you can bypass gatekeepers by finding other points of entry into the research community—your community. The shared identities allow for points of connection, even in cold contacts. With the shared survivor standpoint, there was always something to talk about.

In conclusion, method can be recovery when the role of objective researcher is transformed to the role of an embedded, community researcher—where work can be completed with sensitivity, rather than exploitation. While the goal of objectivity in research is logical, within the landscape of trauma the insensitivity of an objective stance can lead to a sense of exploitation, one which I personally felt as a participant in another scholar's Katrina research study. By contrast, the subjective stance of being a fellow survivor becomes an asset for gleaning more accurate, contextualized information as the goal becomes learning about the social world through an interview with a person. We interview and survey *with* people—they are not our subjects; they are not required to help us. Following a disaster, making the interview request is asking a lot. In short, how we approach an interview can shape the texture and richness of descriptions of lived experiences. Finally, for future scholar-survivors embarking upon studies of their own trauma, it is imperative to anticipate that, and then how, the work will affect you on a more intimate level than expected. Plan for it and be willing to feel that pain, because in the end, those shared experiences and the sensitivities which arise from them will inform the research. It will help you describe the context with richness and sensitivity, to understand the importance of the experiences to your participants' lives. And as a survivor, it might even be a form of recovery—through sociological activism—that creates meaning from a situation otherwise incomprehensible to the soul.

NOTES

1. I would like to acknowledge and thank Deborah Blizzard for her support and emotional work. Deb, you are the definition of an amazing colleague.
2. In Pardee and Blizzard (2014), we examine the mechanisms we engaged to process traumatic information and experiences in the research process during the data collection and dissemination stages of our work. Comparing my work on Hurricane Katrina to Blizzard's work on fetal surgery, we were astonished by the high level of overlap in our organic coping mechanisms during two research processes separated in time by over five years. See also Haney and Barber (2013).
3. Some women who shared their experiences with me indicated they were "Black" and specifically not "African American." Out of respect for their self-identity I use both terms in my work. Additionally, I purposefully capitalize "Black" in reference to race as a form of respect, given I am a white researcher.
4. Due to mass faculty turnover in my graduate department after the storm, my committee changed composition multiple times.

Chapter Eleven

Housing Market Mayhem

Studying Discrimination Post-Disaster

Jeannie Haubert

I was lucky. People usually look at me funny and think it's strange for me to say, given that my home and all its contents were demolished in the storm, but a lot of us say that. Yes, living in Mississippi in a flood zone, I had experienced much more destruction of property than my friends who lived on high ground in uptown New Orleans. And I was technically homeless for a bit, although it never felt like what I imagine homelessness to be like for the millions of people who experience it daily. When I explain to friends, family, and the occasional acquaintance that I was never hungry, covered in filthy waters, didn't see anyone die, didn't have to sleep on the streets or on a cot or worry about my safety, and didn't even have to go a day without electricity, the lucky comment sinks in. I got out ahead of Katrina, and I was "fortunate enough" to find a series of places to live as I figured out my new path.

After hearing all that, they come to understand that, as far as experiencing the storm and being displaced, I was lucky. Or was I? I've come to see my experience as amounting to more than just "luck"; rather, I see my post–Katrina story as a series of privileges, some of which were given to me based on my middle class status and white skin and what people assumed that indicated about my character (see chapter 6 in this volume). In my opinion, my membership in those groups helped me find a place to live, survive, and thrive post–Katrina. I "beat out" others in the competition for housing only because I had substantial savings to be able to put down a large sum of money for a deposit and because my skin color, dress, and speech suggested I would not be a problem tenant. And if we are being real about what white privilege or class privilege is—unfair rewards given out simply based on an individual's membership in a social category—then we have to admit that the flip side of that coin is discrimination. Class-based discrimination is not illegal but discrimination based on race, color, or national origin certainly is, and class and race are inextricably intertwined in the Deep South. With hundreds of thousands of racial minorities left homeless by Katrina, I worried about whether they would get a fair shake in the housing market because, for me, finding a new place to call home represented the cornerstone of my mental and physical recovery from disaster.

My experiences after Katrina, along with my sociological training, made me question what displacement and recovery was like for the hundreds of thousands of non-white evacuees. Landlords could afford to be picky and jack up prices post–Katrina, which could have easily had a negative impact on non-white people looking for a place to live. I wanted to find out if this was a problem and, if so, how big the problem was. As a specialist in racial and ethnic relations, I study these things in hopes of raising awareness when there are systemic inequalities and to do my small part to change it. But given the disaster's impact on the housing market, was it even possible to study whether discrimination was occurring? If we could systematically uncover it, would there even be repercussions for those who engaged in discrimination?

The chapter that follows reveals important methodological and legal loopholes that open up in housing markets following a disaster. These loopholes must be closed for the United States to make good on its promise of fair access to housing for all and for disaster victims to have any hope for a speedy recovery. Simply put, it is more difficult for minority disaster victims to recover at the same rate as their white counterparts because housing discrimination is *more likely, less detectable,* and *less regulated* in a post-disaster context than under normal circumstances. When paired with the lack of affordable housing, a true housing crisis, arises.[1]

FINDING THE "IDEAL TENANT"

Housing discrimination is not only unfair and counter to the American dream, but it has the important consequence of contributing to patterns of residential segregation. Segregation rates were high in New Orleans to start with and patterns of resegregation are ensuing post–Katrina (Campanella 2013). This restricts minority households' access to neighborhoods with quality schooling and other important neighborhood amenities that affect health and quality of life. Fair housing enforcement efforts, usually carried out by local non-profit fair housing organizations following victim complaints, help uncover discriminatory behavior, but in a post-disaster scenario, these local nonprofits have limited capabilities and local residents have much more pressing matters to deal with than filing complaints. Despite a lack of complaints, I argue that race-based housing discrimination is more likely following a disaster. To understand why, it is important to explore what influences rental agent behavior.

A wide variety of factors can influence how rental agents—defined as private landlords and apartment complex managers—treat potential renters. Are potential tenants courted or simply tolerated as they inquire about an available unit? Are they treated fairly, turned away, or exploited for higher rents? Are they seen as "ideal tenants" or viewed with suspicion?

In general, the housing literature finds that racial and ethnic minorities, single women, families with children, and members of religious minorities face a harder time renting or buying homes and often incur more costly housing searches. These home-seekers put their best foot forward when interacting with housing agents, sometimes altering their dress or speech or highlighting parts of their background that they think will make them seem more attractive to a rental agent (Weil 2009), but race/ethnicity-based housing discrimination still occurs. For example, the most recent nationally representative housing discrimination study from the U.S. Department of Housing and Urban Development (USD HUD) revealed that minority renters, across twenty-eight metropolitan areas, were told about and shown fewer available rental units than their white counterparts (Turner et al. 2013). African Americans were told about 11.4 percent fewer units, Hispanics 12.5 percent fewer units, and Asians 9.8 percent fewer units, and the authors of the study admitted that this quasi-experimental methodology (discussed in more depth later), is likely an *underestimation* of actual rates of discrimination against minorities due to real world differences in average incomes between racial and ethnic groups (ibid.). Results were significant for discrimination in home buying as well as renting and do not include well-documented lending discrimination that is also a part of the home buying process. In other words, despite the promises of the Fair Housing Act, discrimination rates remain high resulting in an unfair and likely exhausting search for minority home-seekers.

Not only do the characteristics of the potential tenant matter in how home-seekers are treated, but rental agent characteristics matter too. For example, studies have found that private landlords discriminated much more often than professional rental agents (Massey and Lundy 2001; Fischer and Massey 2004).[2] This is important because, due to limitations on the Fair Housing Act, discrimination tests typically include only apartment complexes run by professional rental agents. Unfortunately, when the Fair Housing Act was passed, it *excluded landlords with fewer than four units* meaning that anti-discrimination laws are unenforceable in cases involving such landlords. At the time that the Fair Housing Act was being considered (1968), this concession for "mom and pop" landlords was made in order to overcome opposition to the proposed legislation and simply get the law passed. The law was controversial at the time, but was finally passed in the days following MLK Jr.'s assassination as a way to ease national tensions and to honor his legacy. As I will explain in this chapter, excluding individual landlords from complying with fair housing laws is particularly devastating in a post-disaster context and there is an urgent need to finally close this loophole in civil rights legislation.

SOCIAL FORCES THAT AFFECT RENTAL AGENT PRACTICES

While the most emphasis is typically placed on the personal characteristics of the renter, several studies have found higher rates of discrimination against racial minorities in predominantly white neighborhoods as compared to predominantly minority neighborhoods (Purnell, Idsardi, and Baughs 1999; Massey and Lundy 2001; Fischer and Massey 2004) indicating that neighborhood characteristics also matter. One study, for example, found that black testers were more likely to experience discrimination in the suburbs than in the central city (Fischer and Massey 2004). Interestingly, the areas with the highest rates of discrimination were those that residents considered "in transition" meaning that they were not overwhelmingly white or black in their resident composition. These studies are important because they acknowledge that rental agents do not operate in a vacuum. Their interactions with others are structured by the social and historical context of the area. Certainly economic factors, the history of race relations in the area, as well as current racial group dynamics could all influence rental agent behavior. For example, perceived group threat theory extended to the housing market would imply that white rental agents may perceive black or Latino renters as threatening the status quo in a neighborhood if the size of the black or Latino populations relative to the white population is large and if economic conditions create scarcity (Quillian 1995). The same prejudice could also apply to other minority groups if they are large enough relative to the local white population.

Even though it is essential to understanding post–Katrina housing dynamics, one external factor that is typically ignored in the housing discrimination literature is the level of supply and demand in the local housing market. Researchers have overlooked this larger market force that either enables or constrains the ability of rental agents to be selective in their choice of tenants. Post-Katrina, rental agents had every opportunity to selectively choose their ideal renter as demand for housing far exceeded supply and rental agents had little chance of facing consequences if their actions were discriminatory since regulatory agencies were similarly damaged. Fair Housing centers such as the Greater New Orleans Fair Housing Action Center and the Gulf Coast Fair

Housing Center experienced interruptions in service due to both physical damage to the nonprofits and the displacement period for employees.[3]

Moreover, the nature of the tight housing market made the traditional methods of detecting discrimination much less effective than they are under normal circumstances. Thus, in a post-disaster context, rental agents are operating relatively unfettered.

Although neoclassical economic theories of supply and demand have not been tested in the housing market literature, labor market researchers often focus on supply and demand dynamics. There is a natural parallel between housing markets and labor markets in that housing agents are in a power position similar to employers wherein they control access to the desired commodity be it a job or a home. Housing agents, like employers, fill vacancies in the market by making selections from a pool of applicants who must meet certain criteria to be eligible; thus labor market theories can be usefully used to infer how changes in supply and demand likely affect housing markets.

Neoclassical theories of discrimination posit that competition in the marketplace—such as when housing complexes compete with one another to attract renters—eliminates "tastes for discrimination" against certain groups (Becker 1971). This perspective suggests that rates of discrimination should be lower in what I call "loose markets," in which housing supply exceeds demand and housing agents compete with one another to attract a limited pool of tenants. Conversely, discrimination should be higher in "tight markets," in which home-seekers compete with one another for a limited pool of rental units as they did post–Katrina. Just as levels of unemployment influence hiring decisions, vacancy rates can influence rental agent decisions. When rental housing is at a premium then, as it was post–Katrina, rental agents have more freedom to exercise their preferences or prejudices, leading researchers to suspect that housing discrimination likely increased.

To illustrate the limitations of discrimination audits in post-disaster contexts, the next section briefly discusses some of the housing discrimination literature and details how my study was organized. Following that, I explain the impact of major changes in the housing market on my study, concluding with a discussion of the implications for academics, nonprofits, and government agencies interested in both uncovering and preventing housing discrimination.

THE STUDY: HOUSING DISCRIMINATION IN MISSISSIPPI PRE- AND POST-KATRINA[4]

Prior to Katrina, I was studying the relatively small, but new influx of Latinos to the Mississippi Gulf Coast. There was a local Latino festival that had recently begun in the area, a handful of tiendas (Latino stores) popping up around town, and there was even a Latin American Association that had formed in an area that had long been characterized by a black/white dichotomy. The research I had been reading on immigrant incorporation had much to say about the importance of the "contexts of reception" in new immigrant destinations. In other words, whether natives roll out the welcome mat or slam the door affects how well immigrants are able to adjust and achieve success in their new surroundings. I had to wonder how these newcomers were being received in Mississippi, an area renowned for its racial hierarchies. Because of this, I decided to focus my research on investigating housing market discrimination. The audit study I constructed focused on the early stages of housing searches, the initial phone inquiry. When I began the study in 2004, I had no idea that housing market dynamics would change so drastically through the course of my study nor did I know that housing access would take on such a heightened importance.

Research conducted by linguistics professors have shown that Americans can identify race by voice with incredible accuracy (Purnell et al. 1999). In a study conducted at a university on the East Coast, one word ("hello") was presented to 300 students. Based on that one word, they were able to make positive ethnic identification more than 80 percent of the time. Extending the study to phone-based housing inquiries, the researchers found, after making nearly 1,000 calls, that landlords do discriminate on the basis of racially and ethnically identifiable accents. Other studies have had similar findings and have tested a combination of gender, race, and class as embodied in accents (Massey and Lundy 2001). These researchers found discrimination on all three axes with important interaction effects. Not surprisingly, poor black women were found to be the most vulnerable to discrimination. Importantly, it is not simply whether one has an accent that predicts discrimination, but what that accent is assumed to signify about the speaker (earnings potential or economic stability or responsibility for example). In talking about foreign accents, Lippi-Green (1997) argued that, "only accents which are linked to skin that isn't white or which signals a third world homeland evoke such negative reactions" (238), citing French and British accents as non-stigmatized accents.

Audit studies (also called "paired testing") are by far the most common way that researchers and anti-discrimination organizations investigate housing discrimination (Turner et al. 2002; Massey and Lundy 2001; Fischer and Massey 2004; Yinger 1995; Galster 1990). If an agent is being tested for race/ethnicity-based discrimination for example, audits would match the profiles of non-Hispanic white and minority auditors (also called "testers") on all other pertinent characteristics such as income, occupation, sex, age, and number of family members in the household, even clothing style among other characteristics. Each tester then inquires about advertised housing and records a variety of notes from the interaction such as whether the unit was available, how much it cost what was included in the price, whether there was an application fee, etc. Tests are "blind," meaning that the tester does not know what type of discrimination is being investigated (i.e., sex, age, race, or another status protected by the Fair Housing Act as amended in 1988). These field experiments are designed to reveal differences in treatment and isolate the cause of that difference. Because all other renter characteristics are controlled, if a minority tester is treated worse than a white tester or flatly denied access to available housing, the researcher can infer that race/ethnicity-based discrimination has occurred.

Although researchers using audit methods have received some criticism for ambiguous definitions of disparate treatment and for not adequately accounting for random noise in the data, audit studies are generally regarded as "an essential methodology for assessing levels of discrimination" (U.S. Department of Housing and Urban Development 2014). Academics, HUD, and fair housing organizations throughout the country rely on audits as their primary means of uncovering housing discrimination, and the U.S. courts have repeatedly upheld lawsuits based on audit evidence. Additionally, the real estate and lending industries have begun using audit methods to self-monitor compliance with the Fair Housing Act. In response to critics, researchers have honed audit methods to more precisely define disparate treatment and better account for random error (for example, see Turner et al. 2002).

For my audit, I recruited and carefully trained Hispanic and non-Hispanic white (Anglo) testers with the help of a fair housing agency on the Mississippi Gulf Coast. Testers were interviewed before being selected and were monetarily compensated after completing the audits. Testers were provided a profile of matched background information and standardized training along with a script.[5]

The audits took place in fall 2004, winter 2006, and spring 2006, meaning that one audit was conducted before Katrina hit in August 2005 and two were conducted in the year following the disaster.[6] The advertised rental units were randomly selected from www.apartments.com, a website that merges local newspaper ads with ads placed directly by multiunit apartment complexes and allows individuals to restrict a search by county. Thus, the sample included private landlords as well as apartment complexes of various sizes rented out by professional agents. I restricted my sample to only those listings in Coastal Mississippi where Katrina's impact was most severe.[7] Testers made their calls within hours of one another to minimize the impact of changes in unit availability. When an agent answered, the testers proceeded through a semi-scripted conversation to gather information on the costs, terms for renting, and availability of the advertised unit and other units that the agent might have available. The phone calls were recorded and the testers filled out a summary sheet of notes on their experience (see Weil [2010] for further methodological detail).

Katrina's forceful winds and massive storm surge not only changed the supply and demand for housing on the Mississippi coast, but she changed the way housing agents and home-seekers interacted. For example, pre-Katrina, rental incentives (i.e., first month free or no security deposit) were often offered to Anglo home-seekers and not to the Latino callers (Weil 2010). For obvious reasons, rental incentives were not offered to any caller post–Katrina. Pre-Katrina rental agents often offered to "work with" the caller to negotiate costs. Even five months following Katrina, no such offers were made. Below I describe the rental housing market in each time period and discuss in further detail how housing availability shifted the nature of these interactions and impacted the discrimination audit.

OCTOBER 2004: A "LOOSE MARKET" PRE-KATRINA

The first round of testing took place in what might be called a "loose market" or a "renter's market." In these types of markets, vacancy rates are moderate to high and the onus is on the housing agent to attract and retain a quality renter. Consequently, rental incentives are relatively common particularly among apartment complexes in such markets. Also, agents may express a willingness to negotiate costs to attract renters in such a market. In the pre-Katrina market, this seemed to be more common among larger low-income apartment complexes and trailer parks.

According to interviews with employees of the Gulf Coast Fair Housing Center, a typical rental agent pre-Katrina would receive anywhere from a few calls a day to a few calls a week. These agents often took time to "feel out" the home-seeker over the telephone by asking questions about why the caller was moving, where the caller had lived before, where the caller worked and in what occupation, and how long the caller had lived in the area. The testers received extensive training to prepare them for such questions and ensure that responses were comparable.

Discriminatory acts could range from denying that an advertised unit was still available to requiring more of a minority renter. Extra requirements often included higher deposits, criminal background checks, credit history checks, or simply the omission of a discount that was offered to attract the non-Hispanic white renter. "Application fees" usually cost around $50 and were designed to cover the costs associated with a background check (see Weil [2010] for more on the findings). All of these forms of discrimination add to the challenges of housing searches for minority renters in that they may have to search for longer than non-Hispanic white home-seekers, make more inquiries to find an available unit, be subject to more rigorous and costly application processes, or even pay more for a unit.

FEBRUARY 2006: A "VERY TIGHT HOUSING MARKET" POST-KATRINA

Round two of testing took place five months after the hurricane and both the housing market and housing agent behavior was noticeably different. Not only were there considerably fewer units advertised, but who was advertising had changed. Whereas the pre-Katrina market had many more apartment complex advertisements than private homes, just the opposite was true post–Katrina. Apartment complexes, often built of cheaper materials than single family homes, were disproportionately damaged by the high winds and storm surge that impacted the Mississippi Gulf Coast. When testers called the apartment complexes that were advertising post–Katrina, they discovered that these complexes had long-term running contracts with the apartment guides and were running ads despite the fact that they did not actually have any vacancies. In fact, many of these complexes had been destroyed but the advertisements still circulated even five months later exacerbating the frustration of those still looking for a home. Although single family homes were also heavily damaged post–Katrina, those that survived the storm were able to be repaired more quickly than entire complexes. Homeowners looking to rent worked quickly to take advantage of the high post–Katrina prices they could demand. By February, enough people had repaired damaged houses that these rentals were appearing in the paper with some frequency.

The costs for advertised homes were extremely high; more than double the comparable pre-Katrina rent amounts (Crowley 2006). Although very low housing supply and high demand meant that housing generally became more expensive post–Katrina, it was the *most* expensive vacancies that were advertised in the newspaper because a vacant affordable home could easily and quickly be filled through social networks. In this type of market when vacancy rates are very low, rental incentives and offers to negotiate costs with potential renters disappeared.

With so many people displaced and so few undamaged houses, the number of calls an agent received each day for an available unit skyrocketed. As a result, agent/caller interactions became extremely brief and standardized, so much so that some agents simply stopped answering the phone and used answering machine messages to convey to interested callers the costs of the unit and where to apply. Landlords were clearly overwhelmed by inquiries. Some answered the phone with an exasperated, "Hello! You are my 18th caller today" and continued to rattle off answers to anticipated questions before testers even had an opportunity to speak. Rather than try to "get a feel" for the caller or woo potential applicants as they had done pre-Katrina, they hurried through the interactions and often seemed annoyed at having to answer any questions. Because housing agents were fielding so many calls each day, whether agents used an answering machine or not, their interactions with callers took on a "prerecorded" tone. Contrary to neoclassical economic theory which would predict higher discrimination in tight housing markets, standardized interactions meant that there were minimal differences in how testers were treated over the phone post–Katrina. (There is further discussion later in this chapter on whether more in-depth audits could capture differences in treatment in a post-disaster market.)

MAY 2006: STILL A "TIGHT MARKET" POST-KATRINA

Each week, the housing market "loosened up" ever so slightly as more renovated houses and apartment complexes became available and more displaced individuals had settled in somewhere. However, judging by the prices being asked for advertised units along with anecdotal reports from interviewees, May 2006 still very much represented a tight market. In fact, median rents were slightly higher in May ($1,130) than in February ($1,095), and still more than double the previous October ($485).[8] Interestingly though, offers to negotiate costs reappeared during this time period. Rental agents who were still trying to profit from the inflated post–Katrina rent prices found that demand was slackening somewhat and they were aware that high post–Katrina housing prices were difficult for the average local resident to afford. Demand for a particular unit likely decreased as the housing supply increased—evidenced by the greater number of units appearing in the listings in May 2006 versus February 2006.[9] Rental incentives (i.e., $100 off the first month's rent or no deposit), were still non-existent in this tight housing market.

In sum, once the strain between supply and demand decreased somewhat, rental agents again began to court some tenants. Although some were offered cheaper units than others, the preliminary telephone-based interactions suggested that Latino home-seekers were not turned away. Landlords appeared willing to rent to any tenant willing to pay the high post-disaster prices, assuming that the renter could pass a credit check. Interviews did reveal, however, that the required credit checks did of course block some Latino home-seekers, particularly newly arrived immigrants who operate in a cash rather than credit-based economy (Weil 2007a).

Contrary to what neoclassical economic theories would predict, the audit did not reveal more pronounced housing discrimination after the disaster. That surprising outcome is more about changes in the nature of post-storm interactions than about any actual decline in discrimination. After Katrina, the expectation was that discrimination against Latinos—a category of newcomers that were migrating into the area in large numbers to help with cleanup and rebuilding—would be much higher given the lack of available housing and their "outsider" status; however, the results of the audit showed only modest levels of discrimination that were actually less impactful than pre-hurricane findings. There are two possible explanations: 1) discrimination actually was not worse post–Katrina, or 2) it went undetected by the audits. The second explanation seems most plausible for the following reasons: First, regulatory agencies were also in recovery mode and were less able to be watchdogs. Second, tenants were plentiful and habitable dwellings were in short supply giving rental agents a substantial upper hand. The damage in this particular county (Hancock) was so severe that nearly all, if not all rental dwellings were damaged (U.S. Department of Housing and Urban Development 2006). Many of those were severely damaged or completely destroyed, 1,215 out of 3,450 rental units according to damage estimates as of February 2006 (ibid.). Data shows rental agents substantially increased rents for undamaged or less damaged units, thus, it seems logical that they would also use that upper hand in tenant selection. Given the history of race relations in Southern Mississippi, one would expect that rental agents who are largely white, would also exercise a preference for white tenants if there were no foreseeable consequences.

CONCLUSION

The current focus in housing discrimination research on individual characteristics of either the renter/homebuyer or housing agent is myopic. It is vitally important that we also consider the impact of larger social forces such as neighborhood demographics and vacancy rates that reflect supply and demand. We must realize that housing discrimination is more likely following a massive disaster and the displacement it produces. Unfortunately, when demand is high and supply is low, housing discrimination becomes more difficult to study using traditional methods. As evidenced above, phone audit methodology is unlikely to detect discrimination because standardization of renter-landlord interactions becomes necessary to efficiently handle call volume. Weary of all the inquiries, landlords recited a script they had spit out numerous times before and quickly hung up reducing the possibility of discrimination at this stage in the interaction. The question remains though, is this specific to telephone audits, or does discrimination surface at later stages in the agent/renter interaction? Would the same limitations apply in the subsequent face-to-face audits wherein testers visit the property to inspect the home and apply for the rental?

Face-to-face housing audits are also likely to face difficulties under disaster conditions. Even if the audits went further and testers were to apply in person for an available unit, in a very tight housing market it would be extremely difficult to prove that the agent's choice was based on racial or ethnic discrimination because of the sheer number of applicants for any given unit. An agent could easily argue that, yes, he or she chose a non-Hispanic white applicant over a qualified Latino applicant, but had also turned down forty other qualified non-Hispanic white applicants. Also, with the speed at which homes were renting (see chapter 6 in this volume), if a tester was told at 9:00 a.m. that an apartment was available and another arrived at 9:30 a.m. and was told it was unavailable, it is quite plausible that the house was actually rented that quickly. Whereas in a normal housing market a quick refusal would have inferred discrimination, in a tight housing market, timing is everything making it extremely difficult to design an effective audit. Thus, fair housing advocates and researchers in post-disaster zones face formidable challenges in uncovering any discrimination that may be occurring using audit methods. While this problem is likely most pronounced following a disaster like Katrina or an earthquake that decimates the housing supply, it may also be applicable to other tight housing markets such as those characteristic in and around Manhattan or San Francisco.

Complaint-based data would not be a suitable substitute for audit data because extraneous variables are not able to be controlled, confounding the cause for the disparate treatment. Moreover, extensive research shows that contemporary discrimination methods are often subtle and targets of discrimination may not even be aware that they have been treated differently. Lastly, even if they were aware of differential treatment, following a massive disasters, home-seekers have more pressing concerns than filing discrimination complaints suggesting that discrimination would be severely underestimated.

Given the flaws in audit methodology in a post-disaster context, and given the increasing frequency and intensity of natural disasters as global warming changes the natural landscape, we urgently need to come up with alternative means of studying discrimination in such markets. In the meantime, area fair housing agencies will need to be creative in how they approach their dual mission of education and enforcement. Enforcement post-disaster will be limited, but perhaps educating rental agents (many of whom may be new landlords who quickly buy a damaged house and fix it up to rent) on fair practices should take on even more importance. They may not be aware that the rules don't apply to those with fewer than four units and even if they do, it is useful to provide a set of guidelines to let them know what they should be doing when screening applicants (even if it is not what they *have* to do).

While the above suggestion could help with promoting fair housing practices, the *most* troublesome flaw is not so much in the difficulties detecting discrimination and struggling fair housing agencies limited regulatory abilities, but rather in the fair housing law itself. Following a disaster private landlords dominate the post-disaster rental market as apartment complexes are more susceptible to damage than sturdily built private homes. Moreover, prior studies have found that individual landlords, as opposed to professional agents at apartment complexes, are far more likely to discriminate (Massey and Lundy 2001; Fischer and Massey 2004). This means that even *if* fair housing organizations were not also in recovery mode post-disaster, and even *if* audit methods worked effectively to prove discrimination post-disaster, the vast majority of housing agents operating in this market have free reign to exercise any and all preferences or prejudices because the law does not hold them accountable. Thus, the severe lack of livable housing, while important, is not the only housing problems following a disaster. For a member of marginalized groups, access to the housing is further limited by unregulated discrimination. There is no doubt that this massive legal loophole has a large and disproportionate impact on minorities, families with children, people with a disability, and women following a disaster as all of the above groups face housing barriers even under normal conditions. Under post-disaster conditions, these disparities are magnified. Following a disaster, all residents should have both the right to return and access to inclusive communities. Instead, because of a lack of affordability, failures in leadership, and housing policy, "the people with the fewest resources have the fewest housing opportunities in the rebuilt Gulf Coast" (Crowley 2006, 142).

We need to be creative if we are committed to ensuring equal access to available housing following a disaster. Thinking about housing discrimination processes as similar to employment discrimination processes is one way of rethinking recovery. Perhaps, the U.S. Department of Housing and Urban Development (USDHUD) should consider implementing government sanctioned diversity initiatives in disaster zones that operate in a similar fashion to affirmative action in employment. Such bold steps may be necessary to promote fair housing for all in very tight or disaster-stricken housing markets, particularly if discrimination varies by the type of neighborhood in which the unit is located and if vacancies are filled primarily through segregated social networks.[10] Rather than mandated compliance, such an initiative could come in the form of incentives that encourage stable community integration, such as tax breaks given to complexes that rebuild with a proportional level of racial/ethnic representation in the community or tax incentives to private landlords who promote diversity in neighborhoods. Given the tremendous importance of place in shaping life chances and the continued segregation of neighborhoods and cities in the United States, a post-disaster housing diversity initiative would have important consequences in making sure that neighborhoods and apartment complexes repopulated in a fair and equitable manner.

To make a case for the need for such initiatives, future research should attempt to further investigate the degree to which housing market access is limited for racial and ethnic minorities in post-disaster housing markets. The problem is that without evidence, we cannot push this much needed policy change and the nature of the post-disaster market makes gathering evidence difficult. This chapter has provided some suggested starting points, but much more collaboration amongst housing market researchers is needed to find the most effective way of studying post-disaster housing discrimination and ensuring equitable repopulation and recovery.

NOTES

1. Portions of this chapter were previously published in *How Ethnically Marginalized Americans Cope with Catostrophic Disasters* (2010), Edwin Mellon Press.

2. Professional agents are defined as those who work for a larger organization and are charged with renting out units, for example, workers at property management groups or managers at apartment complexes. These agents typically go through anti-discrimination training in the course of their job training.

3. My husband at the time, Jason Weil, worked for the Gulf Coast Fair Housing Center. Their office building was left uninhabitable by Katrina. Employees could not return to work for nearly two months and when they did it was to set up an entirely new office. James Perry in the Greater New Orleans Fair Housing Action Center did important anti-discrimination work after Katrina, and their office sustained less damage than in Mississippi, but certainly the long displacement period took a toll on employees' ability to get back to work.

4. The study that I briefly describe has been published in a more expanded version so I don't go into extensive detail about the findings here (see Weil [2010] for more detail); however, some methodological detail is necessary to understand the research challenges posed by disaster.

5. The training encouraged testers to stick closely to the required questions and not to volunteer any personal information unless the agent asked. The training also emphasized that the primary responsibilities of the testers were to elicit the necessary information about the unit, to be convincing as a bona fide home-seeker, and not to deviate from the assigned background profile. The profiles and training standardized the agent/client interactions and isolated ethnolinguistic speech patterns as the sole point of variation between callers with one exception. To minimize random error in the data, minority callers were assigned a slightly higher income. In theory, this should give them a slight advantage in the interaction thereby making claims of discrimination more conclusive if they receive less favorable treatment.

6. Because the nature of the housing market varied between rounds of testing, profiles necessarily varied across rounds so that testers would be inquiring about the average advertised housing units (typically larger and more expensive in rounds two and three). This change was necessary because rent amounts increased and almost no one bedroom units were advertised after the hurricane because private homes were generally more available than units in apartment complexes.

7. The randomly selected listings included in my sample covered fifty-two census tracts in Harrison, Jackson, and Hancock counties, with the largest number of selected housing units located in the cities of Gulfport and Biloxi. All three counties were coastal counties and were heavily impacted by Hurricane Katrina in August 2005.

8. Note, however, that some of the difference in median rents between rounds one and three is attributable to the number of bedrooms that the testers were looking for in each round. In round one, only ads for one or two bedrooms qualified for selection, whereas in rounds two and three, only ads for two to three bedrooms qualified. Still, a housing survey done just one

year before Katrina found that average rent for a two-bedroom apartment in that area was only $562 (W. S. Loper et al. 2004)

9. Although it seems most likely that the change in offers to negotiate is a result of change in the housing supply and demand, it is important to note that round two callers were men whereas round one and three callers were women. An alternative explanation then would be that the change was attributable to the gender of the callers. For example, housing agents might have assumed that the unmarried female callers would have more difficulty paying high rents since women earn less than men on average leading them to offer to "work with" female callers by spreading out payments. Or housing agents may view two unmarried women as more desirable tenants than two unmarried men and offer to negotiate costs for that reason. Because I was unable to collect pre-Katrina data using male testers, this hypothesis cannot be tested with these data.

10. Analyses of these Mississippi audit data also used a spatial analysis that added geocoded census data to the audit data to test whether discrimination is influenced by the ecological position of the unit, specifically the racial composition of the neighborhood. Consistent with past literature on the subject, findings suggested that housing agents with units in "integrating" neighborhoods may be more likely to discriminate than those in "whiter" or more heavily minority neighborhoods.

Chapter Twelve

"We're Still in the Trenches, Baby . . ."

Navigating Academia in an Uncertain, Post-Katrina World

Danielle Antoinette Hidalgo and Dana M. Greene

Downtime at the local bar is such a luxury that it often feels like these moments in time occurred in another life. Overwhelmed with teaching four classes, trying to remain relevant and engaged in our disciplines, and committing ourselves to one too many obligations with little or no recognition often feels like wasted effort—nearly two decades of wasted effort. But this night at the bar with friends was a time to forget about all of that, forget about the ongoing worries, the relentless uncertainties, and the tiresome and broken promises. Tonight was going to be a mini-vacation from responsibility, stark realities, and the many frustrations that typically emerge from an uncertain job market—until a local friend and whip-smart colleague took a moment to catch up with me. We caught up on one another's lives, immediately drawing me back to my situation, drawing me out of my moment of freedom and once again into the uncertainty of my academic existence. She lamented, "I just found out that my friend from graduate school got tenure. It's so crazy and such a weird feeling seeing our friends make it, isn't it? We're still in the trenches, baby, we're still in the trenches." Indeed, we are. And it's a battle that has no definitive end date nor conclusion. It's ongoing and relentless and, quite honestly, exhausting, demoralizing, and often falls into blame-gaming (What am I doing wrong? What's wrong with me?) rather than clear reflections on the larger state of things and the global world that has impacted all of us.[1]

This chapter addresses the U.S.-based academic job market post–Katrina and following the 2007–2008 recession. We connect lived post–Katrina experiences in academia to the larger post–Katrina global economy. The narrative detailed in this chapter shifts from one unstable position to the next: from a Katrina evacuee to a relocated graduate student post–Katrina to an unemployed academic post-graduation and to, ultimately, a non-tenure track (NTT) faculty member. We connect the academic tenuousness in this narrative to what we call *normalized uncertainty*, or a state of being in which uncertainty, vulnerability and the temporary become and remain a way of life. Typically, this means that roots are not made or cultivated (i.e., buying a home, investing in any property, even buying a car or any other extended expense is simply unattainable or especially risky), relationships remain fragmented and shifting (i.e., uncertainty about one's job prospects makes creating and sustaining any long-term intimate relationships and friendships very difficult), and any additional long-term decisions such as raising a child or even purchasing or collecting furniture for one's home remain that much more complicated. Further, this list does not even begin to include the incredible lack of time that NTT or "precarious academics" have to devote to their writing and research, especially given their often intense teaching schedules. Finally, while "most Americans interpret these issues as a private matter of making the most of one's opportunities" (Brown et al. 2011, 13), as we consistently remind our undergraduate students, individualistic readings of the situation are simply not sociological and fail to see and, perhaps, come up with solutions that might address how to challenge the larger system and accompanying social practices that are creating these inequalities (see Chomsky 2014).

On March 28, 2014, Mary-Faith Cerasoli stood outside the New York State Department of Education in Albany in an attempt to highlight just how urgent and inexcusable the plight of NTT, and adjunct faculty throughout the nation truly is. In response to her protest, a wave of NTT faculty descended upon Twitter, voicing their concerns, sharing their experiences with unstable academic positions, and showing their support for Mary-Faith, and other NTTs throughout the nation. In solidarity, adjunct professor Dr. Arik Greenberg wrote, "Keep the faith, Mary-Faith. We are with you." Dr. Jeffery Maret of St. Louis, Missouri, added, "anthropologist and another exploited professor but today we stand as one." Echoing their comments, Margaret Hanzimanolis posted, "I am an adjunct. I am tired of legalized discrimination. I am standing in support of Mary-Faith. I am determined to work for equal pay 4 = work" (for an excellent discussion on this issue, see these *PBS Newshour* reports: Greenberg 2014; Steffensen 2014; and Fruscione 2014).

The lead author's post–Katrina recovery narrative is inextricably connected to the precarity of NTT life more generally. Immediately following the storm, universities throughout New Orleans engaged in austerity programs that entailed cutting entire programs, and firing both tenured and non-tenured faculty members. This forced both professors and graduate students into highly unstable positions beyond the already generalized intense instability that they were experiencing in post–Katrina New Orleans:

> [U]nder the cover of a declaration of fiscal exigency, Tulane [University's] president, Scott Cowen, proffered a "Plan of Renewal," which included reorganization or elimination of academic programs and major changes in the curriculum. Some faculty members charged that the plan was an opportunistic effort to implement proposals that had been presented to the faculty and defeated before Katrina. Tulane's administration rejected this interpretation of events, but President Cowen conceded that the hurricane had allowed him to take "bold" actions that could not have succeeded under normal circumstances. "Out of every disaster comes an opportunity," Cowen said. (Ginsberg 2011, 10)

Elizabeth Fussell, a not-yet-tenured (though tenure-track) sociology professor living in New Orleans and working at Tulane before and after Katrina, explains how this "Plan of Renewal" played out for the Tulane University Sociology Department:

> The Sociology Department—which had recently been ranked 25th in terms of high-profile faculty publications—had its graduate program eliminated as a result of the administration's attempt to cope with the fiscal crisis brought on by hurricane- and flood-related damages. Without a graduate program, Tulane's department would not be ranked at all. The new School of Liberal Arts looked more like a liberal arts college and less like a research university. (Fussell 2008, 64)

NARRATING POST-KATRINA UNCERTAINTY

As a sociology graduate student, I found myself squarely in the middle of these post–Katrina changes at Tulane, and was worried about a number of outcomes: Will my committee members leave Tulane, before I finish my dissertation? Given the fact that the PhD program was eliminated, could I get any internal funding for my research? Upon graduating from a now-eliminated PhD program, how competitive will I be on the job market? After weighing all of my options, and, as a backup plan, I spent my winter break (before Spring 2006, and soon after Katrina) applying to three PhD programs that might reasonably support me as I completed my dissertation. I received acceptance letters from all three programs, and subsequently spent the Spring semester deciding which program would be best for my final years of graduate school.

Although I did everything I could to navigate post–Katrina precarity and complete graduate school both successfully and with a strong publication record, unfortunately, my post–Katrina recovery period has entailed a continuation of the instability I experienced at Tulane University in those early months following the storm. Connected to the post–Katrina milieu, I have similarly found myself in the middle of the nationwide, university-based administrative actions that are promoting record numbers of contingent labor (professors with temporary jobs and little or no benefits, for example), increasing fees for students, and a general lack of opportunities and support for junior academics. Between Katrina and the 2007–2008 recession, there is an uncertain future for the vast majority of professors like me.

Since Katrina, I've been in limbo, as if my feet are never solidly on the ground; a deep feeling of normalized uncertainty permeates my everyday life. I was a strong graduate student and good at research, but the fact that I completed my PhD at UC Santa Barbara (UCSB) rather than Tulane is somewhat miraculous given that I switched to another school at such a late stage in my PhD program.

Then, after three additional years at UCSB, I found myself graduating in the middle of the recession. Initially working as an adjunct instructor at UCSB (Summer 2009–January 2011), I never received adequate health insurance and experienced constant uncertainty about exactly how many classes I would teach from one academic quarter to the next. While my health insurance benefits have improved at Montana State University (MSU; August 2012–present), I lived without health insurance during the period of time when I was between universities. And, while I was consistently in the job market, I experienced at least two years of under- and unemployment before I landed in Montana. In fact, the NTT position I managed to get at MSU was completely serendipitous. I had consistently been on the academic job market from Fall 2008 to Spring 2012 (four solid years!) before I started at MSU. While I had other job opportunities, they certainly wouldn't sustain me in expensive San Francisco, one of the only places I could go after losing the ability to continue paying my rent while teaching at UCSB.[2] *Before the Summer of 2012, I had almost thrown up my hands in absolute defeat, unable to get any academic job that could sustain me in California or anywhere, for that matter. I was virtually out of academic options, even though I continued to apply for both NTT and tenure-track positions throughout the United States and beyond.*

Summer 2012 offered a short break from the daily grind of university applications and, perhaps, a re-evaluation of my life goals, especially given the fact that the academic career path I envisioned was absolutely not coming to fruition. Essentially, I dropped everything for a few months, hopped in a car with my boyfriend and his best friend, and ventured off on a wwoofing-inspired cross-country trip (WWOOF is defined as World Wide Opportu-

nities for Organic Farms). My travel partners and I would drive from one farm to another, work on the farm for room and board while chronicling our trip, learn how to grow our own vegetables, experience areas of the country we had never visited, and, more or less, disconnect from the stress of unemployment. Unexpectedly, the trip only lasted about two months as we collectively fell in love with our third farming destination: Livingston, Montana.

Cooling off and relaxing after a few early morning hours of harvesting, I turned to my partner, Mathew, and suggested we spend an entire season in Livingston. Perhaps we could rent our own land and farm next season, I offered. We quickly turned to my ongoing job market debacle when Mathew suggested, "Isn't there a university here? Do some research, see if they have a sociology program and call them. Why not? What do you have to lose?" A few minutes later, I was on the phone with MSU's Sociology and Anthropology Department discussing a job that had just been posted that morning for a visiting assistant professor. A week later, I had a visiting position at MSU. While I finally found an academic job, this position was, again, only temporary or contingent, at best.

Despite the fact that MSU has been incredibly rewarding and I have enjoyed every class and student I have met while in Montana, I have still experienced a number of troubling outcomes associated with NTT life. For example, every academic year I still spend months "not knowing" whether or not I will have a job the following year and I'm often forced to hustle classes in order to remain in Montana. Due to the constant last-minute hustle, I have consistently earned less money every year because my income now comes from a number of different programs and departments, rather than just my home department, sociology and anthropology. In other words, the salary I earned as a visiting assistant professor during my first academic year at MSU has dwindled by thousands of dollars per year. I experienced the same patterns at UCSB where, as a lecturer, my salary consistently decreased as I continued teaching. Further, in addition to my declining salary, I now work more than I ever have, typically teaching four classes per semester. During my first year at MSU, I never taught more than three classes per semester and was, in contrast, paid significantly more per class.

Finally, the level of uncertainty that I've been experiencing does not make sense. I published two co-edited books while in graduate school, attended top university programs in my field, and continue to publish in journals such as the Journal of International Migration and Integration, Journal of Family Issues, Sociological Spectrum, *and* International Migration *among others. I'm told regularly that, in another academic climate, I would certainly have a tenure-track position.*

Given the current academic job market, however, and the state of affairs (described below) at most universities, this situation does, in fact, make sense. This narrative connects to those of *many* other highly qualified academics who have not landed a coveted position. Telling this post–Katrina recovery story is important for a number of reasons: this story connects to and represents the stories of so many other academics (as we address below) and needs to be deeply discussed and urgently addressed; thus, this chapter is both a review of what is going on as well as a call to action. Quite honestly, we are tired of the silence around these major shifts and inequalities, especially given the fact that our colleagues are sociologists! That is, ALL of us should be outraged and committed to addressing this ongoing dilemma. This reality addresses directly what we do, how we can do the work we do, and, the realities of "the precarious academic." This phenomenon is also impacting academics with those coveted positions; for example, tenure-track academics are also feeling the pressure of these shifts, receiving increasingly less support for their work and are also losing opportunities to do important work with their NTT colleagues because of the ongoing squeeze. Furthermore, this recovery story intimately connects to our global landscape, one in which global corporatization is and continues to permeate every aspect of our lives. The next few sections outline how the corporatization of our lives and universities has and continues to be realized.

THE GLOBAL AUCTION

In addressing this ongoing shift or "new normality" of academia, we are also speaking to a larger global shift in the economy, deftly described in Brown et al.'s (2011) *The Global Auction: The Broken Promises of Education, Jobs, and Incomes*. Closely analyzing seven countries across the globe, Brown et al. ask hard questions about a global value system that pressures individuals to invest in their talents and abilities (via advanced education, for example) at the same time that the neoliberal global economy has consistently and increasingly failed to provide adequate employment for the burgeoning numbers of highly educated candidates. The ongoing and intense competitive job market for recent college graduates, often referred to as the "lost generation," certainly points to the inability of the global economy to remedy or somehow address this situation. Brown et al. show how this is not simply a problem playing out in "affluent societies" only but is intensified by the increase of more qualified and educated workers throughout the globe, an "*education explosion* in the supply of college-educated workers in both affluent and emerging economies" (Brown et al. 2011, 7).

Given this education explosion and business practices that value the bottom line over the support of workers, we have seen job competition that is not primarily restricted to national borders but, instead, includes global competition among a larger pool of very qualified workers. In short, "the relationship between learning and earning is being called into question from within the business community" (Brown et al. 2011, 9) and many other impacted communities. In this *reverse auction*, "workers are expected to do more for less" (Brown et al. 2011, 7) in the form of "longer working hours, inferior retirement provision, reduced healthcare coverage, declining career prospects, and greater job insecurity" (Brown et al. 2011, 7). Because global competition is fierce, workers vying for jobs feel pressured to outbid one another on the market; this then gets translated into less security and protection for workers and more vulnerable, willing workers for employers. While Brown et al. point out that this reverse auction squeeze was previously a problem for low-skilled U.S.-based workers, now we can certainly see the squeeze engulfing workers throughout the world.

THE CORPORATIZATION OF UNIVERSITIES

All of these reverse auction trends have and continue to increase in and through academia. We can see this process clearly if we look at how power operates. That is, how are vulnerable workers controlled, disciplined, and silenced in and through our current academic system? Chomsky's (2014) "The Death of American Universities," maps out the ongoing corporatization of universities and shows how professors are increasingly being forced into positions of precarity; both non-tenured and tenured, but especially non-tenured. Some recent cases, for example, illustrate this trend.

Precarious faculty positions appear to be becoming the norm in some universities, where the administration of those schools is opting to force faculty out of their previously safe "ivory towers" where they had once been protected from firing and other personnel actions because they were tenured. Many universities are opting to hire "bean counters" instead of accomplished academics to fill such administrative slots as Deans, Provosts, and Ombudspeople. Along these same lines, Boards of Trustees and Regents are working ardently toward corporatizing the university in much the same way as Wall Street is part of corporate America. If corporatization meant only that colleges and universities were finding ways to be less wasteful, it would be a welcome turn of events. However, a completely different process is going on; one that has saddled us with a higher-education model that is both expensive to run and difficult to reform as a result of its focus on status, its view of students as customers, and its growing reliance on top-down administration. This move toward corporatization is one that the late University of Montreal professor, Bill Readings, noted sixteen years ago in his study, *The University in Ruins*, but what has happened in recent years far exceeds the alarm he sounded in the 1990s. Not surprisingly, those administrators who occupy the highest ranks in our college and university bureaucracies are those who have professionally benefited the most from corporatization.

Running a corporatized college or university is not easy. The professor who takes time out from teaching and research to devote to administration for a few years increasingly is an anachronism. A new, permanent administrative class now dominates higher education. At the top are the college and university presidents who earn a million dollars or more a year, and serve on numerous corporate boards (Shirley Ann Jackson, the president of Rensselaer Polytechnic Institute [RPI], earned a reported $1.38 million in a single year from her multiple directorships). According to the *Chronicle of Higher Education*, thirty-six (36) private college and university presidents fall into the million-dollars-per-year category, and many more are close behind. A still bigger change in how higher education is managed lies in its growing number of administrators in its ranks.

As political scientist Benjamin Ginsberg, a leading authority on this subject, has pointed out, administrators have become a greater presence in colleges and universities while faculty have been in decline. Between 1998 and 2008, private colleges increased their spending on instruction by 22 percent while they increased their spending on administration and staff support by 36 percent. In *The Fall of the Faculty: The Rise of the All-Administrative University and Why It Matters,* Ginsberg (2011) offers a vast array of examples to highlight these trends: between 1947 and 1995, one telling set of figures shows that "administrative spending . . . increased by a whopping 235 percent [while] instructional spending . . . increased by only 128 percent, twenty points less than the overall rate of spending increase" (33); and, further, he highlights a number of administrative trends, practices and talking points such as "a good deal of education occurs outside the classroom" (20), an oft-stated mantra that justifies administrative projects that often have very little to do with academic work. Ginsberg also points to administrators' "invented activities" that often "cost money or take up staff time without doing much to further the university's educational or research goals" (33). A few examples illustrate this trend:

> At one school, an inventive group of administrators created a "committee on traditions," whose mission seemed to be the identification and restoration of forgotten university traditions or, failing that, the creation of new traditions. Another group of deans constituted themselves as the "War Zones Task Force." This group recruited staffers, held many meetings, and prepared a number of reports whose upshot seemed to be that students should be discouraged from traveling to war zones unless, of course, their homes were in war zones. (Ginsberg 2011, 34)

Clearly, administrative projects such as those listed above accomplish only one primary goal: bloated and useless administrative work.

If we go further back in time, the rise in administrators becomes even more striking. In the last forty years the number of full-time faculty at colleges and universities has grown by 50 percent—in line with increases in student enrollment—but in this same period the number of administrators has risen by 85 percent and the number of staffers required to help the administrators has jumped by a massive 240 percent (Ginsberg 2011, 28). It is no small wonder, then, that so many policy decisions at colleges and universities are made without—or despite—faculty input. Much of the current trends at universities like the University of Southern Maine (USM) illustrate this case in point.

Concurrently, neoliberal policy makers and administrators are using "new normality" language (post-2007–2008 recession, a struggling job market, and tightening our belts) to their advantage. In addition to USM austerity measures described below, Hurricane Katrina was used as a green light for a number of austerity-motivated practices embraced by administrators at the University of New Orleans, Loyola University of New Orleans, and Tulane University.

As a graduate student at Tulane University, I had very little information from my university and Sociology Department about exactly what would happen to and for advanced graduate students, post–Katrina. There was very little, if any, transparency with regard to the support that the graduate students in my program would receive after the waters receded. For obvious reasons, and due to the intense lack of transparency, many other graduate students and I began looking elsewhere in a desperate and last-minute attempt to salvage the last few years of our graduate-level education.

Structurally, the administration at Tulane University were never interested in calming my fears and certainly didn't make it easier for me to stay. As an example, we can simply look at how President Scott Cowen handled university-related decisions post–Katrina. President Cowen claimed that Katrina offered "opportunities" for the administration to make some major institutional changes. Consequently, these so-called opportunities meant that my sociology graduate program was suddenly dismantled. En route from Bangkok to San Francisco, and before the winter holiday break, I received an urgent email from Jeannie Haubert that suggested I would no longer have a program to go home to. In making these sweeping changes, there was a clear disregard for the many students and faculty affiliated with these programs. To me, the actions taken by Tulane University's administration entailed a gross lack of support and clear reflection of who and what they valued. The complete reorganization and gutting of many programs and departments also occurred at the University of New Orleans and Loyola University, forever shifting their academic landscape and further displacing my colleagues and friends (see, for example, Donna Bonner in Hidalgo and Barber, eds. 2007).

These trends have reverberated throughout the university landscape. For example, at USM, where the austerity agenda has taken hold, the university has instituted tuition increases while enrollment has decreased. Further, in efforts to save money for the university, departments are being consolidated while faculty and staff are being laid off, regardless of their tenured or vested status. The impact of all of this is that students are paying more money for less of an education, and are no longer being taught by the most qualified people for the job. When departments are consolidated, the number of adjunct faculty is reduced and full-time tenured faculty find themselves teaching the "grunt" classes: the large introductory courses in their discipline (or in a closely aligned discipline), grading for themselves, and finding that their overall research and publication productivity declines. This represents a serious problem, as tenured faculty must undergo post-tenure review every five years, and if a faculty member has not published a specified number of peer-reviewed articles or books, then s/he is subject to disciplinary action, and possibly even dismissal (under the new austerity agenda/corporatized regime).

At USM, following in the vein of the Occupy Wall Street protests in New York City, students, alumni, and faculty came together to shed light on the questionable practices by the USM administration in the form of the writing of the *Debt Resistor's Handbook*. In this way, students and faculty attempted to build solidarity with regard to their shared struggle: the desire and need for the university to follow through on its mission; namely, to provide quality educational and scholarship opportunities to all who entered USM's hallowed halls. Concurrently, however, the bean counter administrators have an alternative agenda; namely, to restructure the university by cutting and consolidating liberal arts departments, and limiting the opportunities for USM students to even focus their studies in liberal studies. Students and faculty continue to fight ardently to preserve the freedom of thought, pedagogy, and intellectualism, while the administrators at USM try to quash these efforts in such a way as to maintain control of a group of intellectuals who refuse to be silenced.

PRECARIOUS PERGATORY

Some additional statistics point to the fact that neoliberal academic trends have gotten increasingly worse. In 1975, tenure-line faculty made up 57 percent of faculty while contingent (NTT and/or part time) faculty made up 43 percent of faculty (see U.S. Department of Education, compiled by AAUP

Research Office; Ginsberg 2011). These figures reversed in 1993: tenure-line faculty now made up 43 percent of workers while contigent faculty made up 57 percent. By 2011, the figures were dramatically worse at only 30 percent for tenure-line faculty and 70 percent for contingent faculty. Since 1975, this represents a 27 percent spike for contingent faculty; that is, there has been an ongoing increase in the presence of contingent faculty. Instead of counting on a plethora of tenure-track lines to choose from upon graduation, recent PhDs are increasingly faced with a choice of far more NTT positions and are often finding themselves (70–75 percent[3] of them!) in a precarious purgatory. If we look at these figures in more detail, contingent faculty are increasingly even more contingent than we might imagine. Part-time faculty made up 30 percent of faculty in 1975, while full-time NTT faculty made up 13 percent. In 2011, these numbers jumped to 19 percent (full-time NTT) and a whopping 51 percent; that is, of all faculty positions, as many as 51 percent of them are part-time faculty, while only 30 percent of them are tenure-line (21 percent are full-time tenured faculty and 9 percent are full-time tenure-track faculty).

If we think sociologically about these cases and the ongoing trend in hiring non-tenure track faculty, we see immediately how the business model has permeated universities throughout the country (Chomsky 2014). That is, rather than companies committing to and supporting workers, the adoption of corporate business model practices by universities and colleges means reducing labor costs; thereby, increasing labor servility (Chomsky 2014). NTT faculty fit this model perfectly as a university has far less obligation to the NTT faculty member than to tenure-track faculty members; thereby, investing fewer resources (time and money) in these members. Since NTT faculty are, and remain vulnerable, universities can, and do, take advantage of them, offering fewer benefits, and generally expecting more of these instructors (offering last-minute classes or expecting them to work more for less money) than other faculty members.

Chomsky makes sense of the business model by pointing to the ongoing division of two groups in our neoliberal world: the "plutonomy" group (globally, those with the most wealth, yet concentrated primarily in places like the United States) and the other group, the "precariat" (the rest of us who experience a precarious existence) (Chomsky 2014). NTT faculty certainly fall into the precariat group, and remain prey to the neoliberal assault on universities. In general, this means that the tenure-track positions will continue to disappear. As Chomsky also notes, this shift intersects with an undeniable increase in administrators over and above faculty and students over the last thirty to forty years (see also Ginsberg 2011). Thus, the increase in administrative positions is simply another amalgamation of the corporate business model in an educational setting: a model that increasingly creates instability and uncertainty for faculty.

NARRATING THE STORM: NORMALIZED UNCERTAINTY FOR A KATRINA SURVIVOR SCHOLAR

When Katrina hit landfall, I was in a liminal space, not quite home but not quite away from home. I had been living and working in New Orleans for two years at this point but had spent my summers in Madison, Wisconsin, and other large chunks of holidays in my hometown of San Francisco, California. I was extremely focused on my academic career and often to the detriment of my personal life, something that I continue to grapple with today. At the same time that I was navigating my public work and personal life, I was coming into my own as an academic, finding my voice while also exploring my personhood. I was sorting out where I felt most comfortable in the world. Given my queer practices[4]*—both within and beyond academia—I always felt bifurcated. I always felt like there was not quite enough that I could do or say within academic spaces, that I was too provocative or too outspoken or too sexually open and explicit to really, truly speak my voice. Queer spaces*[5] *(both real and imagined) provided an escape, a "staycation," a small slice of hope for other possibilities that were rarely offered in academia. I also did my best to disrupt from within academia, and this is where much of my writing and creative thinking happened. I explored my own queer identity and practices via queering sociology, and thus worked tirelessly as I not only navigated the sociological canon, but also stepped further away from generally accepted precepts to imagine an academic world that might finally embrace me, an academic world that might finally speak to the issues that were both important to me as well as to those in my community.*

Ironically, while I was living in an in-between state, I was also very much embedded in a particular academic track, and committed endless hours, blood, sweat, and tears to some vague but unquestioned success and security that I assumed would come when I finally finished my PhD. I was completely committed to a story that read: Upon graduation and those many years of hard work, of course I will land in an academic position that nourishes me and supports me as I continue to do the writing that needs to be done, continue to contribute to the ideas that need to be shared. I was 99 percent confident that this was what my world would look like, even if the end goal looked hazy and vague when I pictured it. The moment that Katrina hit landfall changed my story immeasurably. Although I was well aware of how much had shifted when Katrina happened, I still vaguely hoped that things couldn't really be as screwed up and difficult as they clearly were for emerging academics with PhDs. I still had some investment in the neoliberal model that told me that hard work and my best efforts would eventually land me that dream job and allow me to do what I really loved (and get support for it!).

Katrina was a wake-up call, to say the least, and has continued to reawaken me as I work in and through academic spaces. When I feel over-

whelmed or defeated, I look to Katrina for strength, for the strength that I somehow mustered in those heady days immediately after the storm and then as I continued to navigate my graduate program months after the storm. When I want to take chances or engage in some provocative, intense research and writing, I look to Katrina for guidance, remembering how the intensity of post–Katrina life offered a daily reminder of just how short life is, of how I'd better do this thing now or miss an opportunity. When I feel taken advantage of, undervalued, or simply unhappy (in work or in private life), I reassess my life goals and accomplishments and then act; Katrina left little room for indecision—everything was urgent and required quick, smart decisions. I certainly approach my life in much the same way now. If my job no longer satisfies or fulfills me, I move on. If a partner no longer brings me joy and support, I carry on without them. In short, if my life is not full of loving support, kindness, and the intensity I need to be a radical and challenging professor, I reassess where I stand and move to where I will be fully embraced, Katrina baggage and all.

The final section of this chapter offers a love letter, of sorts, to Katrina. If any of us are really paying attention, we see the productive and the beautiful in every moment in our lives. While Katrina certainly offered a lot of intense transitions and some real heartache, there is no doubt that the storm and its aftermath also offered renewals, reassessments, and reawakenings. This, therefore, is an offer of appreciation and gratitude for the ongoing lessons that Katrina continues to offer up.

GETTING AN EDUCATION FROM KATRINA

Katrina taught us (and continues to remind us) what really matters in life. While we all have different ways of approaching our lives, and some of us embrace life with grace and ease, while many others stumble through the ups and downs, Katrina's intensity, persistence, and unwillingness to step aside forced all of us to work with her and make things right.

As Katrina hit landfall and then continued to wreak havoc on my life and loved ones in New Orleans, I was consistently forced to put down my innumerable worries and attend to the people I loved and the life that I really wanted. I was forced to pay attention to what mattered most in my life. All of the silly, insignificant things that cluttered my mind simply faded away when I pulled together the pieces after Katrina. Similarly, as I continue to navigate the world around me, I am reminded of those early post–Katrina moments and, again, get that wake-up call: Get it together, you will get through this. . . . You're alive and healthy and whatever it is you're experiencing right now is not the end of the world. . . . This hiccup does not really matter. . . . Do something productive with this difficult situation. The ghost of Katrina has a way of speaking to me in those intense moments of defeat and confusion.

Katrina embraces chaos—the end of what was then normal—and reminds us to embrace it, too. Everything about Katrina screamed out "loud and ferocious refusal"[6] in myriad ways we were forced to see—really see—poverty, racial inequality, gender and sexual harassment, neoliberal failure, environmental devastation, and how the precariat citizen was forcefully and relentlessly made even more precarious by the devastation of the storm and its aftermath. In other words, these realities were magnified in the context of Katrina.

In the first few months after the storm, April Brayfield, Danielle Hidalgo, and Kristen Barber (2007) called the "end of normal" our "new normality." We were living in and through a time that definitely looked very different from the "normal" we had experienced and come to know before Katrina. Similarly, Katrina forced us to rethink and reasses what "normal" had looked like to begin with. As sociologists committed to social change and upending inequality, we reflected on the "new normal" with a little bit of fear and uncertainty but also with a lense that allowed us to begin to see how pre-Katrina normality was clearly not working and required a ferocious refusal anyway.

Katrina literally forced us to reconsider success and embrace failure. If success meant neoliberal markets that ensured the ongoing tenuousness of millions of workers, embracing failure meant we would no longer stand for this treatment. If success meant poverty and inequality in and through every fiber of New Orleans, failure meant we would see the insidiousness of poverty and inequality on every TV screen across the nation. If success meant some vague yet persistent goal that held up and supported neoliberalism and everything that it stood for, failure meant literally turning our backs on these goals and embracing imaginative reinvention.

Katrina asks us, begs us, to release ourselves from attachment, to normalize uncertainty, but not at the expense of people. Certainty, predictability, and permanence are illusions, Katrina tells us, and our tendency to attach ourselves to some illusory sense of permanence is misguided and often dangerous. Permanence and attachment often play tricks on us as it gives us a false sense of security and support. It guides us onto a path that does not see disruptions; it encourages us to fail to act when we know something isn't quite right; and it generally keeps us stuck and inert as we move about in the world. It discourages questions and encourages stagnation.

Normalized uncertainty has kept me constantly alert and sensitive to what is actually happening around me, at the same time that it has encouraged me to remain open to new possibilities and change. Given the ongoing uncertainty of NTT academic life, it's how I have creatively navigated this new job market terrain, yet also remained aware of its hard edges, inconsistencies, and inequalities. Normalized uncertainty has also pushed me to think critically about how to shift the landscape, how to scream out loud with ferocious refusals, and how to turn my back on what's not-quite-right. As my friend said at the beginning of my narrative, "we're still in the trenches, baby," and we certainly are. In order to navigate those trenches we must come armed with creative energy, resistance, and the ability to envision a world that looks very different from the one we're currently tolerating.

Embracing normalized uncertainty uncritically or framing it as an individual failure fails to address the larger picture. If, for example, I blame myself entirely for the twists and turns I experienced post–Katrina and for the difficulty I've had on the job market, I would be failing to see how normalized uncertainty is connected to a larger set of social, cultural, and political patterns. I would be embracing uncertainty at the expense of people. Instead, I am consistently encouraged to compassionately and carefully practice non-attachment. And Katrina has encouraged me to do just that: turn my back on what doesn't feel right, stand up for a better, reinvented world, muster the courage to take those radical chances, and navigate my precarity with as much grace and ease as I can.

We know the facts and, quite honestly, we know what needs to be done. Now, let's all start making some serious changes. Katrina is waiting and if we don't get it together soon, her sister will, most likely, be in for a visit.

NOTES

1. The vignettes in this chapter come from Danielle's reflections on changes to her graduate program at Tulane in New Orleans and her recovery processes following Hurricane Katrina. Written from the perspective of intersecting and often vulnerable social locations—as a survivor of Hurricane Katrina, as a displaced academic, as a queer scholar and teacher who often teaches material on the margins (porn studies, for example) and as an ongoing temporary academic worker—her narrative captures a state of ongoing tenuousness.

2. Without a job, Danielle had to move back home for awhile; this meant she moved back into her grandmother's house in the Bay Area and lived with her grandmother and mother.

3. This figure was at 70 percent in 2011. In recent reports, contingent faculty or the "new faculty majority comprises almost 75 percent of professors at both private and public institutions" (Fruscione 2014).

4. Danielle identifies as *queer*. For her, this means that she engages in sexual and intimate relationships with people regardless of their gender identity. She also engages in *queering* academia; this means that she thinks about sexuality and gender as social processes rather than fixed identities, for example, and approaches her research, writing, and teaching with this framework in mind.

5. These are spaces where Danielle felt/feels most comfortable expressing her queer identity and doing queer research. Notably, academic spaces often do not allow her to freely express her queerness and/or do her queer writing and research.

6. In *Gaga Feminism: Sex, Gender, and the End of Normal*, J. Jack Halberstam offers a call to action: "We may not yet be able to find our way out of the economic crisis into which we have crawled and we still may not be able to size up all of its dimensions, but this book reminds us that if the problem is too much acceptance and resignation *then the answer must be loud and ferocious refusal*. This book models the art of going gaga: *a politics of free-falling, wild thinking, and imaginative reinvention* best exemplified by children under the age of eight, women over the age of forty-five, and the vast armies of the marginalized, the abandoned, and the unproductive" (2012, xv; emphasis added).

Chapter Thirteen

Learning from Disaster

Post-Katrina New Orleans as a Sociological Classroom

Timothy J. Haney

Ten years after Katrina, the recovery of New Orleans and the Gulf Coast is popularly understood as slow and incomplete. In an attempt to understand persistent inequalities in post–Katrina New Orleans, and to hopefully contribute to the city's ongoing rebuilding efforts, I took my class of students from Mount Royal University in Calgary, Alberta, Canada, to New Orleans in May 2013 to learn about both Hurricane Katrina and the Deepwater Horizon oil spill disaster. The course focused specifically on recovery efforts and incorporated a service-learning as its main pedagogical approach.

The initiative also had a secondary motivation though; I am a former New Orleanian who experienced Hurricane Katrina. As a graduate student at Tulane University in 2005, the institutional dislocation wrought by Katrina scattered my colleagues and I to far corners of the continent. Yet even today, teaching at a university in Canada, I remain committed to the city's recovery and very much consider myself a New Orleanian (when people ask me where I am from, I say "I live in Calgary; home is New Orleans"). As a former New Orleanian I believe strongly that my teaching can be a tool to aid in the city's recovery. Yet after introducing what I believe is currently the only sociology of disaster course in Canada, I quickly became disillusioned that our classroom conversations seemed so sterile, sanitized, and so far removed from the everyday lived experience in disaster-affected locales such as New Orleans. So, I decided to embark with my class upon what is perhaps the only disaster field course taught within the social sciences. This chapter documents our experiences, using student reflections, and in doing so, shares some important insights into the recovery of New Orleans nearly a decade after Katrina.

SERVICE-LEARNING IN THE POST-KATRINA CONTEXT

Service-learning is "a form of experiential education where learning occurs through a cycle of action and reflection as students work with others through a process of applying what they are learning to community problems and, at the same time, reflecting upon their experience as they seek to achieve real objectives for the community and deeper understanding and skills for themselves" (Eyler and Giles 1999). The literature demonstrates that field courses are one of the most effective ways to achieve such learning outcomes, particularly for environmentally focused content (Alagona and Simon 2010) and in international contexts (Mitussis and Sheehan 2013).

Service-learning connects explicitly to recent calls for social justice-oriented education (Bush and Little 2009) as well as older, more established calls for emancipatory education (Freire [1970] 2007). According to Bush and Little, "connecting our students to the lived experiences of those involved in contemporary social justice activism and social movements is a core task of public sociology" (2009, 13). As such, service-learning explicitly seeks to cultivate social responsibility, embraces the active and participatory student (rather than the passive recipient of knowledge), and welcomes learning through both objectivity and subjectivity (Howard 1998, 25). As Jacoby (2006) argues, we "must enable [students] to develop not just the values and commitment but also the knowledge, skills, and efficacy to address the complex web of social issues that underlie the need for the service they provide" (31).

Service-learning is applied to many contexts including poverty and issues affecting inner-city communities (Webster 2007), international development (Bringle et al. 2011), teacher education (Baise 2002), economics (McGoldrick 1998), and environmental chemistry (Draper 2004), but it has rarely, if ever, been applied to disaster education. Yet, few locations require outside service as much as New Orleans, and the ability of students to immerse themselves in the region's recovery, I hoped, would help them to develop critical yet scholarly insights into that recovery

OBSERVATIONS OF POST-KATRINA NEW ORLEANS

> Heading into this trip, I knew that we would be seeing a city that has not been able to completely rebuild since the flood, but I don't think I really understood what we would see. Seeing destroyed homes in neighborhood after neighborhood that are still standing, boarded-up, with greenery growing out of the chimney, with roofs caving in, and all of the current construction projects.

> Every time we would see these homes I would have to remind myself that it has been eight years. . . . I knew we would see this, but I don't think I really knew. —Student journal entry

Before departing for New Orleans, the class met for several pre-departure logistical meetings, spending approximately twelve hours in the classroom learning about the history and culture of New Orleans, critically examining research findings on Hurricane Katrina and the Deepwater Horizon oil spill, learning about environmental justice and coastal erosion issues that affect the region, and finally, discussing some common findings from the disaster social science literature. We also viewed Spike Lee's excellent film "If God Is Willing and 'Da Creek Don't Rise" (Lee 2010), which focuses less on the Katrina disaster and more on the arduous and politically charged task of rebuilding a city so devastated by disaster. Students also completed a pre-departure paper asking them to discuss their expectations of the experience in the context of their readings in other courses. This approach forced students to use their existing academic knowledge base in order to develop their expectations. While on the ground, students completed daily journaling activities reflecting upon their experiences. Those journaling activities resulted in a final paper which students submitted after their return home. That final paper asked students to connect theories and concepts from other courses to what they experienced while on the ground in New Orleans. It required them to focus on five areas in which they learned lessons about: 1) The overall experience; 2) Social inequalities; 3) New Orleans and the Gulf Coast; 4) Disaster; and 5) Service-Learning. The reflections used below are drawn from two main sources: 1) Student journals written for the purpose of the course and 2) Student final papers. The use of student writing is done with consent of the students and with ethics board approval. All data are treated in a confidential fashion.

UNEQUAL GEOGRAPHIES

The first day of the field course commenced with a driving tour of New Orleans and southeastern Louisiana. The driving tour took students to Uptown/Garden District, Lower Ninth Ward (including the "Brad Pitt Village," of new homes constructed by the Make It Right Foundation), the 17th Street Canal levee breach (the largest levee breach, responsible for flooding much of the city), the Mississippi River levee, Lake Ponchartrain, and a pumping station. Upon leaving the city, we drove across the Lake Ponchartrain Causeway to St. Tammany Parish, visited the wetlands near Manchac, Louisiana, and the Bonnet Carre Spillway. These visits helped students to appreciate the monumental feat of engineering that it takes to keep a city dry that largely sits below sea level.

After seeing the Central Business District, French Quarter, Magazine Street, and St. Charles Avenue, some students remarked that the city did not look as bad as they had expected (i.e., there were no apparent signs of hurricane or flood damage). Yet as we drove through heavily damaged parts of eastern New Orleans, including St. Roch and the Lower Ninth Ward, the tone changed noticeably. Quietness and a sense of disbelief filled our vehicle as the group took in the myriad flooded and abandoned houses, foundations long missing a home, and derelict cars not touched since 2005. The stark contrast between the ante-bellum mansions and boutiques of uptown and the languishing remains of the Lower Ninth Ward were clearly puzzling to a group from a place lacking these severe inequalities.

Relatedly, my students noticed the unique residential development patterns of the city. One student commented that "there was a very obvious physical division between spaces occupied by different classes. . . . Generally in cities one can see a gradual change in landscape, driving over blocks things start to shift but I have never seen such a drastic, immediate change." Other students noticed the unevenness with regard to those neighborhoods affected by flooding (i.e., the Lower Ninth Ward) and those neighborhoods untouched by flooding (i.e., the Garden District). One student remarked that it was striking "In certain neighbourhoods [i.e., Uptown] . . . people could choose to ignore what happened" because such neighborhoods were nearly untouched by Katrina. This unevenness connects to pre-disaster differences in both economic and social capital (Elliott et al. 2010) and has lasted well beyond the initial recovery, making New Orleans today a whiter, older, and higher-income city than it was pre-Katrina, as younger, African American, and lower-income residents were disproportionately unable to return (Groen and Polivka 2020). In other words, though New Orleans neighborhoods demonstrated high levels of economic inequality, a product of strict racial segregation and political neglect, Katrina further exacerbated these preexisting inequalities. More broadly, students were intrigued by the residential development patterns, whereby wealthier neighborhoods occupied higher, less vulnerable land (see Campanella 2002). Another student remarked that "In essence, property size and the neighbourhood in which a house was located in New Orleans was a true indication of the social class which they belonged to. My perception of inequality was challenged, [in discovering] the importance that was associated to the [elevation] of a neighbourhood."

Students were particularly struck by the engineering required to keep New Orleans dry (see Colten 2006). After visiting the Lower Ninth Ward, the 17th Street Canal levee breach, a pumping station, and the Mississippi River levee, most felt a sense of disbelief in the continued inadequacy of the flood protection system. One student felt that "Even though [the levees are] quite high, the levees don't seem as imposing as I was expecting them to. I think the width [of the floodwalls on the canals] makes them seem . . . less [imposing]. . . . The walls in New Orleans did not inspire . . . faith from me." Another commented "I have little faith partly because it was reconstructed by the same Army Corps of Engineers who failed in their earlier construction." These concerns echo local residents' continuing worries that the flood protection system may not withstand future hurricanes (Lam et al. 2012).

PACE OF RECOVERY

Perhaps most notably, my class was struck by the slow pace of recovery in neighborhoods such as the Lower Ninth Ward (see Chamlee-Wright and Storr 2009; Finch, Emrich, and Cutter 2010). Research indicates that this pace was slowed considerably by the privatization of recovery programs, which systematically advantaged wealthier households while denying assistance to lower-income households (Adams 2013). As Gotham and Greenberg (2014) note, the Louisiana Recovery Authority (LRA) (modeled after the Lower Manhattan Development Corporation in New York) handled much post–Katrina assistance, and entrusted the private sector with distributing the funding. LRA's contracted firm, ICF International, "incorrectly calculated

May 2013—17th Street Canal in New Orleans. Photo by volume contributor Timothy J. Haney.

grant awards, [used] bogus calculations to appraise pre-storm home values, [demonstrated] slow progress in awarding grants to needy homeowners, [mismanaged] a program to help mom-and-pop landlords repair damaged rentals, and [utilized] demeaning antifraud rules that required applicants to be fingerprinted before they received funds."

In this privatized relief system, some might say that New Orleanians fell through the cracks. However, as Adams (2013, 121) says, that analogy "is a handy way of making it seem as if the system works for almost everyone and that those whom it did not work for are either the minority who *found* the cracks in the system or were themselves to blame because they *fell through* the cracks instead of avoiding them." The end result of these delays, of course, is the nearly complete inability for residents of New Orleans's poorer neighborhoods to return and rebuild. This inability continues to manifest itself visually if one visits neighborhoods such as the Lower Ninth Ward. One of my students remarked that "Driving through the Lower Ninth Ward, it was absolutely amazing to see all of the empty lots and so many houses that are still so dilapidated. I found myself noticing all of the current con-

May 2013—Dilapidated housing in the Ninth Ward. Photo by volume contributor Timothy J. Haney.

struction projects happening and realizing this is a sight we should have seen eight months post-disaster, not eight years!"

DISASTER TOURISM

We worried that driving through the Lower Ninth Ward and other devastated neighborhoods in our van, clearly labeled "Big Easy Limos" may mark us as disaster tourists. As Recuber (2013) points out, disaster can be pornographic in the sense that viewing the pain and anguish of others can result in pleasure for the viewer (evidenced by films such as "Twister" and TV series such as "It Could Happen Tomorrow"). This is a particularly sensitive issue in New Orleans with the recent popularity of "devastation tours" (Pezzullo 2009), whereby companies offer bus tours through devastated neighborhoods, often drawing the ire of residents who wish to retain privacy. One viral post–Katrina image featured a sign in front of a devastated house that read "Tourists—shame on you. Paying to see my pain. 1,600+ died here." Even nearly a decade later, these images created a feeling of uneasiness as we toured the city; we hoped that our purpose was nobler—to learn primarily by serving the city—but would locals realize that? Many of the students commented about this tension, with remarks such as "Even a week and a half into this trip I worry that we are upsetting people, driving around in our New Orleans Limos bus looking as touristy as humanly possible." Yet I was reassured that our group considered this possibility and I suspect that many traditional tourists do not consider the ways in which these tours may objectify local residents. At the very least, we seemed more reflexive than run-of-the-mill tourists; perhaps a testament to my ability, as a former New Orleanian, to appropriately prime them.

To understand the New Orleans that most tourists see, the class spent a great deal of time wandering the French Quarter. We also embarked on a swamp tour and a dinner jazz cruise, common activities for tourists visiting the region. On the dinner cruise, one student considered the differential relationships that tourists and locals maintain with nearby bodies of water, commenting that:

> It was being on the river that also got me thinking about the dynamics of the river itself. The people of New Orleans and North America depend on this river for imports, transportation, livelihood, and a source of food, and at the same time, it is something that creates so much fear in people at the thought of a hurricane coming. Yet there we were [on the dinner jazz cruise] using this river for our *entertainment.* (emphasis added)

Students felt as though this tension between water as a source of entertainment and as a potential threat was something not usually considered by visitors to the area. After seeing other parts of the city, however, students were quick to "realize that what most tourists see is not . . . the reality of New Orleans. They only see one side." This observation connects directly to arguments by local researchers that "political and economic elites and powerful organizations model disasters as a form of amusement where tragic events are abstracted from the reality of human loss and suffering, and transformed into images that viewers passively consume" (Gotham 2007, 95). Yet as Gotham (2007) also points out, the spectacle of Hurricane Katrina also cannot help but reveal important contradictions related to the U.S. government's failure to properly handle the initial response or long-term recovery. In that sense, tourism both shelters visitors from the material disparities in post–Katrina New Orleans (by providing a standardized, sanitized, commercialized experience typified by the French Quarter) while also almost necessarily revealing these political and economic inequalities to many visitors. Still, the remainder of our experiences in New Orleans sought to specifically highlight the parts of New Orleans and disaster recovery that most tourists do not see.

UNDERSTANDING KATRINA'S LIVED EXPERIENCE

As a former New Orleanian, I worried that my class, having not experienced Katrina firsthand, would view their visit as solely an academic exercise instead of a profound human tragedy with lingering consequences. After all, the literature suggests that to *understand* disaster, one must also *experience* disaster. Erikson's (1976, 11) classic book *Everything in Its Path* documents how he, as an outsider, struggled to comprehend what a flood-affected community had experienced. He wrote that the people of Buffalo Creek, West Virginia (following a devastating flood) were "so wounded in spirit that they almost constituted a different culture, as though the language we shared in common was simply not sufficient to overcome the enormous gap in experience that separated us." More recently, Marks (2008) wrote in the context of Hurricane Katrina that, "It was clear to me that words, no matter how descriptive or genuinely expressed, were not sufficient to 'tell the story.' They were like a small two-dimensional photograph or post-card of the Grand Canyon which can never convey the majesty and full ambiance of that place" (14). Therefore, although it is possible to read research on disaster recovery (i.e., Vale and Campanella 2005; Pais and Elliott 2008; Aldrich 2012) and this work is valuable to our understanding, the richest learning experiences will logically take place on the ground, amidst the recovery, thus providing students with firsthand experience.

Although my students were outsiders to the region who had learned about Katrina only through the literature and media, being on the ground in New

Orleans helped them to immediately notice the severity and immediacy of the storm's lived experience. Students discussed new perspectives on common arguments they had heard about Katrina, particularly discourses that blame local residents for not evacuating in advance of the storm. Although research demonstrates how lower-income individuals struggled to evacuate from Hurricane Katrina as it approached (Haney et al. 2007; Litt 2008), working and spending time in the Lower Ninth Ward helped students to appreciate why that may have been the case. According to one student, "Feeling the isolation of being in the Lower Ninth Ward, it became really clear how hard it would be to go anywhere without resources. Before the storm, where would you go and how would you get there? If you didn't own a vehicle and no one in your social network was able to help you with a ride, it would be difficult [to evacuate]." As a neighborhood nearly surrounded by water (the Lower Ninth Ward and its neighbor, Holy Cross, are bordered on three sides by the Industrial Canal, the Mississippi River, and the Intracoastal Waterway), the isolation and marginalization experienced by residents of this neighborhood must be felt firsthand and likely cannot be fully understood by simply reading accounts of the neighborhood's history (i.e., Landphair 1999).

Students also felt as though the experience helped them to understand the emotionality and enormity of these catastrophic events such as Katrina, in ways that textbooks never could. As the student remarked earlier in the chapter ("I knew we would see this, but I don't think I really knew"), there is an epistemic chasm between *knowing* and *understanding* that feminist researchers have pointed out for decades (see Smith 1987). One can have knowledge about a phenomenon in a detached, purportedly objective way, but truly understanding that phenomenon in a way that connects directly to emotion and human experience is a very distinct process; although students knew empirically, even before their arrival, that the disaster recovery in New Orleans had been slow, it took visiting the region to fully understand the lived experience of this slow and unequal recovery.

Students also noticed "just how much [Katrina brought] people together. Yes it [caused] major damage, hurt and pain, but the one good thing that can come out of it is the amount of love and support" that it fostered. Despite their dismay at the slow recovery, students were also pleasantly surprised by the resilience of the people and local culture, despite both recent disasters and despite many everyday pressing social problems. In particular, one student said "I think there was an expectation of there being a sort of sadness or anger among the people but that was just completely wrong." They noticed a level of engagement in local issues quite atypical in other cities, with one student remarking that "overall, the city seems to have a level of civic engagement that I have never seen before." Echoing common sentiments in the literature, that disasters uncover existing social dynamics that were previously concealed (Tierney 2007), a student concluded that "I have learned that times of disaster tend to unveil and magnify social problems lurking just beneath the surface of everyday life."

Our second and third days were largely occupied by a lecture series (that we helped to organize), hosted by Xavier University of Louisiana, a historically black college heavily damaged by Hurricane Katrina. The series brought in six of the leading disaster researchers in North America to speak about various aspects of Hurricane Katrina or the Deepwater Horizon oil spill. For the students, hearing the speakers discuss issues such as disaster-induced migration, ethnographic research in a devastated middle-class black neighborhood, and the patriarchal practices of relief organizations, helped them to understand many of the issues facing post–Katrina New Orleans. Perhaps most importantly, as all of the speakers had ties to New Orleans, it helped them realize the emotionality involved in conducting research on one's city following such devastation as well as the difficulties in conducting research both *on* and *in* a disaster recovery (see Haney and Elliott 2013).

Our group was privileged to welcome a number of guest speakers, including Farrah Gafford Cambrice of Xavier University. Her talk was particularly useful for understanding how difficult it is to both do research on and to live within post–Katrina New Orleans. At one point during her talk, for instance, she broke out into tears. In discussing how she considered dropping her Katrina research, but ultimately came back to the work, she remarked powerfully that "I'm back with Katrina—we didn't break up for very long" (Gafford 2013a; see also Gafford 2013b). This speaker (and all of the speakers) conveyed enormous love for the city that our group came to appreciate. As one student pointed out, "[Dr. Gafford] ignited my sociological passions and reminded me of the reasons why I love sociology in the first place." In scanning the audience, many of the students began to cry, as did I. These signs of emotion felt oddly out of place in an academic setting. As Barber (2007) argues, emotions are carefully managed in academic environments, so much so that it is difficult to perform academic and disaster survivor at the same time. Beyond that, the emotionality of the event revealed that the "recovery" in New Orleans is a thin veneer, residing directly atop lingering trauma (Oltenau et al. 2011) and a continued disruption of daily patterns and routines which residents find emotionally troubling (Hawkins and Maurer 2011) but that visitors may not fully understand.

These sentiments were echoed in my students' papers, with one student commenting that living through a disaster in your city "makes being objective and unattached to the research more difficult." This student comment echoes Haney and Barber (2013), who argue that researchers who are themselves affected by a disaster live a "double consciousness" while trying to cope with the disaster and also meet the expectations of colleagues, reviewers, and journal editors—individuals who quite often did not experience the disaster firsthand yet demand detached objectivity. We learned that so many scholars in New Orleans struggle to be the detached observers that their profession often demands while, at the same time, viewing the continuing struggles of their neighbors, coworkers, and friends.

The group was also struck by the ways in which Katrina, even a decade later, continues to permeate the consciousness of local residents, the news media, and political climate, with one student remarking that "I was unprepared for the extent to which New Orleanians incorporated Katrina into their understanding of their lives." All of these observations about the lived experience of post–Katrina New Orleans are observations that can only be gleaned from firsthand, on-the-ground experience and are much harder to grasp without immersion in the city.

LINGERING EFFECTS OF THE DEEPWATER HORIZON OIL SPILL

The field course also involved a day-trip to Plaquemines Parish, Louisiana, a region of the state affected by Hurricane Katrina (2005), the Deepwater Horizon oil spill (2010), and Hurricane Isaac (2012). While we were visiting Plaquemines Parish, we listened to guest lectures from several local people. One of the local families even invited us into their home to talk about the oil spill. People we spoke with discussed the worsening health effects of the oil spill, which included children with breathing problems, rashes, and cancers—potentially related to either the oil spill or the use of chemical dispersants such as Corexit (see Anderson et al. 2011). Hearing about these health effects, while meeting the very same people experiencing them, proved emotionally very powerful for the group. Families in the area discussed wanting to leave, but not being able to sell their homes. At the same time, their usual livelihoods (fishing, shrimping, etc.) were becoming harder and harder as fish populations were in steep decline (though for some, such as shrimpers, the decline started even before Katrina due to a "pink tsunami" of cheap farmed shrimp from Asia that depressed world prices—see Harrison 2012).

Local people said many interesting things such as referring to their region as a "sacrifice zone," or a region in which the health of local people and environmental sustainability are sacrificed for profit or economic growth (see Lerner 2010). They also argued powerfully that the region is not recovering from an oil spill, but still living in an oil spill. Some locals even referred to the "accidental activism" in which they are forced to engage. In other words, although an individual may not conceive of themself as an activist nor want that sort of public role, compelling circumstances often require activism if one is to protect their home, family, or community. Women, in particular, framed their activism in terms of family obligations, engaging in what Bell (2013) calls "activist mothering"—a discursive positioning of one's activism primarily in terms of one's responsibility to the family. This type of activism is a particularly effective strategy, as it is difficult for opponents to construct competing discourses that better capture public sympathies. All of these dynamics were quite salient at the time of our visit; only after our visit was BP forced to pay for some of the medical problems associated with the spill and its cleanup (McGill 2014).

Talking about these issues was very traumatic for some members of our group, and perhaps made worse in cases where we discussed them in someone's home and watched their children playing. On the bus ride back to New Orleans, some students wept. One later wrote, "It disrupts me to my core." Another remarked that, "After meeting with [the people of Plaquemines Parish], I was in a pretty dark place. I imagined I would be confronting contradictions in this place, but I never imagined it would be *so* hard. The unfairness of it all is weighing heavily on my mind" (emphasis in original).

Finally, our time in Plaquemines Parish forced my students to question the quality of media coverage they receive. We know that media coverage of disasters tends to be ephemeral and tends to focus on spectacularized imagery, rather than the experiences of everyday people (Gotham 2007), often focusing on images of social disorder rather than grassroots efforts to care for one another (Tierney et al. 2006). Most of the students arrived in southeastern Louisiana with little idea that people in Plaquemines Parish were becoming ill from the oil spill and use of dispersants (despite empirical evidence; see D'Andrea and Reddy 2013). Therefore, the experience made them ask new questions about the ongoing health, financial, and social issues confronted by victims of the oil spill and other disasters such as September 11.

Students ultimately hoped that the people of the region would be successful in their ongoing legal action against BP, but harbored some doubt. One student remarked in her final course paper that "unfortunately [they] may not win, but as Rachel Luft [Luft 2013] alluded in her guest lecture . . . sometimes it's just as important that you fight."

POLITICAL ECONOMY OF KATRINA RECOVERY

For two days during the field course, we partnered with a local non-profit, the Urban Conservancy, on their StayLocal! campaign, focused on helping locally owned businesses thrive in the post–Katrina business climate. The experience helped students appreciate "the importance of supporting the local economy. I definitely plan on shopping more local than I was before within my own city." Another student took a similar lesson away, saying "something like $0.75 out of every dollar remains in the community. This is incredibly important in this region, because another thing that kept coming up on this trip is the discussion of [Louisiana] basically being a colony rather than a state. [Brinkley (2006, 32) calls it a "colony rather than a capital"]. Resources and money continually get stripped from the area without anything being reinvested."

For about the last decade, scholars have written about disaster capitalism, or the tendency for disasters to spawn not only opportunity, but also opportunism. In the most popular iteration of this argument, Klein (2007) finds that political and economic elites maintain plans for neoliberal reforms (privatization, austerity measures, etc.) that may normally be politically unfeasible. Then, when a disaster or crisis strikes, they are able to usher in these changes while locals are otherwise occupied. In the context of hurricanes, Pais and Elliott (2008) examine how elites use disasters to generate income, often through real estate (re)development, a process that pushes lower-income and more socially vulnerable residents into more disaster prone locations. My students noticed some of these opportunistic tendencies in post–Katrina New Orleans; one student reflected that "It would seem that disaster capitalism was responsible for the turnaround in many places in New Orleans and was empowered by the administration; one such example was Freret Street. [A local] on this street explained that one 'white guy' had a vision for the entire street and bought up all the property." Therefore, the experience helped students to better understand the politics and economic inequalities at play during a protracted disaster recovery such as Hurricane Katrina's.

After having been familiarized with Klein's (2007) work on the political economy of disaster recovery, as well as work by others, many students found the political and demographic changes particularly problematic. Despite not being familiar with New Orleans prior to Katrina, my students seemed to understand and appreciate the processes of gentrification that were occurring, predominantly through the replacement of public housing projects with private housing arrangements (Arena 2012). Through seeing public housing projects turned into posh condominiums, one student remarked "we talked before we left about how things get done after disasters that people have wanted done all along but finally now have a chance to do, but it took going to New Orleans and seeing it to realize how true that is." Another student noticed the tony, natural-foods supermarkets, and other boutique shops and wondered, "[Are government officials] trying to just replace [displaced black people] with young modern white folks?" This astute observation dovetails with empirical findings that New Orleans's neighborhoods are recovering unevenly (Elliott et al. 2009) often through aid programs that undervalued homes in predominantly African American neighborhoods, thus preventing many lower-income black residents from returning and rebuilding (Adams 2013, 38–39). Students wondered about the ethics of this post-disaster decision-making process, with one student saying "Decisions like those [closing public housing projects and Charity Hospital] are made immediately after a disaster because no one is around to fight it or propose other ideas; it is sneaky and immoral, but nonetheless it happens."

One of our group's guest speakers was Pamela Jenkins of the University of New Orleans. She led the students in a brilliant philosophical discussion of what exactly constitutes "help" following a disaster (Jenkins 2013). One student remarked that "she said something that had a deep impact: people impose what help is. All these agencies went into New Orleans thinking they knew what was best and never really asked what [New Orelanians] wanted, for example a sense of community." Following Katrina, international organizations descended upon New Orleans, imposing their vision of the city's needs without asking locals about how to best rebuild their city (Jenkins 2013; Jenkins, Gremillion, and Nowell 2010, 7–10). One example that often arises is that of Brad Pitt's "Make It Right Foundation," which has built approximately eighty homes in the Lower Ninth Ward. Many of these eco-friendly homes utilize space-age architectural designs in a city that prides itself on its history. For instance, "Many residents of the MIR houses have expressed some difficulty in relating to their new house. Some have stated that they would have preferred for their new house to look more like their 'old' house. This familiarity bias on the part of returnees presumably is grounded in a wish for things to return to how they were before August 2005" (Verderber 2010), not surprising given the tendency for those affected by disaster to seek a return of their ontological security, or their security of surroundings and familiar routines (Hawkins and Maurer 2011). Further, "while the MIR project undeniably expresses a deeply grounded concern for social re-engagement, it also boldly, and at least equally, operates as a purveyor of a clear-cut top-down—some would say elitist—environmental and esthetic agenda" (Verderber 2010). This failure to ask returning residents about their desires and their envisioned community highlights Jenkins's (2013) point about top-down "help," while illuminating to visitors such as ourselves how outside organizations are transforming New Orleans. Responding to these realizations, students expressed surprise that agencies failed to first connect to like-minded local organizations. It also prompted them to consider how they, as outsiders, can best aid in the recovery process.

RECONSTRUCTING THE LOWER NINTH WARD

Following all of the knowledge that we had taken from New Orleans, I felt it important that we give something material and concrete back to the community. As such, I arranged for us to spend a week working with the local chapter of Habitat for Humanity, building a house in the Lower Ninth Ward. Each day that we worked, temperatures hovered around 95°F/35°C, extreme heat for Canadian students accustomed to a very mild summer. During that

May 2013—House from "Brad Pitt Village" stands as an example of newly constructed housing in the Ninth Ward of New Orleans. Photo by volume contributor Timothy J. Haney.

week, students were struck with the level of devastation in the Lower Ninth Ward. As one student noticed, "To stand beside our Habitat house on Tricou [Street] and realize that there had been 12 feet of water submerging the place where I was standing was unreal."

Although students reflect on this experience below, it is worth first mentioning that building the house helped them appreciate the very hard work of disaster recovery. Hurricane Katrina damaged or destroyed an estimated 130,000 homes in New Orleans alone (GNOCDC 2013a). We spent a week of very difficult labor and finished only the siding and painting of one house. This realization helped them see the sheer magnitude of the work that must take place in rebuilding the Lower Ninth Ward, not to mention the greater New Orleans area. It takes billions of dollars and millions of volunteer hours to make a small dent in that work. As one student remarked, "It made all of us realize that we were only building one part of a house, and that this is the type of work it takes to build thousands. . . . [It] would be more difficult for people living anywhere else [to] understand." Another student felt discouraged by the difficulty of the work itself, saying:

> I knew it was going to be hard work and it definitely was, especially in the heat and sun and I was happy it ended when it did. Near the end some of us were feeling frustrated and I know personally when I get frustrated with a task I need to step back from it otherwise it will only get worse. However, due to our circumstances, it was a weird idea to want to stop working and almost give up knowing that you are volunteering and building a home for someone. . . . We were very fortunate to be able to help in these efforts but near the end it was taking a toll on me physically.

The students soon realized that disaster recovery is not cheap nor easy nor immediate. They saw how many empty lots remained, and the task at hand seemed daunting. It also helped them develop rebuttals for comments they hear at home such as "It's been eight years! Why isn't New Orleans all rebuilt yet?" A student wrote eloquently that "I worked so hard during those four days, and I saw what progress we made in that short of time, but I also saw how many empty lots there were in the Lower Ninth Ward, and it made me appreciate how hard it is to rebuild a city. . . . I cannot imagine how many people it would take to completely [re]build New Orleans."

Many students commented about the quality of their work, which was often lacking as inexperienced home-builders. One student wondered "what would it feel like to have a bunch of strangers building a house for you? I would be concerned that the future costs of fixing the problems would be expensive and overwhelming" due to the work of inexperienced builders. As such, they wondered about the best way for outsiders to help in disaster recovery: to donate money so that high-quality work can be performed by professionals? Or to travel to the location and provide needed and cheaper (though admittedly lower quality) labor? Which approach provides the most just, humane disaster recovery?

Despite this nagging question, most of the students also felt a sense of accomplishment. One "became really attached to the house. I'm happy someone will call this place home and I hope it stands against future hurricane threats." Most of the students, of course, considered in their writings the very real possibility that it may not survive these future events.

One of the immediate realizations upon commencing work on the house in the Lower Ninth Ward was the difficulty of the labor. According to one student:

> This was the most difficult work any of us have done in a long time, especially in the heat and humidity. It made me realize that the only way of rebuilding NOLA was mainly through community service if locals were having insurance problems, ownership problems, and lack of funds available. I realized how important it was that we participate in service-learning while we were in NOLA, it was the least we could do considering how much NOLA had given to us.

Another student was particularly pleased with her or his hard work, saying "If I would have told myself what I did the last four days even a week ago I wouldn't have believed myself."

TAKING NEW ORLEANS HOME

Students in my class felt that spending time learning and serving in New Orleans changed the way they thought about catastrophic events, about sociological issues, and about their own lives. Upon return home students possessed a new lens through which they filtered comments they heard about disaster and about New Orleans. One student remarked that:

> [My hair stylist] asked me how New Orleans was seeing how "they had that storm or something." I suppose I should not be surprised by her comment but again, it reminded me that most people have forgotten about Katrina, and simply view New Orleans as a place to get drunk and party. The people I met there were so much more than that, the culture was so rich, and the city had a certain magical feeling to it that makes my heart cringe when I heard comments like the ones I hear these last few weeks.

Reflections such as this reveal how students had become sensitized about issues related to disaster and more critical about offhand comments that misunderstood or downplayed the significance of the event.

Many students remarked that they would seek out organizations in their home community doing work similar to New Orleans Area Habitat for Humanity. One said that "participating in this field school has motivated me to volunteer more of my time to this organization and to contribute to community service projects in my own backyard" while another said "I feel really inspired to pursue working with Habitat in Calgary and plan to get involved with them this summer." These connections are particularly inspiring and appropriate given that many communities in Southern Alberta, including our home community of Calgary, were inundated by flooding in June 2013, only a month after the group returned from New Orleans. This event is now considered the costliest disaster in Canadian history (Canadian Broadcasting Corporation 2013). As a result, many communities in Alberta desperately need precisely the sort of work that students learned how to do while we visited New Orleans.

Most importantly, visiting and serving New Orleans helped the students to see their home community in a new way. In particular, it helped them understand the dynamics of oil production in their home province and country in a more critical light. Many students connected the experience to their own lives in Alberta, home to a well-known but empirically debated cancer cluster in the town of Fort Chipewyan, Alberta, a First Nations community downstream from the tar-sands (Kelly et al. 2009). One student remarked, "I feel guilt in not knowing more of the environmental and social effects of the oil sands, which I am largely complicit in." That same student continued, commenting that, "Given what I have learned about the importance of local service, I want to become engaged in policy and social change in Alberta regarding the oil sands and the resulting health effects felt by those disproportionately affected through environmental racism." A different student remarked that she or he wants "to be involved within my own province's oil industry and to be aware about the realities of the industry. . . . In this way, I see myself approaching my life differently because I want to be more involved with environmental justice in my region."

As a former New Orleanian, comments like these help me to better see and articulate the enduring legacy of Katrina; though surely Katrina will be remembered for its devastation and dislocation, over the longer-term, the disaster may be remembered for rekindling an interest in environmental inequalities and motivating a new generation of young people concerned with issues of social and environmental justice. By traveling to the region, immersing themselves in the city (albeit to greatly varying degrees), and seeing the slow pace of recovery, students from around North America return home newly sensitized and highly motivated. If this pattern continues I have confidence that Katrina's enduring legacy will be this new generation of thinkers, activists, and global citizens.

It is my hope that more members of the Katrina diaspora return "home," bringing with them their students, coworkers, and friends. At the start of our work in New Orleans, I wondered: How can instructors and researchers working in post–Katrina New Orleans be sure that they are contributing in a way that is ethical and sensitive to local concerns? As one of my students since pointed out, "I think that service must always take the knowledge and understanding of locals above those of the understandings brought into an area by those wanting to do service," an approach that has not always been applied in post–Katrina New Orleans, even by those who come with good intentions. In other words, those from outside the region must actively work to involve community members in activities and decision-making processes, continually asking them about their needs and wants.

It is inspiring to see so many survivor scholars, many contributing to this volume, continuing to do work that benefits New Orleans and its people. Although many local academics have since left New Orleans and now live elsewhere, we each continue to contribute to the city's rebuilding through our teaching, our research, and our service to the community. As part of a large and enduring diaspora (Weber and Peek 2012), I know that we each feel committed to ensuring the city's future as a safer, more prosperous, and more sustainable place to live, work, and play.

PostScript

Notes on the Buildup to Katrina and the Future of the Gulf Coast

Dana M. Greene

At every level, individuals, universities, and agencies who were asked to shoulder the responsibility for the Katrina debacle had varying degrees of plausible deniability. However, while this may be true for the specific failures surrounding Hurricane Katrina, this was not simply a tragic case of many balls being dropped all at once. The indirect racism, impotent federal leadership, and persistent failure to prepare for the inevitable all have common and deeply structural roots in neoliberal ideology. Adding insult to injury, while the United States both requested and accepted foreign aid in the immediate aftermath of the combined natural and technological "na-tech" disaster for the first time in modern history, much of the donated aid and resources never reached the people who were most in need of those items. Trucks filled with water, healthcare supplies, tents, food, and tarps (to name just a few) sat in wait or were turned away as a result of bureaucratic mismanagement of funds and resources. In essence, it appears that the governmental attempts to "manage" the disaster ended up doing the opposite; namely, actively contributing to the continued victimization of those who were trying their very best to survive "by any means, necessary." Perhaps this occurrence can be attributed to the lack of necessary ad hoc networks to coordinate the acceptance of both domestic and international aid donations, but this does not excuse the fact that bureaucratic incompetence contributed not only to the primary victimization of those who survived Hurricane Katrina, but also to the continuing (ten plus years after the fact) secondary trauma that continues to be the reason for governmental distrust, illness, death, and discouragement among survivors in New Orleans.

Neoliberalism is defned simply by a rejection of free-market capitalism, and advocates, instead a more limited role for federal government. One of the basic assumptions of neoliberalism remains the idea that people should be free to work and benefit from the global economy and free enterprise. Further, Stuart Varner (2006) notes that "neoliberalism has a basic distrust of government bureaucracy and maintains faith in the efficiency of the private sector. This is responsible for the deregulation and privatization that have revolutionized such disparate industries as household utilities, healthcare, and airline travel in the United States." When applying this concept to that which occurred during and immediately following Hurricane Katrina, it is clear that neoliberalism had significant consequences for the storm's victims. George Lakoff, professor of Linguistics at the University of California, Berkeley, wrote in a piece for AlterNet that:

> . . . eliminating as much as possible of the role of government accounts for the demotion of FEMA from cabinet rank, for Michael Brown's view that FEMA was a federal entitlement program to be cut, for the budget cuts in levee repair, for placing more responsibility on state and local government than they could handle, for the failure to fully employ the military, and for the lax regulation of toxic waste dumps contributing to a "toxic stew." (Lakoff 2005)

GLOBALIZING NEOLIBERALISM

Neoliberalism is not without its problems. Varner notes that neoliberalism might have a homogenizing effect, through which the drive to decentralize big government's involvement in disaster response will have the unintended consequence of creating further problems for victims of the primary and secondary disasters (the initial storm, and the continued aftermath) (2006). Following Hurricane Katrina, new problems were significantly associated with neoliberalist implications; namely, isolation from mainstream sources of capital combined with the "neoliberal drive to decentralize and privatize the federal government, local governments frequently find that their top priority is to figure out how to connect to the global flows of mobile capital. Isolation from the flow would means no jobs, no investment and rapid decline (Sites). The impact of this problem is significant: social programs are sacrificed in favor of job creation in big business: a process that is typically associated with the perception of "selling out" by those most impacted by Hurricane Katrina: the victims who lost everything, including a means by which to make a living in their own city. Ultimately, Sites argues "that the nation-state, often characterized as all but irrelevant in today's global society, is actually central to the creation of the global neoliberal economy. Yet, despite its centrality, this process is essentially a self-destructive one for the nation-state because it means that all levels of government have to relinquish their powers and duties to the private sector." The end result of all of this, however, has been for those most vulnerable to the storm being stuck in low-paying jobs in the service industry, while monies rooted in tourism have benefited the middle and upper-middle classes in the City (Lambert Strether, "*Naked Capitalism*"). The bottom line with regard to the impact of neoliberalism in New Orleans is quite simple; namely, vulnerable populations who were disproportionately affected by the Hurricane Katrina lacked both the structural, political, social, economic, and even personal resources from which to recover. The very fact that the only jobs available to those who lost everything do not yield enough income to rebuild lives or make houses home again. The local, state, and federal political systems add insult to injury by neglecting to fund social programs to aid those most in need following the Storm; opting instead to focus on big business, profits from tourism and gambling, thereby, keeping the focus on the almighty dollar.[1] The changes in the labor market that are linked to the tourism-led gentrification give rise to Sassen's concept of the "casualization of labor": inadequately paid jobs that further divided the city's population. In fact, as housing costs increased, they did so at the benefit of the local bourgeoisie who were both economically and culturally privileged, while the proletariat (racial and ethnic minorities, single parent households, older adults, non-native speakers of English, etc.) continue to find themselves struggling to make ends meet in an "Alcatraz-type" situation wherein the proletariat can *see* the benefits of what the power elite is reaping, but those resources and the socio-economic benefits contained therein remain beyond their reach (Gotham and Greenberg (2008)).

Following Hurricane Katrina, the reach of neoliberalist policies has grown beyond simple economic effects that privileged the middle class over the poor. Instead, gentrification led to an increased disenfranchised racial and ethnic hierarchy in New Orleans. From being cast as "refugees" in mainstream media immediately following the storm, to being so economically disadvantaged in spite of "programs that were supposed to help," has increased the stark negative race relations in the city. Beyond finding themselves politically and economically isolated, racial and ethnic minorities continue to be physically isolated from areas of New Orleans that reaped the benefits of significant economic prosperity.

TEN YEARS AFTER KATRINA

Incredible inequality existed in New Orleans prior to Hurricane Katrina, and was simply exacerbated for vulnerable populations following the storm. The fact that local, state, and federal representatives and agencies failed to respond with the relief necessary to actually aid those most impacted by the storm remains an unfortunate reality and reminder of white privilege in the face of disaster. Should those who fought for their lives in the immediate aftermath of the storm continue to be angry? Absolutely. Their realities today remain no better than those within which they lived prior to the storm. What has become more stark, however, is the racial and ethnic inequalities that continue to pervade every aspect of the survivor existence. Sadly, the socio-economic situation and racial and ethnic discrimination that continues to pervade the everyday existence for Katrina victims. Even ten years after the storm, the situation is steadily growing worse, and not better. Neoliberalist strategies have not benefited anyone other than the white power elite.

Certainly, the "relief strategies such as 'charter schools,' the elimination of Charity Hospital, public housing 'reforms,' etc., were rooted in neoliberalist ideology" (Varner, 2006). There is also no denying that private entities and faith based organizations worked hard to mobilize resources, funds, clothing, water, and volunteers (myself included) to aid the victims of the storm. Unfortunately, as a direct result of government bureaucracy and the inefficient and mismanagement of the emergency situation by local, state, and federal authorities, donations of goods, funds, and physical labor were not only delayed in getting to the victims, but, in several cases, were turned away by those more interested in "following rules" and "working through bureaucratic red tape. The War on Terror necessitated that FEMA be subsumed under the Department of Homeland Security (DHS), and, as a result, requests for aid even with State and Federal Declarations of Emergency became "stuck" in the bureaucratic quagmire. It was only recently that policies for "fast-tracking" emergency aid to afflicted regions of the United States have been put into place. At the time that Katrina struck New Orleans and the Gulf Coast, however, tunnels through the required paperwork were not yet in place. In fact, with Hurricane Rita following closely on the footsteps of Katrina, it was almost as though the region had been hit by three (3) distinct storms: Katrina, Rita, and Ka-FEMA. As such, and as has become clear with more recent natural and technological disasters, FEMA is a good idea; it just needs strong leadership, full funding and independence from an agency—Homeland Security—that is preoccupied with the war on terrorism.

Certainly, there is a difference betweeen disaster preparedness and disaster preparation, just as there is a difference between emergency management plans and emergency management. Hurricane Katrina provided a tangible example within which those affected directly and indirectly could note the problems and issues inherent within the current system in the United States. One would think that the days of highlighting racial and ethnic minority citizens affected by natural and technological disasters labeled as "refugees" and as dispensible were long gone. However, this has not been the case. Disaster recovery is slow if one is poor, but is fast-tracked if an area is predominately White or if there is money involved or if the area can benefit from disaster capitalism and tourism (Klein 2008). Racial and economic inequity continues to plague disaster recovery in New Orleans and around the world. One need only look to the Lower Ninth Ward in New Orleans and see the continued devastation and lack of necessary resources there to Haiti where the scourge of racism and economic despair continues to impede recovery efforts. It seems that being black and poor continues to be problem numero uno. Following Superstorm Sandy, repair and reconstruction was hurried, the victims were predominately white, and cleanup and floodzone buy-outs were swift. What we have here is a problem: race and class continue to impede assistance efforts. We began this volume with the idea of "rethinking disaster recovery." As the essays contained herein depict, the suffering continues beyond the current disaster dialectic of primary and secondary victimization. Instead, recovery efforts need to be reinvigorated in such a way as to promote and initiate emergency management plans during phases of emergency management. This can be done by re-thinking both how we prepare, mitigate, and respond to disasters, as well as by re-evaluating the recovery process.

Disaster recovery is a process on which greater emphasis must be placed in governmental, academic, and NGO research. It is only by noting what doesn't work in disaster response that we can effect positive social change in recovery. While eliminating the race/class/gender dynamic would be the utopian ideal, sadly, such is too broad a problem when evaluating disaster recovery as a process. Instead, we must focus on affecting the race problem by focusing on increasing prompt assistance to all areas affected by na-tech disasters, including, but not limited to prompt evacuation, appropriate and adequate sheltering, healthcare and medical assistance, transportation, and rebuilding. The rebuilding effort in particular, as has been the focus of this volume, must be done with fairness and justice for all affected residents in mind if we have any hope of upholding the core ideals of our nation. It must be done with the awareness that not all affected voices are necessarily sitting at the rebuilding table and must make a concerted effort to include those marginalized voices. It should also be done with recognition that private businesses are self-interested entities and sometimes government, nonprofits, and volunteers must step in to ensure the public good. This must be the essence of rethinking disaster recovery.

NOTE

1. Varner cites Saskia Sassen's work that "describes intensified gentrification as a consequence of trying to compete in the global market in *The Global City*. This process often takes place in previously underserved sections of a city and leads to a kind of consumer oriented homogenization (Molotch 1976) and, if "successful," generally produces a dramatic increase in both commercial and residential property values. As a result, any economic—and, by common

extension, racial—diversity that existed, or was possible is greatly diminished and geographic segregation is exacerbated. While none of this is exactly new, Sassen argues that its scale is and that contemporary gentrification "represents a massive appropriation of public resources and urban space" (2001, 3; 2006).

REFERENCES

Bond-Graham, Darwin. 2007. "The New Orleans That Race Built: Racism, Disaster, and Urban Spatial Relationships." *Souls: A Critical Journal of Black Politics, Culture, and Society* 9 (1).

Brief, Arthur P., Robin Reizenstein Cohen, S. Douglas Pugh, and Joel B. Vaslow. 2000. "Just Doing Business: Modern Racism and Obedience to Authority as Explanations for Employment Discrimination." *Organizational Behavior and Human Decision Processes* 8 (1): 72–97.

Gotham, Kevin Fox, and Miriam Greenberg. 2008. "From 9/11 to 8/29: Post-Disaster Recovery and Rebuilding in New York and New Orleans." *Social Forces* 87 (2): 1039–1062.

Klein, Naomi. 2008. *The Shock Doctrine: The Rise of Disaster Capitalism*. New York: Picador Press.

Lakoff, George. 2005. "The Post Katrina Era." Alternet: http://www.alternet.org/story/25099/the_post-katrina_era.

Molotch, Harvey. 1976. "The City as a Growth Machine: Toward a Political Economy of Place." *American Journal of Sociology* 82 (2): 309–332.

Muro, M., A. Lieu, R. Sohmer, D. Warren, D. Park, et al. 2005. "New Orleans After the Storm: Lessons from the Past, a Plan for the Future." The Brookings Institution. Special Analysis. October. http://www.brookings.edu/~/media/research/files/reports/2005/10/metropolitan-policy/20051012_neworleans.pdf.

Sassen, Saskia. 2001. *The Global City: New York, London, Tokyo*. Princeton University Press.

Varner, Stewart. 2006. "Hurricane Katrina: Neoliberal Globalization and the Global City" in *HypheNation: An Interdisciplinary Journal for the Study of Critical Moments Discourse*. Volume 1, Number 1.

References

Adamo, Ralph. 2007. "Squeezing Public Education: History and Ideology Gang Up on New Orleans." *Dissent* 54 (3): 44–51.

Adams, R. E., E. J. Bromet, N. Panina, E. Golovakha, D. Goldgaber, and S. Gluzman. 2002. "Stress and Well-Being in Mothers of Young Children 11 Years after the Chernobyl Nuclear Power Plant Accident." *Psychological Medicine* 32: 143–156.

Adams, Vincanne. 2013. *Markets of Sorrow, Labors of Faith: New Orleans in the Wake of Katrina.* Durham: Duke University Press.

Alagona, P. S. and G. L. Simon. 2010. "The Role of Field Study in Humanistic and Interdisciplinary Environmental Education." *Journal of Experiential Education* 32 (3): 191–206.

Aldrich, Daniel P. 2012. *Building Resilience: Social Capital in Post-Disaster Recovery.* Chicago: University of Chicago Press.

Anastario, Michael P., Ryan Larrance, and Lynn Lawry. 2008. "Using Mental Health Indicators to Identify Postdisaster Gender-Based Violence among Women Displaced by Hurricane Katrina." *Journal of Women's Health* 17 (9): 1437–1444.

Anderson, Nick. 2010. "Education Secretary Duncan Calls Hurricane Katrina Good for New Orleans Schools." *Washington Post*, January 30. http://www.washingtonpost.com/wp-dyn/content/article/2010/01/29/AR2010012903259.html.

Anderson, Stacey E., Jennifer Franko, and Ewa Lukomska. 2011. "Potential Immunotoxicological Health Effects Following Exposure to COREXIT 9500A during Cleanup of the Deepwater Horizon Oil Spill." *Journal of Toxicology and Environmental Health* 74 (21): 1419–1430.

Arena, John. 2012. *Driven from New Orleans: How Nonprofits Betray Public Housing and Promote Privatization.* Minneapolis: University of Minnesota Press.

Arnett, Jeffrey. 2000. "Emerging Adulthood: A Theory of Development from Late Teens through the Twenties." *American Psychologist* 55 (5): 469–480. doi:10.1037//0003-066X.55.5.469.

Babbie, E. 2001. *The Practice of Social Research.* Belmont: Wadsworth.

Baise, Marilynne Boyle. 2002. *Multicultural Service Learning: Educating Teachers in Diverse Communities.* New York: Teacher's College Press.

Barber, Kristen. 2007. "The Emotional Management of a Stranger: Negotiating Class Privilege and Masculine Academics as a Hurricane Katrina Evacuee." In *Narrating the Storm: Sociological Stories of Hurricane Katrina*, edited by Danielle A. Hidalgo and Kristen Barber, 78–89. Newcastle, UK: Cambridge Scholars Press.

———. 2013. "Review of 'The Women of Katrina: How Gender, Race, and Class Matter in an American Disaster,' and 'Women Confronting Natural Disaster: From Vulnerability to Resistance.'" *SIGNS: Journal of Women in Culture and Society* 38 (3): 763–767.

Barber, Kristen, Danielle Antoinette Hidalgo, Timothy J. Haney, Stan Weeber, Jessica W. Pardee, and Jennifer Day. 2007. "Narrating the Storm: Storytelling as a Methodological Approach to Understanding Hurricane Katrina." *Journal of Public Management & Social Policy* 13 (2): 99–120.

Barnshaw, John, and Joseph Trainor. 2010. "Race, Class, and Capital amidst the Hurricane Katrina Diaspora," 2nd ed. In *The Sociology of Katrina: Perspectives on a Modern Catastrophe*, edited by David L. Brunsma, David Overfelt, and J. Steven Picou, 103–118. Lanham: Rowman & Littlefield.

Barrow, B. 2010. "Louisiana children have a hard road ahead, statistical review suggests." *Times-Picayume*, July 27. http://www.nola.com/health/index.ssf/2010/07/louisiana_children_have_a_hard.html.

Bartky, S. 1990. *Femininity and Domination: Studies in the Phenomenology of Oppression*. New York: Routledge.

Batlan, Felice. 2008. "Weathering the Storm Together (Torn Apart by Race, Gender, and Class)." *NWSA Journal* 20 (3): 163–184.

Becker, G. S. 1971. *The Economics of Discrimination*, 2nd ed. Chicago: University of Chicago.

Belkhir, Jean Ait, and Christiane Charlemaine. 2007. "Race, Gender and Class Lessons from Hurricane Katrina." *Race, Gender & Class* 14 (1–2): 120–152.

Bell, Shannon Elizabeth. 2013. *Our Roots Run Deep as Ironweed: Appalachian Women and the Fight for Environmental Justice*. Urbana: University of Illinois Press.

Berg, B. L. 2009. *Qualitative Research Methods for the Social Sciences*, 7th ed. Boston: Allyn & Bacon.

Bertrand, Marianne, and Sendhil Mullainathan. 2004. "Are Emily and Greg More Employable Than Lakisha and Jamal? A Field Experiment on Labor Market Discrimination." *American Economic Review* 94 (4): 991–1013.

Berube, Alan, and Bruce Katz. 2005. "Katrina's Window: Confronting Concentrated Poverty across America." The Brookings Institution. October. http://www.brookings.edu/research/reports/2005/10/poverty-berube.

Bevc, Christine A., Keith Nicholls, and J. Stephen Picou. 2010. "Community Recovery from Hurricane Katrina: Storm Experiences, Property Damage, and the Human Condition," 2nd ed. In *The Sociology of Katrina: Perspectives on a Modern Catastrophe,* edited by David L. Brunsma, David Overfelt, and J. Steven Picou, 157–176. Lanham: Rowman & Littlefield.

Blaikie, P., T. Cannon, I. Davis, and B. Wisner. 2004. *At Risk: Natural Hazards, People's Vulnerability, and Disasters,* 2nd ed. New York: Routledge.

Blizzard, D. 2007. *Looking within: A Sociocultural Examination of Fetoscopy*. Cambridge: MIT Press.

Blumer, Herbert. 1958. "Race Prejudice as a Sense of Group Position." *Pacific Sociological Review*: 3–7.

Bobo, Lawrence, and Vincent L. Hutchings. 1996. "Perceptions of Racial Group Competition: Extending Blumer's Theory of Group Position to a Multiracial Social Context." *American Sociological Review*: 951–972.

Boisseau, T. J., K. Feltey, K. Flynn, L. Gelfand, and M. Triece. 2008. "New Orleans: A Special Issue on the Gender Politics of Place and Displacement." *NWSA Journal* 20 (3): vii–xiv.

Bonacich, Edna. 1972. "A Theory of Ethnic Antagonism." *American Sociological Review* 37: 547–559.

Bond-Graham, Darwin. 2007. "The New Orleans That Race Built: Racism, Disaster, and Urban Spatial Relationships." *Souls: A Critical Journal of Black Politics, Culture, and Society* 9 (1).

Bonner, Donna. 2007. "A Bricolage of Loss." In *Narrating the Storm: Sociological Stories of Hurricane Katrina,* edited by Danielle Antoinette Hidalgo and Kristen Barber, 206–217. Newcastle, UK: Cambridge Scholars Publishing.

Bordo, Susan. 1993. *Unbearable Weight: Feminism, Western Culture, and the Body*. Berkeley: University of California Press.

Borjas, George. J. 1987. "Immigrants, Minorities, and Labor Market Competition." *Industrial and Labor Relations Review* 40 (3): 382–392.

Brief, Arthur P., Robin Reizenstein Cohen, S. Douglas Pugh, and Joel B. Vaslow. 2000. "Just Doing Business: Modern Racism and Obedience to Authority as Explanations for Employment Discrimination." *Organizational Behavior and Human Decision Processes* 8 (1): 72–97.

Bringle, Robert G., Patty H. Clayton, and Julie A. Hatcher. 2013. "Research on Service Learning: An Introduction." In *Research in Service Learning* (volume 2a), edited by Patti H. Clayton, Robert G. Bringle, and Julie A. Hatcher, 3–29. Sterling: Stylus Publishing.

Brinkley, Douglas. 2006. *The Great Deluge: Hurricane Katrina, New Orleans, and the Mississippi Gulf Coast*. New York: Harper.

Brown, Bethany L. 2012. "Battered Women's Shelters in New Orleans: Recovery and Transformation." In *The Women of Katrina: How Gender, Race, and Class Matter in an American Disaster*, edited by Emmanuel David and Elaine Enarson, 179–189. Nashville: Vanderbilt University Press.

Brown, Bethany L., and Pamela Jenkins. 2011. "The Public Health Crisis of Violence Against Women in the Aftermath of Katrina." Paper presented at the annual meeting for the American Sociological Association, Las Vegas, Nevada, August 20–23.

Brown, Bethany L., Pamela J. Jenkins, and Tricia Wachtendorf. 2010. "Shelter in the Storm: A Battered Women's Shelter and Catastrophe." *International Journal of Mass Emergencies and Disasters* 28 (2): 226–245.

Brown, Michael K., Martin Carnoy, Troy Duster, and David B. Oppenheimer. 2003. *Whitewashing Race: The Myth of a Color-Blind Society*. Oakland: University of California Press.

Brown, Phillip, Hugh Lauder, and David Ashton. 2011. *The Global Auction: The Broken Promises of Education, Jobs, and Incomes*. New York: Oxford University Press.

Bullard, Robert, and Beverly Wright, eds. 2009. *Race, Place and Environmental Justice after Hurricane Katrina: Struggles to Reclaim, Rebuild, and Revitalize New Orleans and the Gulf Coast*. Boulder: Westview Press.

Buras, Kristen. 2011. "Race, Charter Schools and Conscious Capitalism: On the Spatial Politics of Whiteness as Property and the Unconscionable Assault on Black New Orleans." *Harvard Educational Review* 81 (2): 296–330.

Bush, Melanie E. L., and Deborah Little. 2009. "Teaching toward Praxis and Political Engagement." In *Engaging Social Justice: Critical Studies of 21st Century Transformation*, edited by David Fasenfest, 11–36. Leiden, Netherlands: Brill.

Butterbaugh, Laura. 2005. "Why Did Hurricane Katrina Hit Women So Hard?" *Off Our Backs* 35 (9–10): 17–19.

Caldwell, Robert. (2005) 2006. "New Orleans: The Making of an Urban Catastrophe." *MRZine*, December 9. http://mrzine.monthlyreview.org/2005/caldwell120905.html.

Caldwell, Jr., James H., and Theodore J. Dubinsky. 2005. "New Orleans: The Making of a Social Catastrophe." *New Socialist Magazine*, January 2006.

Calefati, Jessica. 2008. "The High School That Beat Katrina." *U.S. News & World Report*. December 4. http://www.usnews.com/education/high-schools/articles/2008/12/04/the-high-school-that-beat-katrina.

Callaghan, William M., Sonja A. Rasmussen, Denise J. Jamieson, Stephanie J. Ventura, Sherry L. Farr, Paul D. Sutton, Thomas J. Mathew, Brady E. Hamilton, Katherine R. Shealy, Dabo Brantley, and Sam F. Posner. 2007. "Health Concerns of Women and Infants in Times of Natural Disasters: Lessons Learned from Hurricane Katrina." *Maternal and Child Health Journal* 11 (4): 307–311.

Campanella, Richard. 2002. *Time and Place in New Orleans: Past Geographies in the Present Day*. Gretna, LA: Pelican Publishing.

———. 2007. "An Ethnic Geography of New Orleans." *Journal of American History* 94 (3): 704–715.

———. 2013. "Gentrification and Its Discontents: Notes from New Orleans." *New Geography*, March 1. http://www.newgeography.com/content/003526-gentrification-and-its-discontents-notes-new-orleans.

Campo-Flores, Arian. 2005. "How Latino Workers Could Change New Orleans: Will Latino Day Laborers Locating in New Orleans Change Its Complexion?" *Newsweek*, December 5.

Canadian Broadcasting Corporation (CBC). 2013. "Alberta Floods Costliest Natural Disaster in Canadian History." September 23. Available at: http://www.cbc.ca/news/canada/calgary/alberta-floods-costliest-natural-disaster-in-canadian-history-1.1864599.

Card, David. 1990. "The Impact of the Mariel Boatlift on the Miami Labor Market." *Industrial and Labor Relations Review* 43 (2): 245–257.

———. 2005. "Is the New Immigration Really so Bad?" *The Economic Journal* 115 (507): F300–F323.

Card, David, and John DiNardo. 2000. "Do Immigrant Inflows Lead to Native Outflows?" *The American Economic Review* 90 (2): 360–367.

Catanzarite, Lisa. 2000. "Brown-Collar Jobs: Occupational Segregation and Earnings of Recent-Immigrant Latinos." *Sociological Perspectives* 43 (1): 45–75.

———. 2003. "Occupational Context and Wage Competition of New Immigrant Latinos with Minorities and Whites." *Review of Black Political Economy* 31 (1): 77–94.

Centers for Disease Control and Prevention (CDC). 2013. "Effects of Disasters on Pregnant Women." *Emergency Preparedness and Response for Special Groups,* March 14. http://www.cdc.gov/ncbddd/disasters/women.html.

Chamlee-Wright, Emily, and Virgil Henry Storr. 2009. "'There's No Place Like New Orleans': Sense of Place and Community Recovery in the Ninth Ward after Hurricane Katrina." *Journal of Urban Affairs* 31 (5): 615–634.

Chomsky, Noam. 2014. "The Death of American Universities." *Jacobin: A Magazine of Culture and Polemic.* https://www.jacobinmag.com/2014/03/the-death-of-american-universities/.

Clark, Candice. 1987. "Sympathy Biography and Sympathy Margin." *American Journal of Sociology* 93 (2): 290–321.

Clark, Rebecca. 2006. "Eight Months Later: Hurricane Katrina Aftermath Challenges Facing the Infectious Diseases Section of the Louisiana State University Health Science Center. *Clinical Infectious Diseases* 43 (4): 485–489.

Cohen, Rick. 2014. "New Orleans Becomes Nation's First All-Charter School System." *Non Profit Quarterly*, June 2. https://nonprofitquarterly.org/policysocial-context/24284-new-orleans-becomes-nation-s-first-all-charter-school-system.html.

Collins, Patricia Hill. 1990. *Black Feminist Thought.* New York: Routledge.

Colten, Craig. 2006. *Unnatural Metropolis: Wresting New Orleans from Nature.* Baton Rouge: Louisiana State University Press.

Colten, Craig E., Robert W. Kates, and Shirley B. Laska. 2008. "Three Years: Lessons for Community Resilience." *Environment* 50 (5): 36–47.

Converse, Jean M., and Stanley Presser. 1986. *Survey Questions: Handcrafting the Standardized Questionnaire.* Thousand Oaks: Sage Publications, Inc.

Couch, Stephen R. 1996. "Environmental Contamination, Community Transformation and the Central Mine Fire." In *The Long Road to Recovery: Community Responses to Industrial Disaster*, edited by James K. Mitchell, 60–84. New York: United Nations University Press.

Cowen Institute. 2010. "The State of Public Education in New Orleans: Five Years after Hurricane Katrina." http://www.coweninstitute.com/wp-content/uploads/2010/07/katrina-book.final_.CIpageSmaller.pdf.

Croom, Carolyn, Pamela Jenkins, and Abigail Eddy. 2007. "The Story of the Senior Center: Meeting Immediate Needs." *Generations* 31 (4): 47–48.

Crowley, Sheila. 2006. "Where Is Home? Housing for Low-Income People after the 2005 Hurricanes." In *There Is No Such Thing as a Natural Disaster,* edited by Chester Hartman and Gregory D. Squires, 121–166. New York: Routledge.

Cvetkovich, Ann. 2003. *An Archive of Feelings: Trauma, Sexuality, and Lesbian Public Culture*. Durham: Duke University Press.

D'Andrea, Mark A., and G. Kesava Reddy. 2013. "Health Consequences among Subjects Involved in Gulf Oil Spill Clean-up Activities." *The American Journal of Medicine* 126 (11): 966–974.

David, Emmanuel, and Elaine Enarson, eds. 2012. *The Women of Katrina: How Gender, Race, and Class Matter in an American Disaster.* Nashville, TN: Vanderbilt University Press.

D'ooge, Charlotte. 2006. "Queer Katrina: Gender and Sexual Orientation Matters in the Aftermath of the Disaster." In *Katrina and the Women of New Orleans: Executive Report & Summary of Findings*, edited by Beth Willinger, 22–23. Newcomb College Center for Research on Women.

Dale, Charles V. 2005. Katrina Relief: U.S. Labor Department Exemption of Contractors from Written Affirmative Action Requirements. Congressional Research Service Report for Congress. Order Code RS22282, September 27, 2005.

Davis, Elizabeth, and Kelly Rouba. 2012. "Out of Sight, Out of Mind: Women's Abilities and Disabilities in Crisis." In *The Women of Katrina: How Gender, Race, and Class Matter in an American Disaster,* edited by Emmanuel David and Elaine Enarson, 76–89. Nashville: Vanderbilt University Press.

Davis, Ophera A., and Marie Land. 2007. "Southern Women Survivors Speak about Hurricane Katrina, the Children and the What Needs to Happen Next." *Race, Gender & Class* 14 (1–2): 69–86.

Day, Kristen. 1994. "Conceptualizing Women's Fear of Sexual Assault on Campus: A Review of Causes and Recommendations for Change." *Environment and Behavior* 26: 742–765.

Delp, Linda, Laura Podolsky, and Tomás Aguilar. 2009. "Risk Amid Recovery: Occupational Health and Safety of Latino Day Laborers in the Aftermath of the Gulf Coast Hurricanes." *Organization and Environment* 22 (4): 479–490.

Denzin, N. K., and Y. S. Lincoln, eds. 2011. *The SAGE Handbook of Qualitative Research, Fourth Edition.* Thousand Oaks: Sage Publications Inc.

Dequine, Kari. 2011. "St. Augustine High School Paddling Policy is 'not broken,' Marchers Say." *Times-Picayune,* March 26. http://www.nola.com/education/index.ssf/2011/03/st_augustine_high_school_paddl.html.

DeVault, M. 1999. *Liberating Method: Feminism and Social Research.* Philadelphia: Temple University Press.

Donato, Katharine, Nicole Trujillo-Pagán, Carl Bankston, and Audrey Singer. 2007. "Reconstructing New Orleans after Katrina: The Emergence of an Immigrant Labor Market." In *The Sociology of Katrina: Perspectives on a Modern Catastrophe*, edited by David Brunsma, David L. Overfelt , and J. Steven Picou, 217–234. Lanham: Rowman & Littlefield.

Draper, Alison J. 2004. "Integrating Project-Based Service-Learning into an Advanced Environmental Chemistry Course." *Journal of Chemical Education* 81 (2): 221–224.

Dreier, Peter, John Mollenkopf, and Todd Swanstrom. 2001. *Place Matters: Metropolitics for the Twenty-first Century.* Lawrence: University of Kansas Press.

Drever, Anita I., and Sarah A. Blue. 2011. "Surviving Sin Papeles in Post-Katrina New Orleans: An Exploration of the Challenges Facing Undocumented Latino Immigrants in New and Re-emerging Latino Destinations." *Population, Space and Place* 17 (1): 89–102.

DuBois, W. E. B. 1903. *The Souls of Black Folk.* Chicago: A. C. McClurg & Co.

Duneier, Mitchell, and Harvey Molotch. 1999. "Talking City Trouble: Interactional Vandalism, Social Inequality, and the 'Urban Interaction Problem.'" *American Journal of Sociology* 104 (5): 1263–1295.

Dynes, Russell R., and Havidán Rodríguez. 2010. "Finding and Framing Katrina: The Social Construction of Disaster," 2nd ed. In *The Sociology of Katrina: Perspectives on a Modern Catastrophe*, edited by David L. Brunsma, David Overfelt, and J. Steven Picou, 25–36. Lanham: Rowman & Littlefield.

Edelstein, Michael R. 2004. *Contaminated Communities: Coping with Residential Toxic Exposure*, 2nd ed. Cambridge: Westview Press.

Edin, Kathryn, and Laura Lein. 1997. *Making Ends Meet: How Single Mothers Survive Welfare and Low-Wage Work.* New York: Russell Sage Foundation.

Elliott, James R., Amy Bellone-Hite, and Joel A. Devine. 2009. "Unequal Return: The Uneven Resettlements of New Orleans' Uptown Neighborhoods." *Organization and Environment* 22 (4): 410–421.

Elliott, James R., Timothy J. Haney, and Petrice Sams-Abiodun. 2010. "Limits to Social Capital: Comparing Network Assistance in Two New Orleans Neighborhoods Devastated by Hurricane Katrina." *The Sociological Quarterly* 51 (4): 624–648.

Enarson, Elaine. 1997. "Responding to Domestic Violence in Disaster: Guidelines for Women's Services and Disaster Practitioners." November. http://gdnonline.org/resources/dv-and-disaster.doc.

———. 1998. "Through Women's Eyes: A Gendered Research Agenda for Disasters" *Disasters* 22 (2):157–173.

———. 1999. "Violence Against Women in Disasters: A Study of Domestic Violence Programs in the United States and Canada." *Violence Against Women* 5 (7): 742–768.

———. 2002. "Building Disaster Resilient Communities: Learning from Community Women." Statement for the UN Commission for the Status of Women [46th Session] Panel Discussion on Environmental Management and Mitigation of Natural Disasters: A Gender Perspective. Available through DAW: http://www.un.org/womenwatch/daw/csw/csw46/panel-Enarson.pdf.

———. 2006. "Women and Girls Last?: Averting the Second Post-Katrina Disaster." *Understanding Katrina*, June 11. http://understandingkatrina.ssrc.org/Enarson/

———. 2009. "Preface." In *Women, Gender and Disaster: Global Issues and Initiatives,* edited by Elaine Enarson and P. G. Dhar Chakrabarti, xiv-xviii. London: SAGE Publications Ltd.

———. 2012a. *Women Confronting Natural Disaster: From Vulnerability to Resilience.* Boulder: Rienner Publishers.

———. 2012b. "Women and Girls Last?: Averting the Second Post-Katrina Disaster." In *The Women of Katrina: How Gender, Race, and Class Matter in an American Disaster,* edited by Emmanuel David and Elaine Enarson, 7–14. Nashville: Vanderbilt University Press.

Enarson, Elaine, and Betty Hearn Morrow, eds. 1998. *The Gendered Terrain of Disaster: Through Women's Eyes*. Westport: Praeger.

Enarson, Elaine, and Emmanuel David. 2012. "Introduction." In *The Women of Katrina: How Gender, Race, and Class Matter in an American Disaster,* edited by Emmanuel David and Elaine Enarson, xvii-xxv. Nashville: Vanderbilt University Press.

Erikson, Kai. 1976. *Everything in Its Path: Destruction of Community in the Buffalo Creek Flood*. New York: Simon and Schuster.

———. 1994. *A New Species of Trouble: The Human Experience of Modern Disasters*. New York: W.W. Norton.

Eyler, J., and D. E. Giles. 1999. *Where's the Learning in Service-Learning?* San Francisco: Jossey-Bass.

Finch, Christina, Christopher T. Emrich, and Susan L. Cutter. 2010. "Disaster Disparities and Differential Recovery in New Orleans." *Population and Environment* 31: 179–202.

Fischer, M. J., and D. Massey. 2004. "The Ecology of Racial Discrimination." *City & Community* 3: 221–241.

Fordham, Maureen. 1998. "Making Women Visible in Disasters: Problematizing the Public Domain." *Disasters* 22: 126–143.

Fordham, M., W. Lovekamp, D. S. K. Thomas, and B. D. Phillips. 2013. "Understanding Social Vulnerability," 2nd ed. In *Social Vulnerability to Disasters,* edited by D. S. Thomas, A. Fothergill, and L. Blinn-Pike. Boca Raton: CRC Press.

Fothergill, Alice. 1996. "Gender, Risk, and Disaster." *International Journal of Mass Emergencies and Disasters* 14 (1): 33–56.

———. 1998. "The Neglect of Gender in Disaster Work: An Overview of the Literature." In *The Gendered Terrain of Disaster: Through Women's Eye*s, edited by Betty Hearn Morrow and Elaine Enarson, 11–25. Westport: Praeger.

———. 1999a. "An exploratory study of woman battering in the Grand Forks flood disaster: Implications for community responses and policies." *International Journal of Mass Emergencies and Disasters* 17 (1): 79–98.

———. 1999b. "Women's Roles in a Disaster." *Applied Behavioral Science Review* 7 (2): 125–143.

Fothergill, Alice. 2003. "The Stigma of Charity: Gender, Class, and Disaster Assistance." *The Sociological Quarterly* 44 (4): 659–680.

Freire, Paolo. (1970) 2007. *Pedagogy of the Oppressed.* New York: Continuum.

———. 2004. *EPZ Pedagogy of Hope: Reliving Pedagogy of the Oppressed.* New York: Continuum Book.

Freudenberg, William R. 1993. "Risk and Recreancy: Weber, the Division of Labor, and the Rationality of Risk Perceptions." *Social Forces* 71 (4): 909–932.

———. 1997. "Contamination, Corrosion, and the Social Order: An Overview." *Current Sociology* 45 (3): 19–39.

Frey, William H., Audrey Singer, and David Park. 2007. *Resettling New Orleans: The First Full Picture from the Census*. The Brookings Institution, Metropolitan Policy Program. http://www.brookings.edu/~/media/research/files/reports/2007/9/07katrinafreysinger/2007 0912_katrinafreysinger.pdf.

Fruscione, Joseph. 2014. "When a college contracts 'adjunctivitis,' it's the students who lose." *PBS Newshour*. http://www.pbs.org/newshour/making-sense/when-a-college-contracts-adjunctivitis-its-the-students-who-lose/.

Fussell, Elizabeth. 2006. "Leaving New Orleans: Social Stratification, Networks, and Hurricane Evacuation." *Understanding Katrina: Perspectives from the Social Sciences,* June 11. http://understandingkatrina.ssrc.org/Fussell/.

———. 2007. "Constructing New Orleans, Constructing Race: A Population History of New Orleans." *Journal of American History* 94 (3): 846–855.

———. 2008. "Leaving New Orleans, Again." *Traumatology* 14 (4): 63–66.

———. 2009a. "Hurricane Chasers in New Orleans Latino Immigrants as a Source of a Rapid Response Labor Force." *Hispanic Journal of Behavioral Sciences* 31 (3): 375–394.

———. 2009b. "Post-Katrina New Orleans as a New Migrant Destination." *Organization and Environment* 22 (4): 458–469.

———. 2011. "The Deportation Threat Dynamic and Victimization of Latino Migrants: Wage Theft and Robbery." *Sociological Quarterly* 52 (4): 593–615.

———. 2012. "Help from Family, Friends, and Strangers during Hurricane Katrina: Finding the Limits of Social Networks." In *Displaced: Life in the Katrina Diaspora,* edited by Lynn Weber and Lori Peek, 150–166. Austin: University of Texas Press.

———. 2013. "Population Change in New Orleans after Hurricane Katrina." Paper presented at the annual meeting of the Population Association of American, New Orleans, Louisiana, April 11–13.

Fussell, Elizabeth, and Abel Valenzuela. 2010. "Getting a Construction Job in Post-Katrina New Orleans: Race, Nativity, and Luck." Paper presented at the annual meeting of the Southern Sociological Society, New Orleans, LA. http://tulane.edu/liberal-arts/political-economy/new-orleans/upload/Fussell-and-Valenzuela-Getting-a-construction-job-in-New-Orleans.pdf.

Fussell, Elizabeth, and James R. Elliott. 2009. "Introduction: Social Organization of Demographic Responses to Disaster: Studying Population—Environment Interactions in the Case of Hurricane Katrina." *Organization and Environment* 22 (4): 379–394.

Fussell, Elizabeth, Narayan Sastry, and Mark VanLandingham. 2010. "Race, Socioeconomic Status, and Return Migration to New Orleans after Hurricane Katrina." *Population and Environment* 31 (1–3): 20–42.

Gaarder, Emily. 2011. "Where the Boys Aren't: The Predominance of Women in Animal Rights Activism." *Feminist Formations* 23 (2): 54–76.

Gabor, Andrea. 2013. "Disaster Capitalism and Charter Schools: Revisiting New Orleans Post-Katrina." *The Becoming Radical,* September 24. http://radicalscholarship.wordpress.com/2013/09/24/disaster-capitalism-and-charter-schools-revisiting-new-orleans-post-katrina/.

Gafford, Farrah. 2013a. "Re-Building Community in a Post-Katrina Neighborhood: Reflections from an Ethnographer." Disaster Speaker Series, Hosted by Xavier University of Louisiana, May 9.

———. 2013b. "It Was a Real Village: Community Identity Formation among Black Middle-Class Residents in Ponchartrain Park." *Journal of Urban History* 39 (1): 36–58.

Galster, G. C. 1990. "Racial Steering in Housing Markets during the 1980s: A Review of the Audit Evidence." *Journal of Planning Education and Research* 9: 165–175.

Gardner, Carol. 1995. *Passing By: Gender and Public Harassment.* Berkeley: University of California Press.

Gault, Barbara, Heidi Hartmann, Avis Jones-DeWeever, Misha Werschkul, and Erica Williams. 2005. *The Women of New Orleans and the Gulf Coast: Multiple Disadvantages and Key Assets for Recovery. Part 1. Poverty, Race, Gender, and Class.* Institute for Women's Policy Research, September. http://www.iwpr.org/publications/pubs/the-women-of-new-orleans-and-the-gulf-coast-multiple-disadvantages-and-key-assets-for-recovery-part-i.-poverty-race-gender-and-class.

GazetteXtra. 2012. "New Orleans' Post-Katrina Gentrification Is Touchy." August 28. http://www.gazettextra.com/news/2012/aug/28/new-orleans-post-katrina-gentrification-touchy/.

Gehman, Mary. 2012. "Surviving Hurricane Katrina." In *The Women of Katrina: How Gender, Race, and Class Matter in an American Disaster,* edited by Emmanuel David and Elaine Enarson, 27–29. Nashville: Vanderbilt University Press.

Ginsberg, Benjamin. 2011. *The Fall of the Faculty: The Rise of the All-Administrative University and Why It Matters*. New York: Oxford University Press.

Gleber, Anke. 1998. *The Art of Taking a Walk: Flanerie, Literature, and Film in Weimar Culture.* Princeton: Princeton University Press.

Goodall, H. Lloyd. 2000. *Writing the New Ethnography*. Lanham: AltaMira Press/Rowman & Littlefield Publishers.

Gorman, Leo. 2010. "Latino Migrant Labor Strife and Solidarity in Post-Katrina New Orleans, 2005–2007." *The Latinamericanist* 54 (1): 1–33.

Gotham, Kevin. 2007. "Critical Theory and Katrina: Disaster, Spectacle, and Immanent Critique." *City* 11 (1): 81–99.

Gotham, Kevin Fox, and Miriam Greenberg. 2008. "From 9/11 to 8/29: Post-Disaster Recovery and Rebuilding in New York and New Orleans." *Social Forces* 87 (2): 1039–1062.

———. 2014. *Crisis Cities: Disaster and Redevelopment in New York and New Orleans.* New York: Oxford University Press.

Gould, Virginia Mecham, ed. 1998. *Chained to the Rock of Adversity: To Be Free, Black & Female in the Old South.* Athens: University of Georgia Press.

Gratz, Roberta Brandes. 2011. "Why Was New Orleans's Charity Hospital Allowed to Die?" *The Nation*, May 16. http://www.thenation.com/article/160241/why-was-new-orleanss-charity-hospital-allowed-die#.

Greater New Orleans Community Data Center (GNOCDC). 2009. "Post-Katrina housing affordability challenges continue in 2008, worsening among Orleans Parish very low income renters." https://gnocdc.s3.amazonaws.com/reports/GNOCDC_NewOrleansMetroArea HousingAffordability2004-2008.pdf.

———. 2013a. "Facts for Features: Hurricane Katrina Impact." Available at: http://www.gnocdc.org/Factsforfeatures/HurricaneKatrinaImpact/.

———. 2013b. *The New Orleans Index at Eight: Executive Summary*. http://www.datacenterresearch.org/reports_analysis/the-new-orleans-index-at-eight/.

———. 2013c. The New Orleans Index at Eight: Measuring Greater New Orleans's Progress toward Prosperity. https://gnocdc.s3.amazonaws.com/reports/GNOCDC_NewOrleans IndexAtEight.pdf.

Greeley, Meghan. 2008. "Sexual Health of Young Women." In *Katrina and the Women of New Orleans,* edited by Beth Willinger, 70–72. New Orleans: Newcomb College Center for Research on Women.

Greenberg, Arik. 2014. "How one professor's American dream — teaching — turned into the American nightmare." *PBS Newshour.* http://www.pbs.org/newshour/making-sense/one-professors-american-dream-teaching-turned-american-nightmare/.

Griffin, E. M. 2009. *Communication: A First Look at Communication Theory*, 7th ed. New York: McGraw-Hill.

Groen, Jeffrey A., and Anne E. Polivka. 2010. "Going Home after Hurricane Katrina: Determinants of Return Migration and Changes in Affected Areas." *Demography* 47 (4): 821–844.

Guba, Egon G., and Yvonna S. Lincoln. 1994. "Competing Paradigms in Qualitative Research." In *The Handbook of Qualitative Research,* edited by Norman Denzin, and Yvonna Lincoln, 105–117. Thousand Oaks: Sage Publications, Inc.

Hafiz, Amina. 2005. "The Disaster Continues." *Off Our Backs* 35 (9–10): 16.

Halberstam, J. Jack. 2012. *Gaga Feminism: Sex, Gender, and the End of Normal.* Boston: Beacon Press.

Halberstam, Judith. 2005. *In a Queer Time and Place*. New York: New York University Press.

Hamilton, Stephen, and Mary Agnes Hamilton. 2006. "School, Work and Emerging Adulthood." In *Emerging Adults in America: Coming of Age in the 21st Century*, edited by Jeffrey Arnett and Jennifer Tanner, 257–277. Washington, DC: American Psychological Association.

Haney, Timothy J., and James R. Elliott. 2013. "The Sociological Determination: A Reflexive Look at Conducting Local Disaster Research after Hurricane Katrina." *Sociology Mind* 3 (1): 7–15.

Haney, Timothy J., and Kristen Barber. 2013. "Reconciling Academic Objectivity and Subjective Trauma: The Double Consciousness of Sociologists who Experienced Hurricane Katrina." *Critical Sociology* 39 (1): 105–122.

Haney, Timothy J., James R. Elliott, and Elizabeth Fussell. 2007. "Families and Hurricane Response: Evacuation, Separation, and the Emotional Toll of Hurricane Katrina," 1st ed. In *The Sociology of Katrina: Perspectives on a Modern Catastrophe*, edited by David Brunsma, Dave Overfeldt, and J. Steven Picou, 71–90. Lanham: Rowman & Littlefield.

———. 2010. "Families and Hurricane Response: Risk, Roles, Resources, Race, and Religion: A Framework for Understanding Family Evacuation Strategies, Stress, and Return Migration," 2nd ed. In *The Sociology of Katrina: Perspectives on a Modern Catastrophe*, edited by David L. Brunsma, David Overfelt, and J. Steven Picou, 77–102. Lanham: Rowman & Littlefield.

Harding, Sandra. 2004. *The Feminist Standpoint Theory Reader: Intellectual and Political Controversies*. New York: Routledge.

Harrison, Jill Ann. 2012. *Buoyancy on the Bayou: Shrimpers Face the Rising Tide of Globalization*. Ithaca, NY: Cornell University Press.

Hartman, Chester, and Gregory D. Squires. 2006. *There Is No Such Thing as a Natural Disaster*. New York: Taylor and Francis Group.

Harville, E. W., C. A. Taylor, H. Tesfai, X. Xiong, and P. Buekens. 2010. "Experience of Hurricane Katrina and Reported Intimate Partner Violence." *Journal of Interpersonal Violence* 26 (4).

Hauser, C., and T. J. Lueck. 2005. "Mandatory Evacuation Ordered for New Orleans as Storm Nears." *New York Times*, August 28. http://www.nytimes.com/2005/08/28/national/29katrinacnd.html?_r=0.

Hawkins, Robert L,. and Katherine Maurer. 2011. "'You Fix My Community, You Have Fixed My Life': The Disruption and Rebuilding of Ontological Security in New Orleans." *Disasters* 35 (1): 143–159.

Hawkins, Robert, and Katherine Maurer. 2012. "Waiting for the White Man to Fix Things: Rebuilding Black Poverty in New Orleans." *Journal of Sociology & Social Welfare* 39 (1): 111–139.

Henrici, Jane M., Allison Suppan Helmuth, and Angela Carlberg. 2012. "Doubly Displaced: Women, Public Housing, and Spatial Access after Katrina." In *The Women of Katrina: How Gender, Race, and Class Matter in an American Disaster,* edited by Emmanuel David and Elaine Enarson, 142–154. Nashville: Vanderbilt University Press.

Hesse-Biber, S. 2011. *Handbook of Feminist Research: Theory and Praxis,* 2nd ed. Thousand Oaks, CA: Sage Publications.

Hetzler, Olivia, Veronica Medina, and David Overfelt. 2007. "Race, Immigration and Economic Restructuring in New Urbanism: New Orleans as a Case Study." *Sociation Today* 5 (1). http://www.ncsociology.org/sociationtoday/v51/second.htm.

Hidalgo, Danielle Antoinette, and Kristen Barber, eds. 2007. *Narrating the Storm: Sociological Stories of Hurricane Katrina*. Newcastle, UK: Cambridge Scholars Publishing.

Hill Collins, Patricia. 1990. *Black Feminist Thought: Knowledge, Consciousness and the Politics of Empowerment*. New York: Harper Collins.

Hochschild, Arlie. 1979. "Emotion Work, Feeling Rules, and Social Structure." *American Journal of Sociology* 85: 551–575.

———. 1983. *The Managed Heart: Commericalization of Human Feeling*. Berkeley: University of California Press.

Hollander, Jocelyn. 2001. "Vulnerability and Dangerousness: The Construction of Gender through Conversations about Violence." *Gender and Society* 15: 83–109.

Holzer, Harry, and Robert Lerman. 2006. "Employment Issues and Challenges in Post-Katrina New Orleans." The Urban Institute. http://www.urban.org/publications/900921.html.

Honeycombe, Beth. 1993. "Special Needs of Women in Emergency Situations." Symposium: Women in Emergencies and Disasters. Queensland Bureau of Emergency Services. Brisbane: Queensland.

Howard, Jeffrey P. F. 1998. "Academic Service Learning: A Counternormative Pedagogy." *New Directions for Teaching and Learning* 73: 21–29.

Hsu, Spencer S. 2006. "2 Million Displaced by Storms." *Washington Post*, January 13.

Idakula, Ruth S. (2007) 2011. "Cataclysm in New Orleans: Story of a Black Single Mother." In *Narrating the Storm: Sociological Stories of Hurricane Katrina*, edited by Danielle A. Hidalgo and Kristen Barber, 33–46. Newcastle: Cambridge Scholar Publishing.

INCITE! Women of Color Against Violence. 2012. "INCITE! Statement on Katrina." In *The Women of Katrina: How Gender, Race, and Class Matter in an American Disaster,* edited by Emmanuel David and Elaine Enarson, 3–6. Nashville: Vanderbilt University Press.

Institute for Women's Policy Research. 2010. "Women, Disasters, and Hurricane Katrina." Available at www.iwpr.org.

Jacoby, Barbara. 2006. "Bottom Line—Making Politics Matter to Students." *About Campus* 11 (4): 30–32.

Jeffrey, Julie Roy. 1998. *Frontier Women: "Civilizing" the West? 1840–1880?* New York: Hill and Wang.

Jenkins, P. (forthcoming 2015). "When Resilience Is Not Enough: Recovery, Privilege, and Hurricane Katrina." In *Sociologists in Action on Inequalities: Race, Class, Gender, and Sexuality*, 18–35.

Jenkins, Pamela. 2012a. "Faith in Exile." In *Displaced: Life in the Katrina Diaspora*, edited by L. Weber and L. Peek. Austin: University of Texas Press.

———. 2012b. "Gender and the Landscape of Community Work before and after Katrina." In *The Women of Katrina: How Gender, Race, and Class Matter in an American Disaster,* edited by Emmanuel David and Elaine Enarson, 169–178. Nashville: Vanderbilt University Press.

———. 2013. "Disasters and Help: The Role and Impact of Local Non-profit Organizations." Disaster Speaker Series, Hosted by Xavier University of Louisiana, 10 May 2013.

Jenkins, Pam, and Brenda Phillips. 2008. "When Catastrophe Strikes (Battered) Women: Domestic Violence in the Context of Disaster." *National Women's Studies Journal Special Issue on Katrina* 20 (3): 49–68.

Jenkins, P., B. Brown, and K. Mosby. 2012. "Rebuilding and Reframing: Non-profit Organizations Respond to Hurricane Katrina," 2nd ed. In *Crime and Criminal Justice in Disaster,* edited by D. Harper and K. Frailing, 339–357. Durham: Carolina Academic Press.

Jenkins, P., J. Renne, and J. Keifer. 2011. "Gender Differences in Self-Reported Evacuation Experiences: An Analysis of the City Assisted Evacuation Program during Hurricane Gustav." Proceedings of the TRB Women's Issues in Transportation, Washington, DC: Transportation Research Board of the National Academies. *Women's Issues in Transportation,* Volume 2: Technical Papers, 127–133.

Jenkins, Pamela, Michelle Gremillion, and Branda Nowell. 2010. "Achieving Successful Long-Term Recovery and Safety from a Catastrophe: Recommendations for Human Recovery." *CHART Publications.* Paper 5. http://scholarworks.uno.edu/chart_pubs/5.

Jones-DeWeever, Avis A., and Heidi Hartmann. 2006. "Abandoned before the Storms: The Glaring Disaster of Gender, Race and Class Disparities in the Gulf." In *There Is No Such Thing as a Natural Disaster,* edited Chester Hartman and Gregory D. Squires, 85–101. New York: Taylor and Francis Group.

Jordan, Flaherty. 2011. "Battle for New Orleans, 6 Years after Katrina, Political Power has Shifted to Whites, But Blacks Have Not Given Up Their Struggle for a Voice—and Justice." *TheRoot.com*, August 27. http://www.theroot.com/articles/culture/2011/08/katrina_6th_anniversary_battle_for_new_orleans_continues.html.

Kalleberg, Arne L., Barbara F. Reskin, and Ken Hudson. 2000. "Bad Jobs in America: Standard and Nonstandard Employment Relations and Job Quality in the United States." *American Sociological Review* 65 (2): 256–278.

Kates, Robert W., Craig E. Colten, Shirley Laska, and S. P. Leatherman. 2006. "Reconstruction of New Orleans after Hurricane Katrina: A Research Perspective." *Proceedings of the National Academy of Sciences* 103 (4): 14653–14660.

Kearl, Holly. 2010. *Stop Street Harassment: Making Public Places Safe and Welcoming for Women*. California: Praeger.

Kelly, Erin N., Jeffrey W. Short, David W. Schindler, Peter V. Hodson, Mingsheng Ma, Alvin K. Kwan, and Barbara L. Fortin. 2009. "Oil Sands Development Contributes Polycyclic Aromatic Compounds to the Athabasca River and Its Tributaries." *Proceedings of the National Academy of Sciences of the United States of America* 106 (52): 22346–22351.

Kirschenmen, Joleen, and Kathryn M. Neckerman. 1991. "'We'd Love to Hire Them, But . . .': The Meaning of Race for Employers." In *The Urban Underclass,* edited by Christopher Jencks and Paul Pertson, 203–234. Washington, DC: The Brookings Institution.

Kissling, E., and C. Kramaral. 1991. "Stranger Complaints: The Interpretation of Street Remarks." *Women's Studies in Communication* 4 (1): 75–95.

Klein, Naomi. 2007. *Shock Doctrine: The Rise of Disaster Capitalism.* New York: Picador.

Kroll-Smith, S., V. Baxter, and P. Jenkins (forthcoming 2015). *The Authority of Chance*. Austin: University of Texas.

Kugler, Adriana, and Mutlu Yuksel. 2008. "Effects of Low-Skilled Immigration on U.S. Natives: Evidence from Hurricane Mitch." NBER Working Paper No. 14293. http://www.nber.org/papers/w14293.pdf.

———. 2011. "Do Recent Latino Immigrants Compete for Jobs with Native Hispanics and Earlier Latino Immigrants?" In *Latinos and the Economy*, edited by David. L. Leal and Stephen. J. Trejo, 213–231. New York: Springer New York.

Lakoff, George. 2005. "The Post Katrina Era." Alternet. http://www.alternet.org/story/25099/the_post-katrina_era.

Lam, Nina S., Helbert Arenas, James LeSage, and Richard Campanella. 2012. "Predictors of Business Return in New Orleans after Hurricane Katrina." *PLoS One.* doi: 10.1371/journal.pone.0047935.

Landphair, Juliette. 1999. "Sewerage, Sidewalks, and Schools: The New Orleans Ninth Ward and Public School Desegregation. *Louisiana History* 40 (1): 35–62.

Landry, M.C. 2006. *2006 Self Study*. Crescent House/DV/SA Services, Catholic Charities Archdiocese of New Orleans. Written for the Governor's Office on Women's Policy.

Larkin, June. 1997. "Sexual Terrorism on the Street: The Moulding of Young Women into Subordination." In *Sexual Harassment: Contemporary Feminist Perspectives,* edited by A. Thomas and C. Kitzinger. Philadelphia: Open University Press.

Laska, Shirley. 2007. "The 'Mother of All Rorschachs': Katrina Recovery in New Orleans." *Sociological Inquiry* 78 (4): 580–591.

Laudisio, G. 1993. "Disaster Aftermath: Redefining Response—Hurricane Andrew's Impact on I & R." *Alliance of Information and Referral Systems* 15: 13–32.

Lawson, Erma. 2010. "A Gender Comparison of Resiliency among Older African American Katrina Survivors." *Western Journal of Black Studies* 34 (4): 457–470.

Layne, L. L. 1996. "Never such Innocence Again: Irony, Nature and Technoscience in Narratives of Pregnancy Loss," edited by R. Cecil, 131–152. *Comparative Studies in Pregnancy Loss*. Oxford: Berg Publishers.

Layton, Lyndsey. 2014. "In New Orleans, Major School District Closes Traditional Public Schools for Good." *Washington Post*, May 28. http://www.washingtonpost.com/local/education/in-new-orleans-traditional-public-schools-close-for-good/2014/05/28/ae4f5724-e5de-11e3-8f90-73e071f3d637_story.html.

Lee, Spike (Director). 2010. "If God Is Willing and 'Da Creek Don't Rise." HBO and 40 Acres and a Mule Filmworks.

Leonardo, Michaela di. 1981. "The Political Economy of Street Harassment." *Aegis* (Summer): 51–57.

Lerner, Steve. 2010. *Sacrifice Zones: The Front Lines of Toxic Chemical Exposure in the United States*. Cambridge, MA: MIT Press.

Levitt, Jeremy I., and Matthew Whitaker. 2009. *Hurricane Katrina: America's Unnatural Disaster.* Washington, DC: Library of Congress Cataloging.

Lilliedahl, Erika. 2009. "The Impact of Hurricane Katrina Migration on Low-Wage Labor Markets." Master's thesis, Georgetown University.

Lippi-Green, Rosina. 1997. *English with an Accent: Language, Ideology, and Discrimination in the United States*. New York: Routledge.

Lister, Sarah A. 2005. "Hurricane Katrina: The Public Health and Medical Response." *CRS Report for Congress.* September 21. http://fpc.state.gov/documents/Organization/54255.pdf.

Litt, Jacquelyn. 2008. "Getting Out or Staying Put: An African American Women's Network in Evacuation from Katrina." *NWSA Journal* 20 (3): 32–48.

Litt, Jacquelyn. 2012. "'We Need to Get Together with Each Other': Women's Narratives of Help in Katrina's Displacement." In *Displaced: Life in the Katrina Diaspora,* edited by Lynn Weber and Lori Peek, 167–82. Austin: University of Texas Press.

Litt, Jacquelyn, Althea Skinner, and Kelley Robinson. 2012. "The Katrina Difference: African American Women's Networks and Poverty in New Orleans after Katrina." In *The Women of Katrina: How Gender, Race, and Class Matter in an American Disaster,* edited by Emmanuel David and Elaine Enarson, 130–141. Nashville: Vanderbilt University Press.

Liu, Amy, and Allison Plyer. 2010. "An Overview of Greater New Orleans: From Recovery to Transformation." Brookings Institution and Greater New Orleans Data Center. August. http://www.brookings.edu/~/media/research/files/reports/2011/8/29percent20newpercent20orleans percent20index/08neworleansindex.pdf.

Liu, Cathy. 2011. "Employment Concentration and Job Quality for Low-Skilled Latino Immigrants." *Journal of Urban Affairs* 33 (2): 117–142.

Logan, John. 2005. "The Impact of Katrina: Race and Class in Storm-Damaged Neighborhoods." Spatial Structures in the Social Sciences Initiative. Brown University. http://www.s4.brown.edu/katrina/report.pdf.

Long, Alecia P. 2004. *The Great Southern Babylon.* Baton Rouge: Louisiana State University Press.

———. 2007. "Poverty Is the New Prostitution: Race, Poverty, and Public Housing in Post-Katrina New Orleans." *Journal of American History* 94: 795–803. http://www.journalofamericanhistory.org/projects/katrina/Long.html?link_id=lan_poverty.

Loper, W. S., and Associates. 2004. *Mississippi Gulf Coast Apartment Survey.* Gulfport, MS: Gulf Regional Planning Commission.

Lorde, Audre. 1984. *Sister Outsider*. Freedom, CA: Crossing Press.

Louisiana Department of Health and Hospitals (LDHH). 2004. "Louisiana HIV/AIDS Epidemiological Profile and Annual Report." *HIV/AIDS Surveillance Program*. Baton Rouge: Office of Public Health.

———. 2007. "Louisiana HIV/AIDS Surveillance Quarterly Report." Office of Public Health, June 30. http://hiv.dhh.louisiana.gov/.

Lovell, Anne M. 2011. "Who cares about care? Health care rationalization and the demise of a public hospital after Katrina." *Metro Politiques*, June 14. http://www.metropolitiques.eu/spip.php?page=print&id_article=166.

Luckey, John R., and Jon O. Shimabukuro. 2005. "Prevailing Wage Requirements and the Emergency Suspension of the Davis-Bacon Act." Congressional Research Service Report for Congress. Order Code RS22265, September 16, 2005.

Luft, Rachel. 2013. "Disaster Patriarchy: The Race and Gender Politics of the Movement for a Just Reconstruction after Katrina." Disaster Speaker Series, Hosted by Xavier University of Louisiana, May 9.

Mack, Vicki, and Elaine Ortiz. 2013. "Who Lives in New Orleans and the Metro Now?" *The Data Center Research,* September 26. http://www.datacenterresearch.org/data-resources/who-lives-in-new-orleans-now/.

MacKinnon, Catherine A. 1989. *Toward a Feminist Theory of the State*. Cambridge: Harvard University Press.

Macmillan, Ross, Annette Nierobisz, and Sandy Welsh. 2000. "Experiencing the Streets: Harassment and Perceptions of Safety Among Women." *Journal of Research in Crime and Delinquency* 37: 306–322.

Madison, D. S. 2005. *Critical Ethnography: Method, Ethics, and Performance*. Thousand Oaks: Sage Publications, Inc.

Madriz, Esther I. 1997. "Images of Criminals and Victims: A Study on Women's Fear and Social Control." *Gender and Society* 11: 342–356.

Marks, Ronald E. 2008. "Canoeing Home: A Personal and Professional Journey through Murky Waters." *Traumatology* 14 (4): 14–20.

Martin, Joan M. 2000. "Placage and the Louisiana Gens de Couleur Libre," in *Creole*, edited by Sybil Kein, Louisiana State University Press.

Martinez, Michael. 2005. "Big Easy uneasy about migrant wave." *Chicago Tribune*, November 3.

Massey, D., and Lundy, G. 2001. "Use of Black English and Racial Discrimination in Urban Housing Markets: New Methods and Findings." *Urban Affairs Review* 36: 452–469.

Massey, Douglas S., and Nancy A. Denton. 1993. *American Apartheid: Segregation and the Making of the Underclass*. Cambridge: Harvard University Press.

McGill, Kevin. 2014. "Way Cleared for Medical Claims in 2010 BP Spill." *ABC News* online, February 14. http://abcnews.go.com/m/story?id=22504976&sid=81.

McGoldrick, KimMarie. 1998. "Service-Learning in Economics: A Detailed Application." *Journal of Economic Education* 29 (4): 365–376.

McIntosh, Molly. 2008. "Measuring the Labor Market Impacts of Hurricane Katrina Migration: Evidence from Houston, TX." *American Economic Review* 98 (2): 54–57.

Melbin, Murray. 1987. *Night as Frontier: Colonizing the World of after Dark.* New York: Free Press.

Merton, Robert. 1969. Foreword to *Communities in Disaster: A Sociological Analysis of Collective Stress Situations*, edited by Allen H. Barton. New York: Doubleday.

Miller, DeMond Shondell, and Jason David Rivera. 2007. "Landscapes of Disaster and Place Orientation in the Aftermath of Hurricane Katrina." In *The Sociology of Katrina: Perspectives on a Modern Catastrophe*, edited by David L. Brunsma, David Overfelt, and J. Steven Picou, 141–154. Lanham: Rowman & Littlefield Publishers.

Miller, Lee M. 2012. "Katrina Evacuee Reception in Rural East Texas: Rethinking Disaster "Recovery." In *Displaced: Life in the Katrina Diaspora,* edited by Lynn Weber and Lori Peek, 104–118. Austin: University of Texas Press.

Mills, C. Wright. 1959. *The Sociological Imagination*. London: Oxford University Press.

Mitussis, Darryn, and Jackie Sheehan. 2013. "Reflections on the Pedagogy of International Field Schools: Experiential Learning and Emotional Engagement." *Enhancing Learning in the Social Sciences* 5 (3): 41–54.

Molotch, Harvey. 1976. "The City as a Growth Machine: Toward a Political Economy of Place." *American Journal of Sociology* 82 (2): 309–332.

Molpus, Jim, and Gary Baldwin. 2006. "Patching New Orleans." Health Leaders, August. http://www.healthleadersmedia.com/content/MAG-82377/Patching-New-Orleans.

Morrison, Derrick. 2010. "Post-Katrina New Orleans: A Third Reconstruction?" *Solidarity*, October 26. http://www.solidarity-us.org/site/node/2610.

Moss, Philip, and Chris Tilly. 1996. "Soft Skills and Race: An Investigation of Black Men's Employment Problems." *Work and Occupations* 23: 252–276.

———. 2001. *Stories Employers Tell, Race, Skill, and Hiring in America*. New York: Russell Sage Foundation.

Mulcahy, Matthew. 2006. "Hurricanes, Poverty, and Vulnerability: An Historical Perspective." *Understanding Katrina*, June 11. http://understandingkatrina.ssrc.org/Mulcahy/.

Mullins, Dexter. 2014. "New Orleans to be home to nation's first all-charter school district." *Aljazeera America*, April 4. http://america.aljazeera.com/articles/2014/4/4/new-orleans-charterschoolseducationreformracesegregation.html.

Munson, Elizabeth. 2002. "Walking on the Periphery: Gender and the Discourse of Modernization." *Journal of Social History* 36: 63–75.

Muro, M., A. Lieu, R. Sohmer, D. Warren, D. Park, et al. 2005. "New Orleans after the Storm: Lessons from the Past, a Plan for the Future." The Brookings Institution. Special Analysis. October. http://www.brookings.edu/~/media/research/files/reports/2005/10/metropolitanpolicy/20051012_neworleans.pdf.

Murray, Charles. (1984) 1994. *Losing Ground*. Reprint, New York: Basic Books.

Murray, Robert. 2005. *Hurricane Katrina: Implications for the Construction Industry*. McGraw-Hill Construction Research and Analytics. Lexington, MA. http://www.siteforless.com/customer336/upload/breaking/percent20news,percent209-05.pdf.

National Climatic Data Center (NCDC). 2014. "Billion-Dollar Weather/Climate Disasters: Overview." National Oceanic and Atmospheric Administration. http://www.ncdc.noaa.gov/billions.

National Sexual Violence Resource Center. 2006. *Hurricanes Katrina/Rita and Sexual Violence: Report on Database of Sexual Violence Prevalence and Incidence Related to Hurricanes Katrina and Rita*. http://www.nsvrc.org/sites/default/files/Publications_NSVRC_Reports_Report-on-Database-of-Sexual-Violence-Prevalence-and-Incidence-Related-to-Hurricane-Katrina-and-Rita.pdf.

New Orleans Family Justice Center (NOFJC). 2013. *2013 Summary Report*. New Orleans.

New Orleans Family Justice Center Alliance. 2014. *Case for Support*. New Orleans.

Newcomb College Center for Research on Women. 2010. "New Orleans Women Pre- and Post-Katrina: A demographic profile of age, race/ethnicity, and family and non-family households." Fact Sheet NOLA #1. http://tulane.edu/nccrow/upload/Fact-sheet-NOLA-1.pdf.

Newmark, Kathryn, and Veronique De Rugy. 2006. "Hope After Katrina: Will New Orleans Become the New City of Choice?" *Education Next* 6 (4): 13–21.

Nguyen, Gennie Thi. 2012. "Building Coalitions and Rebuilding Versailles: Vietnamese American Women's Environmental Work after Hurricane Katrina." In *The Women of Katrina: How Gender, Race, and Class Matter in an American Disaster,* edited by Emmanuel David and Elaine Enarson, 198–209. Nashville: Vanderbilt University Press.

NOPD Consent Decree - 12-1924. 2014. *NOPD Consent Decree - 12-1924,* September 16. http://www.laed.uscourts.gov/consent/consent.htm.

NOVA. 2005. *Hurricane Katina: The Storm That Drowned a City*. Documentary. WGBH Boston Video.

NPR. 2006. "Nearly 100,000 Spend Thanksgiving in FEMA Trailers." November 23. http://www.npr.org/templates/story/story.php?storyId=6529452.

O'Leary-Kelly, Anne, Ramona L. Paetzold, and Ricky W. Griffen. 2000. "Sexual Harassment as Aggressive Behavior: An Actor-Based Perspective." *Academy of Management Review* 25: 372–388.

Oltenau, Alina, Ruth Arnberger, Roy Grant, Caroline Davis, David Abramson, and Jaya Asola. 2011. "Persistence of Mental Health Needs among Children Affected by Hurricane Katrina in New Orleans." *Prehospital and Disaster Medicine* 26 (1): 3–6.

Ott, Kenneth Brad. 2012. "The Closure of New Orleans' Charity Hospital after Katrina: A Case of Disaster Capitalism." Master thesis, University of New Orleans. http://scholarworks.uno.edu/cgi/viewcontent.cgi?article=2488&context=td.

Ottaviano, Gianmarco I. P., and Giovanni Peri. 2006. "Rethinking the Effects of Immigration on Wages." National Bureau of Economic Research. Working Paper No. 12497. http://www.nber.org/papers/w12497.

Pain, Rachel. 2001. "Gender, Race, Age and Fear in the City." *Urban Studies* 38: 899–913.

Pais, Jeremy F., and James R. Elliott. 2008. "Places as Recovery Machines: Vulnerability and Neighborhood Change after Major Hurricanes." *Social Forces* 86 (4): 1415–1453.

Pardee, Jessica Warner. (2007) 2011. "Using Simmel to Survive: The Blasé Attitude as a Disaster Reaction and Response." In *Narrating the Storm: Sociological Stories of Hurricane Katrina,* edited by Danielle A. Hidalgo and Kristen Barber, 151–168. Newcastle: Cambridge Scholar Publishing.

———. 2012. "Living through Displacement: Housing Insecurity among Low-Income Evacuees." In *Displaced: Life in the Katrina Diaspora*, edited by Lynn Weber and Lori Peek, 63–78. Austin: University of Texas Press.

———. 2014. *Surviving Katrina: The Experiences of Low-Income African American Women*. Boulder: FirstForumPress/Lynne Rienner Publishers.

Pardee, Jessica, and Deborah Blizzard. 2014. "The Methodology of Trauma: A Comparative Case Study of Researcher Reactions in the Data Collection Process." Presented at the 2014 Annual Meeting of the Eastern Sociological Society. Baltimore, MD. February 20–23, 2014.

Pastor, Manuel, Robert Bullard, James K. Boyce, Alice Fothergill, Rachel Morello-Frosch, and Beverly Wright. 2006. "*In the Wake of the Storm: Environment, Disaster and Race after Katrina.*" New York: Russell Sage Foundation.

Paxson, Christina, Elizabeth Fussell, Jean Rhodes, and Mary Waters. 2012. "Five Years Later: Recovery from Post-Traumatic Stress and Psychological Distress among Low-Income Mothers Affected by Hurricane Katrina." *Social Science & Medicine* 74 (2): 150–157.

PBS Newshour. 2006. "New Orleans Health Care Struggles after Hurricane Katrina." February 27. http://www.pbs.org/newshour/bb/health-jan-june06-nolahealth_2-27/.

Pearce, Diana. 1978. "The Feminization of Poverty: Women, Work, and Welfare." *Urban & Social Change Review* 11 (1–2): 28–36.

Peek, Lori. 2012. "They Call It Katrina Fatigue: Displaced Families and Discrimination in Colorado." In *Displaced: Life in the Katrina Diaspora,* edited by Lynn Weber and Lori Peek, 31–46. Austin: University of Texas Press.

Peek, Lori, and Alice Fothergill. 2008. "Displacement, Gender, and the Challenges of Parenting after Hurricane Katrina." *NWSA Journal* 20 (3): 69–106. doi: 10.1353/nwsa.0.0044.

Peek, Lori, and Kai Erikson. 2008. "Hurricane Katrina." *Blackwell Encyclopedia of Sociology.* Oxford: Blackwell.

Peek, Lori, Bridget Morrissey, and Holly Marlatt. 2011. "Disaster Hits Home: A Model of Displaced Family Adjustment after Hurricane Katrina." *Journal of Family Issues* 32 (10): 1371–1396. doi: 10.1177/0192513X11412496.

Perry, Andre, and Franz Reneau. 2012. "The Path of Education Reform toward Higher Education for African Americans in New Orleans." *Equilibrium: The State of Black New Orleans.* Houma: Morgan Hill Publishing. http://urbanleague.morganhillpublishing.com/wp-content/uploads/2013/11/StateofBlackNewOrleans2012-11.pdf.

Perry, Andre, and Michael Schwam-Baird. 2010. "School by School: The Transformation of New Orleans Public Education." *The New Orleans Index at Five: Reviewing Key Reforms after Hurricane Katrina*, August. http://cis.uchicago.edu/outreach/summerinstitute/2013/documents/sti2013_perry_thetransformationofneworleanspubliceducation.pdf.

Peterson, Kristina J., and Richard Krajeski. 2012. "Grounded in Faith, Inspired to Action: Bayou Women Own Their Recovery." In *The Women of Katrina: How Gender, Race, and Class Matter in an American Disaster,* edited by Emmanuel David and Elaine Enarson, 220–229. Nashville: Vanderbilt University Press.

Pew Hispanic Center. 2007. Construction jobs expand for Latinos despite slump in housing market. Fact Sheet. March 7, 2007. http://pewhispanic.org/factsheets.

Pezzullo, Phaedra C. 2009. "Tourists and/as Disasters: Rebuilding, Remembering, and Responsibility in New Orleans." *Tourist Studies* 9 (1): 23–41.

Picou, J. Steven, Brent K Marshall, and Duane A. Gill. 2004. "Disaster, Litigation and the Corrosive Community." *Social Forces* 82 (4): 1493–1522.

Plyer, Allison. 2014. "Facts for Features: Katrina Impact." The Data Center. August 28th. http://www.datacenterresearch.org/data-resources/katrina/facts-for-impact/.

Plyer, Allison, Elaine Ortiz, Ben Horwitz, and George Hobor. 2013. "The New Orleans Index at Eight." The Data Center. http://www.datacenterresearch.org/reports_analysis/the-new-orleans-index-at-eight/.

Polaski, Adam. 2012. "Queer New Orleans after the Storm." Ithaca College. http://www.ithaca.edu/parkscholars/blogs/park_scholars_in_new_orleans:_service,_learning,_m/queer_new_orleans_after_the_storm_-_by:_adam_polas/#.VCihOfldWa8.

Potter, Hillary. 2007. *Racing the Storm: Racial Implications and Lessons Learned from Hurricane Katrina.* Lanham: Lexington.

powell, john a., Hasan Kwame Jeffries, Daniel W. Newhart, and Eric Stiens. 2006. "Toward a Transformative View of Race: The Crisis and Opportunity of Katrina." In *There Is No Such Thing as a Natural Disaster,* edited by Chester Hartman and Gregory D. Squires, 59–84. New York: Taylor and Francis Group.

Purnell, T., W. Idsardi, and J. Baughs. 1999. "Perceptual and Phonetic Experiments on American English Dialect Identification." *Journal of Language and Social Psychology* 18: 10–30.

Quarantelli, E. L. 2005. "Catastrophes are different from disasters: some implications for crisis planning and managing drawn from Katrina." *Understanding Katrina: Perspectives from the Social Sciences.* Social Science Research Counsel. http://understandingkatrina.ssrc.org.

Quigley, Bill. 2007. "Feeding 18,000 Families a Month in One Neighborhood, The Right to Return to New Orleans." *Counter Punch,* February 26. http://www.counterpunch.org/2007/02/26/the-right-to-return-to-new-orleans/.

———. 2011. "Katrina Pain Index 2011: Race, Gender, Poverty." *Bridge the Gulf Project,* August 22. http://bridgethegulfproject.org/blog/2011/katrina-pain-index-2011-race-gender-poverty.

———. 2013. "*New Orleans Eight Years Later, The Katrina Pain Index.*" *Counter Punch,* August 27. http://www.counterpunch.org/2013/08/27/the-katrina-pain-index-2013/.

Quigley, Bill, and Davida Finger. 2011. "Katrina Pain Index 2011: Race, Gender, Poverty." *New America Media,* August 25. http://newamericamedia.org/2011/08/katrina-pain-index-2011-race-gender-poverty.php.

Quillian, Lincoln. 1995. "Prejudice as a Response to Perceived Group Threat: Population Composition and Anti-immigrant and Racial Prejudice in Europe." *American Sociological Review* 60: 586–611.

Quinn, Beth A. 2002. "Sexual Harassment and Masculinity: The Power and Meaning of 'Girl Watching.'" *Gender and Society* 16: 386–402.

Raines, Howell. 2005. "'I'm Just Glad I Saw It.'" *The Guardian,* August 31. theguardian.com/world/2005/sep/01/hurricanekatrina.naturaldisasters.

Rainwater, Lee, and William L. Yancey. 1967. *The Moynihan Report and the Politics of Controversy.* Cambridge: MIT Press.

Randall, Kate. 2006. "City Residents Denounce 'Bring New Orleans Back' Rebuilding Plan." *World Socialist Web Site,* January 14. http://www.wsws.org/en/articles/2006/01/newo-j14.html.

Readings, Bill. 1997. *The University in Ruins.* Cambridge, MA: Harvard University Press.

Reckdahl, Katy. 2011. "New C.J. Peete Complex Is Solid, Shiny—But Not As Social, Some Residents Say." *Times-Picayune*, August 21. http://www.nola.com/politics/index.ssf/2011/08/new_cj_peete_complex_is_solid.html.

Recuber, Timothy. 2013. "Disaster Porn!" *Contexts* 12 (2): 28–33.

Reid, Megan, and Corinne Reczek. 2011. "Stress and Support in Family Relationships after Hurricane Katrina." *Journal of Family Issues* 32 (10): 1397–1418.

Reinharz, S. 1992. *Feminist Methods in Social Research*. New York: Oxford University Press.

Roberts, J. Timmons, and Melissa M. Toffolon-Weiss. 2001. *Chronicles from the Environmental Justice Frontline*. New York: Cambridge University Press.

Roberts, Jonathan, and Thomas J. Durant. 2010. *A History of the Charity Hospitals of Louisiana: A Study of Poverty, Politics, Public Health, and the Public Interest.* Lewiston: Edward Mellen Press.

Robichaux, Brenda Dardar, and the Ms. Foundation for Women. 2012. "We Like to Think Houma Women Are Very Strong." In *The Women of Katrina: How Gender, Race, and Class Matter in an American Disaster,* edited by Emmanuel David and Elaine Enarson, 43–46. Nashville: Vanderbilt University Press.

Robinson, Eugene. 2005. "No longer invisible." *Washington Post*, September 9. http://www.washingtonpost.com/wp-dyn/content/article/2005/09/08/AR2005090801535.html.

Roderick, Anne Marie. 2010. "After the Flood." *Dissent* 57 (2) 34–37.

Rose, Chris. 2005. *1 Dead in Attic.* New Orleans: Chris Rose Books.

Rose, Kalima, and Laura Tuggle. 2010. "Community Action: Bringing People Home to Stronger Neighborhoods." New Orleans, LA and Washington, DC: Greater New Orleans Data Center and the Brookings Institution, August. http://community-wealth.org/content/community-action-bringing-people-home-stronger-neighborhoods.

Rosenbaum, Judith. 2012. "Listening for Gender in Katrina's Jewish Voices." In *The Women of Katrina: How Gender, Race, and Class Matter in an American Disaster,* edited by Emmanuel David and Elaine Enarson, 190–197. Nashville: Vanderbilt University Press.

Rosewarne, Lauren. 2005. "The Men's Gallery: Outdoor Advertising and Public Space: Gender, Fear, and Feminism." *Women's International Forum* 28: 67–78.

Ross, Loretta. 2012. "A Feminist Perspective on Katrina." In *The Women of Katrina: How Gender, Race, and Class Matter in an American Disaster,* edited by Emmanuel David and Elaine Enarson, 15–23. Nashville: Vanderbilt University Press.

Ross-Sheriff, Fariyal. 2007. "Women and Disasters: Reflections on the Anniversary of Katrina and Rita." *Affilia: Journal of Women and Social Work* 22 (1): 5–8.

Rubin, Gayle. 1984. "Thinking Sex: Notes for a Radical Theory of the Politics of Sexuality." In *Pleasure and Danger: Exploring Female Sexuality*, edited by Carole S. Vance, 267–319. London: Pandora.

Rudowitz, Robin, Diane Rowland, and Adele Shartzer, 2006. "Health Care before and after Hurricane Katrina." *Health Affairs* 25: 393–406. http://content.healthaffairs.org/content/25/5/w393.full.

Sams-Abiodun, Petrice, and Gregory Rattler. 2013. "Recognizing the Underutilized Economic Potential of Black Men in New Orleans." Lindy Boggs National Center on Community Literacy. June 14. http://allthingslocalnola.info/yahoo_site_admin/assets/docs/Recognizing-Potential.170111053.pdf.

Sassen, Saskia. 2001. *The Global City: New York, London, Tokyo*. Princeton: Princeton University Press.

Schippers, Mimi. 2002. *Rockin' Out of the Box: Gender Maveuvering in Alternative Hard Rock*. New Brunswick: Rutgers University Press.

———. Forthcoming. *Polyqueer: The Monogamous Couple, Gender, and the Queer Potential of Plural Sexualities*. New York: New York University Press.

Schumacher, Julie A., Scott F. Coffey, Fran H. Norris, Melissa Tracy, Kahni Clements, and Sandro Galea. 2010. "Intimate Partner Violence and Hurricane Katrina: Predictors and Associated Mental Health Outcomes." *Violence and Victims* 25 (5): 588–603.

Schutt, R. 2009. *Investigating the Social World: The Process and Practice of Research,* 6th ed. Thousand Oaks: Pine Forge Press.

Scott, Jerome, and Walda Katz-Fishman. 2007. "American through the Eye of Hurricane Katrina—Capitalism at Its 'Best' What Are We Prepared to Do?" *Race, Gender & Class* 14 (1–2): 7–16.

Seager, Joni. 2012. "Noticing Gender (or Not) in Disasters." In *The Women of Katrina: How Gender, Race, and Class Matter in an American Disaster,* edited by Emmanuel David and Elaine Enarson, 7–9. Nashville: Vanderbilt University Press.

Sellers, Susan, Andre Perry, Petrice Sams-Abiodun, Alison Plyer, and Elaine Ortiz. 2012. "Building an Inclusive, High Skilled Workforce for New Orleans' Next Economy." The Greater New Orleans Community Data Center. March 27. https://gnocdc.s3.amazonaws.com/reports/GNOCDC_BuildingAnInclusiveHigh-SkilledWorkforceForNewOrleansNextEconomy.pdf.

Settersten, Richard, and Barbara Ray. 2010. "What's Going on with Young People Today?: The Long and Twisting Path to Adulthood." *Future of the Children* 20 (1): 19–41.

Sexual Assault Response Assistance (SARA) Center. 2006. Unpublished lecture material, New Orleans: Tulane University.

Singleton, R. A., and B. C. Straits. 1999. *Approaches to Social Research,* 3rd ed. New York: Oxford University Press.

Smith, Dorothy E. 1987. *The Everyday World as Problematic: A Feminist Sociology.* Boston: Northeastern University Press.

Smith, G. 2012. *Planning for post-disaster recovery: A review of the United States disaster assistance framework*. Washington, DC: Island Press.

Smith, Kenneth J., and Linda Liska Belgrave. 1995. "The Reconstruction of Everyday Life: Experiencing Hurricane Andrew." *Journal of Contemporary Ethnography* 24: 244–269.

Smith, Ryan A., and James R. Elliott. 2002. "Does Ethnic Concentration Influence Employees' Access to Authority? An Examination of Contemporary Urban Labor Markets." *Social Forces* 81 (1): 255–279.

Sokoloff, N. J., and I. Dupont. 2013. "Examining the Intersections of Race, Class, Gender, and Culture." In *Domestic Violence at the Margins: Readings on Race, Class, Gender, and Culture*, edited by N. J. Sokoloff and I. Dupont, 1. New Brunswick: Rutgers University Press.

Spain, Daphne. 1993. "Gendered Spaces and Women's Status." *Sociological Theory* 11: 137–151.

Spence, Patric R., Kenneth A. Lachlan, and Jennifer M. Burke. 2007. "Adjusting to Uncertainty: Coping Strategies among the Displaced after Hurricane Katrina." *Sociological Spectrum* 27 (6): 653–678.

Stanko, Elizabeth A. 1995. "Women, Crime, and Fear." *Annals of the American Academy of Political and Social Science* 539: 46–58.

Steffensen, Ingrid. 2014. "Two loves: An adjunct's journey from the classroom to the racetrack." *PBS Newshour*. http://www.pbs.org/newshour/making-sense/two-lovers-adjuncts-journey-classroom-racetrack/.

Stockemer, Daniel. 2006. "Gender Inequalities and Hurricane Katrina." *International Journal of Diversity* 6 (1): 138–142.

Stone, Gregory, Arina Lekht, Nancy Burris, and Clayton Williams. 2007. "Data Collection and Communications in the Public Health Response to a Disaster: Rapid Population Estimate Surveys and the Daily Dashboard in Post-Katrina New Orleans." *Journal of Public Health Management Practice* 13 (5): 453–460.

Strange, Jackie. 2006. "Gone with Katrina's Wind." *Southern Quarterly* 43 (3): 79–83.

Strolovitch, Dara, Dorian Warren, and Paul Frymer. 2006. "Katrina's political roots and divisions: Race, class and federalism in American politics." *Understanding Katrina,* June 11. http://understandingkatrina.ssrc.org/FrymerStrolovitchWarren//.

Sullivan, Laura. 2005. "How New Orleans' Evacuation Plan Fell Apart." *NPR*, September 23. http://www.npr.org/templates/story/story.php?storyId=4860776.

Swain, A. 2013. "Waiting for Daybreak: A Survivor's Account of Theft and Recovery." *Qualitative Inquiry* 19 (7): 502–504.

Taylor, Guy. 2006. "Hispanics rush in to rebuild New Orleans; Fears raised about city's makeup." *Washington Times*, February 22.

Taylor, Verta. 1998. "Feminist Methodology in Social Movements Research." *Qualitative Sociology* 21 (4): 357–379.

Thornton, W. E., and L. Voigt. 2010. "Disaster Rape: Vulnerability." In *Crime and Criminal Justice in Disaster*, edited by Dee Wood Harper and Kelly Frailing, 107. Durham: Carolina Academic Press.

Tienda, Marta, and Ding-Tzann Lii. 1987. "Minority Concentration and Earnings Inequality: Blacks, Hispanics, and Asians Compared." *American Journal of Sociology* 93 (1): 141–165.

Tierney, Kathleen. 2007. "From the Margins to the Mainstream? Disaster Research at the Crossroads." *Annual Review of Sociology* 33: 503–525.

Tierney, Kathleen, Christine Bevc, and Erica Kuligowski. 2006. "Metaphors Matter: Disaster Myths, Media Frames, and their Consequences in Hurricane Katrina." *Annals of the American Academy of Political and Social Science* 604: 57–81.

Tobin-Gurley, Jennifer, and Lori Peek. 2010. "Displaced Single Mothers in the Aftermath of Hurricane Katrina: Resource Needs and Resource Acquisition." *International Journal of Mass Emergencies and Disasters* 28 (2): 170–206.

Top 101 cities with the highest percentage of single-parent households, population 50,000+. 2014. *City-Data.com*. http://www.city-data.com/top2/h7.html.

Treaster, Joseph B. 2005. "Superdome: Haven Quickly Becomes an Ordeal." *New York Times*, September 1. http://www.nytimes.com/2005/09/01/national/nationalspecial/01dome.html?pagewanted=all.

Trichur, Ganesh K. 2007. "Spectacular Privatizations: Perceptions and Lessons from Privatization of Warfare and the Privatization of Disaster." In *Racing the Storm: Racial Implications and Lessons Learned from Hurricane Katrina*, edited by Hillary Potter, 225–246. Lanham: Lexington Books.

Trujillo-Pagan, Nicole. 2007. "From 'Gateway to the Americas' to the 'Chocolate City': The Racialization of Latinos in New Orleans." In *Racing the Storm: Racial Implications and*

Lessons Learned from Hurricane Katrina, edited by Hillary Potter, 95–113. Lanham: Lexington Books.

———. 2012a. "Neoliberal Disasters and Racialisation: The Case of Post-Katrina Latino Labour." *Race and Class* 53 (4): 54–66.

———. 2012b. "Boundary Work at the New Corner: Latino Workers in New Orleans." *International Review of Modern Sociology* 38 (1): 1–24.

Turner, Margery Austin, Rob Santos, Diane Levy, Doug Wissoker, Claudia Aranda, and Rob Pitingolo. 2013. *Housing Discrimination against Racial and Ethnic Minorities, 2012*. Washington, DC: U.S. Department of Housing and Urban Development, Office of Policy Development and Research, 3.

Turner, Margery Austin, S. Ross, G. C. Galster, and J. Yinger. 2002. *Discrimination in Metropolitan Housing Markets: National Results from Phase I HDS 2000.* The U.S. Department of Housing and Urban Development. http://www.huduser.org/publications/hsgfin/hds_phase1 .html.

Tuzzolo, Ellen, and Damon Hewitt. 2006. "Rebuilding Inequality: The Re-Emergence of the School to Prison Pipeline in New Orleans." *High School Journal* 6: 59–68.

U.S. Bureau of Labor Statistics. 2014. State and Area Employment, Hours, and Earnings. New Orleans-Metairie-Kenner, LA, Louisiana. http://data.bls.gov.

———. 2005. *American Community Survey.* Washington, DC: U.S. Census Bureau's American Community Survey Office.

———. 2006. *American Community Survey.* Washington, DC: U.S. Census Bureau's American Community Survey Office.

———. 2007. *American Community Survey.* Washington, DC: U.S. Census Bureau's American Community Survey Office.

———. 2010. New Orleans Quick Facts. Washington, DC: U.S. Government Printing Office.

———. 2012. *American Community Survey.* Washington, DC: U.S. Census Bureau's American Community Survey Office.

———. 2014. American Factfinder. www.factfinder.census.gov.

U.S. Department of Homeland Security. 2006. Current Housing Unit Damage Estimates: Hurricanes Katrina, Rita, and Wilma. U.S. Department of Housing and Urban Development. February 12. www.huduser.org/publications/pdf/GulfCoast_Hsngdmgest.pdf

UNITY of Greater New Orleans. 2011. *Homelessness in Greater New Orleans: A Report on Progress toward Ending Homelessness in the Years after the Nation's Largest Housing Disaster.* New Orleans. http://unitygno.org/wp-content/uploads/2011/06/PIT-2011-Report.pdf.

US Department of Housing and Urban Development. 2006. "Current Housing Unit Damage Estimates: Hurricanes Katrina, Rita, and Wilma." February 12. https://gnocdc.s3.amazonaws.com/reports/Katrina_Rita_Wilma_Damage_2_12_06___revised.pdf.

———. 2014. "Paired Testing and the Housing Discrimination Studies." *Evidence Matters* Spring/Summer. http://www.huduser.org/portal/periodicals/em/spring14/highlight2.html.

Vale, Lawrence J., and Thomas J. Campanella, eds. 2005. *The Resilient City: How Modern Cities Recover from Disaster.* New York: Oxford University Press.

Valke, Anne, and Leslie Brown. 2010. *Living with Jim Crow: African American Women and Memories of the Segregated South.* New York: Palgrave Macmillan.

Verderber, Stephen. 2010. "Five Years after—Three New Orleans Neighborhoods." *Journal of Architectural Education* 64 (1): 107–120.

Vigil, Jacob M., Adam C. Carle, David C. Geary, Doug A. Granger, Mark V. Flinn, and Patricia Pendleton. 2009. "Maternal Correlates of Children's Stress Functioning Following a Major Natural Disaster." *Journal of Child & Adolescent Trauma* 2 (4): 287–296.

Vinck, Patrick, Phuong Pham, Laurel E. Fletcher, and Eric Stover. 2009. "Inequalities and Prospects: Ethnicity and Legal Status in the Construction Labor Force after Hurricane Katrina." *Organization and Environment* 22 (4): 470–478. doi: 10.1177/1086026609347192.

Waldinger, Roger. 1997. "Black/Immigrant Competition Re-Assessed: New Evidence from Los Angeles." *Sociological Perspectives* 40 (3): 365–386.

Waldinger, Roger, and Thomas Bailey. 1991. "The Continuing Significance of Race: Racial Conflict and Racial Discrimination in Construction." *Politics and Society* 19 (3): 291-323.

Walsh, Joan. 2005. "Flushing Out the Ugly Truth." *Salon*, September 1. http://www.salon.com/2005/09/01/katrina_race/.

Walsh, Lynn. 2005. "Race, Class and Katrina." *Socialist Today*, October. http://www.socialistalternative.org/poor-black-and-left-to-die/race-class-and-katrina/.

Warren, Carol A. B. (with Debora Archer, Beverly Broderick, Sara Collas, Debra Dobbs, Gloria Flores, Robert Futrell, Laurie Grow, Jennifer Hackney, Tracy X. Karner, Douglas Kivett, Richard Johnson, Lourdes Pereira-Nunez, Erin Reilly, and Christine Robinson). 2000. "Writing the Other, Inscribing the Self." *Qualitative Sociology* 23 (2): 183–199.

Wasem, Ruth Ellen. 2005. Hurricane Katrina-Related Immigration Issues and Legislation. Congressional Research Service Report for Congress, Order Code RL33091, September 19, 2005.

Watson, Bruce. 2010. "The Awful Odyssey of FEMA's Hurricane Katrina Trailers." *Daily Finance*. http://www.dailyfinance.com/2010/08/28/the-awful-odyssey-of-femas-hurricane-katrina-trailers/.

Weber, Lynn. 2010. *Race, Class, Gender, and Sexuality: A Conceptual Framework*. New York: Oxford University Press.

———. 2012. "When Demand Exceeds Supply: Disaster Response and the Southern Political Economy." In *Displaced: Life in the Katrina Diaspora,* edited by Lynn Weber and Lori Peek, 79–103. Austin: University of Texas Press.

Weber, Lynn, and Lori Peek, eds. 2012. *Displaced: Voices from the Katrina Diaspora*. Austin: University of Texas Press.

Webster, Nicole. 2007. "Enriching School Connection and Learning in African American Youth: The Impact of a Service-Learning Feasibility Project in Inner-City Philadelphia." In *Service Learning: From Passion to Objectivity*, edited by Sherril B. Gelmon and Shelley H. Billig, 159–176. Charlotte: Information Age Publishing.

Weems, Carol, Leslie Taylor, Melinda Cannon, Reshelle Marino, Dawn Romano, Brandon Scott, Andre Perry, and Vera Triplett. 2008. "Post Traumatic Stress, Context, and Lingering Effects of the Hurricane Katrina Disaster among Ethnic Minority Youth." *Journal of Abnormal Child Psychology* 38: 49–56.

Weil, Jeannie Haubert. 2007a. "Challenging and Circumventing Discrimination and Exploitation: A Study of Latinos in Mississippi's Post-Katrina Housing Market." Paper presented at conference—Disaster and Migration: Hurricane Katrina's effects on New Orleans Population. Conference sponsors: Stone Center for Latin American Studies and the Social Science Research Council. New Orleans, LA.

———. 2007b. "Discrimination, Segregation, and the Racialized Search for Housing Post-Katrina." In *Through the Eye of Katrina: Social Justice in the United States,* edited by Kristin A. Bates and Richelle S. Swan. Durham: Carolina Academic Press.

———. 2009. "Finding Housing: Discrimination and Exploitation of Latinos in the Post-Katrina Rental Market." *Organization and Environment* 22 (4): 491–502. doi: 10.1177/1086026609347194.

———. 2010. "Impediments to Latino Resiliency and Incorporation? A Study of Linguistic Profiling in the Housing Market before and after Hurricane Katrina." In *How Ethnically Marginalized Americans Cope with Catastrophic Disasters: Studies in Suffering and Resiliency,* edited by Jason D. Rivera and DeMond S. Miller. New York: Edwin Mellon Press.

Welsh, Sandy. 1999. "Gender and Sexual Harassment." *Annual Review of Sociology* 25: 169–190.

White, Mia Charlene. 2012. "Gender, Race, and Place Attachment: The Recovery of a Historic Neighborhood in Coastal Mississippi." In *The Women of Katrina: How Gender, Race, and Class Matter in an American Disaster,* edited by Emmanuel David and Elaine Enarson, 157–168. Nashville: Vanderbilt University Press.

Willinger, Beth. 2008. *Katrina and the Women of New Orleans*. New Orleans: Newcomb College Center for Research on Women.

Willinger, Beth, and Janna Knight. 2012. "Setting the Stage for Disaster: Women in New Orleans before and after Katrina." In *The Women of Katrina: How Gender, Race, and Class Matter in an American Disaster,* edited by Emmanuel David and Elaine Enarson, 55–75. Nashville: Vanderbilt University Press.

Willinger, Beth, and Jessica Gerson. 2008. "Demographic and Socio-Economic Change in Relation to Gender and Hurricane Katrina." In *Katrina and the Women of New Orleans,* edited by Beth Willinger, 25–31. New Orleans: Newcomb College Center for Research on Women.

Wilson, Kenneth L., and Alejandro Portes. 1980. "An analysis of the labor market experiences of Cubans in Miami." *American Journal of Sociology* 86 (2): 295–319.

Wilson, William Julius. 1987. *The Truly Disadvantaged.* Chicago: University of Chicago.

———. 1996. *When Work Disappears*. New York: Vintage Books.

———. 2010. *More Than Race: Being Black and Poor in the Inner City*. New York: W. W. Norton & Co.

Wise, S., and L. Stanley. 1987. *Georgie Porgie: Sexual Harassment in Everyday Life*. London: Pandora Press.

Woodward, A. 2013. "New Orleans groups chart response to domestic violence." *Gambit,* October 16. http://www.bestofneworleans.com/blogofneworleans/archives/2013/10/16/new-orleans-groups-chart-response-to-domestic-violence.

World Health Organization. 2002. "Gender and health in disasters." July 2002. http://www.who.int/gender/other_health/disasters/en/.

Yinger, J. 1995. *Closed Doors, Opportunities Lost: The Continuing Costs of Housing Discrimination.* New York: Russell Sage Foundation.

Yukins, Christopher R. 2005. "Hurricane Katrina's Tangled Impact on U.S. Procurement." George Washington University Law School Public Law and Legal Theory Paper, No. 161. http://ssrn.com/abstract=810764.

Zissimopoulos, Julie, and Lynn A. Karoly. 2010. "Employment and Self-Employment in the Wake of Hurricane Katrina." *Demography* 47 (2): 345–367.

Zotti, Marianne E., and Amy M. Williams. 2011. "Reproductive Health Assessment after Disaster: Introduction to the RHAD Toolkit." *Journal of Women's Health* 20 (8): 1123–1127.

Zotti, Marianne E., Van T. Tong, Lyn Kieltyka, and Renee Brown-Bryant. 2012. "Factors Influencing Evacuation Decisions among High-Risk Pregnant and Postpartum Women." In *The Women of Katrina: How Gender, Race, and Class Matter in an American Disaster,* edited by Emmanuel David and Elaine Enarson, 90–104. Nashville: Vanderbilt University Press.

Zúñiga, Victor, and Rubén Hernández-León, eds. 2005. *New Destinations: Mexican Immigration in the United States*. New York: Russell Sage Foundation.

Index

activism, 195; accidental activism, 195; activist mothering, 195; feminist activism, 150; contemporary social justice activism, 186; sociological activism, 151
affirmative action, 159, 165
American Red Cross, 47, 83, 84, 122
audit studies, 158, 163, 164. *See also* discrimination

bias, 10n3, 143, 144, 149, 198
Baker, Richard H., 128
Baton Rouge, 43, 79, 101, 121, 124, 131
Biloxi, 2, 4, 83, 166n7
Blanco, Kathleen, 60
Blueprint for Safety Project, 49
BP oil spill, 4, 8, 50. *See also* Deepwater Horizon oil spill
Buffalo Creek, 192

capitalism, 84, 125, 128, 133, 197, 206; disaster capitalism, 209
Catholic Charities, 48
Central Business District, 188
Charity Hospital, 30, 60, 127, 131, 135n7, 197, 208
civil rights, 10, 18, 33, 131, 133, 156
class: classism, 140; middle class, 17, 30, 72, 75, 79, 83, 105, 117, 119, 129, 153, 194, 207; mobility, 59, 79, 144; upper class, 6, 77, 84, 101, 109; working class, 72, 77, 79, 101, 118, 126, 132, 144. *See also* privilege; stratification
contexts of reception, 158
corporatization, 174, 175; of universities, 175
Cowen, Scott, 171, 177
Crescent House, 45, 46, 48
crime, 18, 33, 98, 106, 132; interpersonal, 42; petty, 66; racially-motivated, 133; rates, 3, 49; violent, 33, 49. *See also* incarceration
criminal justice system, 40, 45

Davis Bacon Act, 95
Deepwater Horizon Oil Spill, 185, 187, 194, 195. *See also* BP oil spill
Department of Education, 106, 108, 115, 178
Department of Health and Human Services, 60
Department of Housing and Urban Development, 46, 83, 155, 159, 163, 165
Department of Justice, 49
Department of Labor, 95
disaster management, 7, 54, 59
disaster preparedness, 8, 62, 126, 208
disaster recovery, xiii, 5, 8, 30, 36, 45, 47, 65, 85, 141, 154, 192, 193, 194, 197, 198, 200, 208, 209

discrimination, 3, 10, 17, 55, 63, 67, 73, 81, 83, 86, 88, 107, 110, 154, 155, 156–157, 158–159, 160, 162, 164, 165, 166n2, 166n3, 166n6, 167n10; heterosexist, 17; housing, 10, 154, 155, 156, 157–159, 162, 163, 165, 166; legalized, 170; neoclassical theories of, 157; organizational, 63; racial, 63, 82, 84, 86, 155, 158, 159; rates of, 155, 156, 157; religious, 83; unregulated, 165
displacement, 7, 8, 10, 17, 20, 56, 59, 71, 73, 79, 85, 86, 91, 99, 147, 154, 156, 163, 166n3
domestic violence, 7, 40, 41, 41–42, 44, 45, 45–46, 48, 49, 50–51, 51n1, 59, 66; domestic abuse, 33, 59; rates, 3, 42, 58

Earl K. Long Hospital, 131
economy, 42, 61, 67, 108, 110, 118, 119, 162, 196; economic inequality, 188; global shift in the, 170, 174; political, 95, 109, 196, 197; post-disaster, 67; tourism-based, 3
education. *See also* schools: educational attainment, 3, 49; educational system, 108, 109, 129, 133; public education, 118, 133; schools; Department of Education
emergency management, 60, 93, 105, 210
emergency period, 92, 98
emergency response, 2, 53, 54, 58
emerging adulthood, 106, 107
empirical research, ix, 41, 103, 142
employment opportunities, 29, 40, 110
entrepreneurship, 3, 10n1, 108
environmental inequalities, 202
environmental justice, 65, 187, 202
ethnographic research, 24, 194
ethnography, 146
evacuation, 16, 17, 28, 41, 43, 44, 47, 55, 62, 63, 67, 77, 78, 115, 119, 121, 125, 133, 209

Fair Housing Act, 155, 159
Family Justice Center, 48, 49, 50
Federal Emergency Management Agency, 60, 93; FEMA, 44, 46, 47, 48, 83, 105, 124, 206, 208
femininity, 25, 33
feminist, 11n5, 22, 24, 141, 142–144, 145, 148, 149, 150, 193; feminist methodology, 141, 143, 149; feminist research, 141, 144, 193
free market, 127, 128, 133. *See also* neoliberalism; capitalism
French Quarter, 27, 28, 57, 64, 93, 103, 112, 129, 132, 188, 191, 192, 210
the frontier, 29–31, 31, 35, 89; frontier culture, 29, 35

Garden District, 129, 132, 187, 188
Gautier, 4
gender: hierarchy, 33; interaction, 25, 35, 36; maneuvering, 25; pay gap, 67; roles, 43. *See also* stratification; inequality
gendered interactions, 25, 35, 36
Gentilly, 122, 123
gentrification, 129, 135n5, 141, 146, 197, 207, 209n1, 210
grassroots movements, 64, 65, 66
grassroots response, 87
group threat theory, 156
group position, 74, 75
Gulf Shores, 81, 83
Gulfport, 4, 166n7

Habitat for Humanity, 198, 201
Harrington, Michael, 127, 134n2, 134n3
harassment: public, 32, 33; sexual, 21, 22, 23, 27, 28, 31, 32, 33, 34, 35, 36, 57, 58, 139, 146, 182; stranger, 32; street, 7, 21, 27, 31, 32, 33, 34, 35, 36–37, 37n2
healthcare: access, 45; facilities, 36, 67; mental, 36, 131; public, 8, 66, 124, 127, 131; pediatric, 61; reproductive, 59, 61, 67; for women, 40, 63
heteronormativity, 17, 25
heterosexism, 17, 25, 76. *See also* discrimination; sexism
Homeless, 16, 40, 50, 71, 72, 74, 81, 134, 153, 154; Homelessness, 50, 133, 153
HOPE VI, 141
housing: affordable, 50, 56, 63, 86, 91, 134, 154; fair, 10, 83, 154, 155–156, 156, 159, 160, 164, 164–165, 166n3;

Greater New Orleans Fair Housing Action Center, 83, 156, 166n3; Gulf Coast Fair Housing Center, 156, 160, 166n3; lack of livable, 165; Housing Act of 1937, 128; mixed income, 46; public, 3, 8, 10, 46, 56, 60, 67, 93, 99, 124, 127, 128, 133, 135n4, 139, 140, 141, 146, 147, 197, 208. *See also* HOPE IV; Fair Housing Act; US Department of Housing and Urban Development; Gulf Coast Fair Housing Center; Greater New Orleans Fair Housing Center; homeless
Houston, 63, 101, 140
Hurricane Andrew, 47, 145
hurricane lovers, 7
Hurricane Mitch, 100
Hurricane Rita, 2, 4, 39, 41, 50, 91

Immigration and Customs Enforcement, 99, 102
incarceration, 3, 49. *See also* crime
income: annual, 77, 132, 135n7; average, 155; gap, 3; higher, 166n5, 188; household, 10n2, 10n3, 189; low/lower, 46, 47, 55, 56, 62, 63, 66, 67, 91, 95, 118, 126, 131, 141–142, 160, 188, 189, 192, 197
inequality/inequalities: class, 36, 55, 124, 125, 126, 127, 188; economic, 55, 125, 182, 188, 192, 197; environmental, 202; gender, 5, 36, 124, 125, 127, 141, 182; intersecting, 72; racial, 36, 55, 73, 110, 124, 125, 126, 127, 182, 188; social, 4, 5, 24, 36, 125, 133, 170, 187; structural, 127
intimate partner violence, 41, 48, 58. *See also* domestic violence
isolation, 48, 81, 193, 206

Jazz Heritage Festival, 132
Johnson, Lyndon B., 134n3

Katrina babies, 61
Katrina-fatigue, 74, 86
Kennedy, John F., 134n2

labor: cost of, 95, 179; force, 91, 92, 95, 96, 97, 99, 102; immigrant, 99, 100; local, 8, 100, 101; manual, 29, 30; market, 8, 82, 88, 91, 92, 95–96, 99–100, 100, 101, 102, 157, 207
laborers: day, 91, 92, 93, 95, 98, 99; erotic, 22
Lakeview, 39, 115, 122
life history interviews, 110
Long Beach, 4, 76
Long, Huey P., 131
Louisiana Recovery Authority, 189
Louisiana Road Home, 47
Louisiana State Legislature, 108
Lower Ninth Ward, 39, 187–188, 189, 190, 191, 193, 198, 200, 201, 209

Make It Right Foundation, 187, 198
Mardi Gras, 19, 22, 132
masculinity, 22, 25
media: coverage, 196; mainstream, 18; portrayals, 84, 87; reports, 57; social, 118
mixed-method research, 142
mononormativity, 25
Morial Convention Center, 78, 106, 111
Morial, Marc, 41
motherwork, 64

Nagin, Ray, 90, 99
narrative case studies, 54
na-tech, 205
National Guard, 35, 123; guardsmen, 146
neoliberal: academic trends, 178, 179; capitalism, 133; global economy, 10, 174; ideology, 205; markets, 182; policymakers, 177; project, 23; reforms, 8, 197
neoliberalism, 131, 182, 206
new normality, 31, 64, 174, 177, 182
New Orleans East, 117
non-monogamy, 17, 19, 20
non-profit, 3, 7, 10n1, 42, 44, 47, 48, 49, 50, 64, 130, 154, 156, 157, 196, 209
normalized uncertainty, 170, 172, 180, 183

objectivity, 143, 145, 149, 186, 194
Occupational Health and Safety Administration, 95

Pass Christian, 1, 4, 76, 83

Perry, James, 83, 166n3
Planned Parenthood, 61
Plaquemines Parish, 10, 94, 195, 196
police, 18, 23, 35, 42, 45, 55, 58, 62, 98, 109, 149; military police, 28, 57; Orleans Police Department, 49; procedures, 42; response, 48, 57; policing, 42, 50, 66
positionality, 140, 142, 150. *See also* social position
positivism, 142–144, 144, 145, 149
poverty, 56, 62, 63, 101, 124, 125, 126, 127, 128, 130, 132, 182, 186; black, 77, 84, 132; concentrated,, 106; cycle of, 125; effects of, 55; feminization of, 56; level, 101; line, 42, 55, 56, 77, 78; pre-Katrina, 63, 77; rates, 42, 54, 106, 127, 130; research, 141; urban, 141; War on, 134n2
prejudice, 55, 75, 76, 80, 81, 156, 157, 165
privatization, 133, 189, 197
privilege, 25, 71, 72, 83, 208; class privilege, 2, 8, 83, 86; hetero-masculine, 22; male, 33; narratives, 73; racial, 75, 86, 121, 124, 153, 208; social position, 10; social status, 71, 72, 86
production of knowledge, 5, 6
prostitution, 25, 31, 61

queer, 16, 17, 18, 180, 183n1, 183n4, 184n5; polyqueer, 17, 25; theorists, 24; time, 17–18, 23

racial hierarchy, 158
racial segregation, 110, 128, 188
racialization, 93, 95, 98, 99
racism, 73, 75, 81, 83, 125, 140, 205, 209; environmental, 202; institutional, viii
rapport, 6, 143, 144
reconstruction period, 93
Recovery School District, 108, 109, 130
reflexivity, ix, 139, 141, 142
relationship ties, 79. *See also* social networks
research methods, 103, 110, 139, 142; participatory methods, 141; qualitative, 5, 7, 110, 143, 148; quantitative, 5, 142–143
resilience, 64, 139, 193
restoration period, 92, 93, 97

Salvation Army, 46
sampling, 111, 159, 166n7; convenience, 103; frame, 103; probability, 103; snowball, 110
schools: charter, 108, 109, 127, 130, 208; private, 119; public, 106, 108, 109, 117, 118, 119, 124, 129, 130
sex negativity, 20
sexism, 35, 125, 140. *See also* heterosexism
sexual assault, 34, 40, 47, 49, 57, 58, 59. *See also* sexual violence
sexual cultures, 7, 19, 20, 23, 24, 25
sexual harassment. *See* harrassment
sexual violence, 47, 58
sexually transmitted diseases, 60, 61
sexually transmitted infections, 7, 20, 23
social capital, 78, 79, 80, 140, 188
social control, 31, 34
social networks, 40, 43, 64, 65, 67–68, 79, 86, 96, 98, 107, 161; concentrated, 77, 79; dispersed, 62, 63; informal, 44, 98; limited, 106; similarly situated, 55. *See also* relationship ties
social organization, 4; of gendered sexuality, 22, 24; of sexuality, 23–24
social position, 10, 56, 72, 74. *See also* positionality
social structure, 18, 19, 23, 148
socially isolated, 79. *See also* isolation
sociological imagination, viii, 72
standpoint, 6, 11n5, 143, 144, 148, 149, 150; of the citizen sociologist, ix; of the discipline, ix; political, 134; solidarity, 144, 148, 150; theory, 11n5
stratification: class, 53; ethnic systems of, 99; gender, 34; systems of, 99
subjectivity, 5, 25, 34, 149, 186
Superdome, 57, 58, 60, 66, 68, 78, 106, 111, 125, 126, 134, 140, 143
sympathy: biography, 74, 75; exchange, 8, 72, 73, 87; sympathy margin, 73, 76, 77, 81, 86, 87

Teach for America, 108, 112, 130
tourism, 3, 4, 10, 102, 114, 115, 125, 192, 207, 209; industry, 93; sex tourism, 20;

disaster tourism, 191
transition into adulthood, 8, 107, 120. *See also* emerging adulthood
transportation, 40, 44, 45, 62, 66, 67, 77, 78, 83, 140, 191, 209
trauma, 7, 10, 17, 19, 20, 24, 33, 56, 139–140, 141, 142, 143, 145, 148, 149, 150, 151, 194; center, 135n7; collective, 15, 24, 140; emotional, 10, 31; of displacement, 17; physical, 41; post-traumatic stress, 33, 35; psychological, 15, 107; retraumatization, 139; recovery from, 20, 24; studies, 19; to cope with, 19

unemployment, 87, 97, 157, 172, 173
The Urban Conservancy, 196
The Urban Land Institute, 67

validity, 141, 143
verstehen, 5, 10n4
victimization, 34, 47, 58, 91, 97, 98, 205, 209
vulnerability, 33, 34, 35, 40, 41, 68, 170; disaster, 40, 55, 56; gendered, 42, 43; of women, 36, 43, 54, 61, 64, 66; workers', 98

wages, 95, 96, 97, 98, 100, 101, 108, 109
Waveland, 4
Weil, Jason, 166n3

youth, 106, 107, 110; African American, 106–107, 119, 120

About the Authors

Kristen Barber is assistant professor of sociology and faculty affiliate with the Women, Gender, and Sexuality Studies Department at Southern Illinois University, Carbondale. Her research focuses on issues of gender, social inequality, work, the body, and qualitative and feminist methodologies. Having lived in New Orleans during Hurricane Katrina while attending graduate school at Tulane University, she expanded her work into the area of disaster. This work emphasizes the sociological insights of local scholars affected by Katrina, and she has been published in the *Journal of Public Management and Social Policy* and *Critical Sociology*, and as an anthology, *Narrating the Storm: Sociological Stories of Hurricane Katrina.*

Jean Ait Belkhir is associate professor of sociology at Southern University at New Orleans (SUNO) and the University of New Orleans (UNO). Belkhir founded the American Sociological Association Section Race, Gender and Class, which he chaired from 1994 to 1998; he was reelected chair in 2005 and 2006. He also created the journal *Race, Gender & Class* in 1993. Since the formation of the journal and the section, several issues of the *Race, Gender & Class* journal have fostered debate and discussion on issues of intersectionality. In 1998, he founded the annual Race, Gender & Class Conference in New Orleans, which he continues to organize on the campus of the University of New Orleans.

Amy Bellone-Hite is the Clarence Jupiter Professor of Sociology at Xavier University of Louisiana, where she also serves as the chairperson of the Division of Social and Behavioral Sciences. In addition to her interest in demographic changes inspired by Katrina, she studies the impacts of economic globalization. Bellone-Hite received her PhD in Latin American studies from Tulane University. She has published several articles and chapters on how rapid population shifts affect local labor markets. She has co-edited, with J. Timmons Roberts, *From Modernization to Globalization* and *The Globalization and Development Reader.* A second edition of the latter volume, co-edited with J. Timmons Roberts and Nitsan Chorev is forthcoming.

Farrah Gafford Cambrice is an urban sociologist who earned her PhD in sociology from Tulane University in New Orleans in 2009. While many of her colleagues were scattered all over the country after the storm, she stayed the course in New Orleans working at Xavier University and observing the long-term recovery of New Orleans first-hand. Her research focuses on race, class, and disaster and has been published in the *Journal of Black Studies*, the *Journal of Global Policy and Resilience*, and the *Journal of Urban History*, among others. Her recent move to Houston, a major receiving-city of Katrina evacuees, affords her the opportunity to begin research on the impact of Katrina on those who were more permanently displaced.

Jennifer Day-Sully received her master's degree in sociology from Tulane University. She was awarded a mayoral fellowship in 2006 and went on to serve as the director for the New Orleans Office of Film & Video before acting as the director of communications and public relations for the New Orleans Convention & Visitors Bureau. While she currently lives in Queensland, Australia, with her husband David and daughter Delta, New Orleans is never far from her heart or mind. Jennifer still speaks weekly with her co-authors and values their friendship and the bond they forged enduring disaster.

Shiloh Deitz is a master's student in the Department of Geography with an emphasis on GIS at Southern Illinois University, Carbondale. She also holds a master's degree in sociology. Currently, she works at the Paul Simon Public Policy Institute as the Celia Howard Fellow. Her interests are in urban design, environmental health, and reducing social vulnerabilities. Dr. Kristen Barber sparked her interest in Hurricane Katrina and the pre-storm vulnerability of New Orleans while she was a student in sociology. In the Spring of 2014 she presented to the Illinois Department of Public Health on the need for gender-sensitive disaster management using the lessons learned from Hurricane Katrina. She is interested in building resilient, socially just, and healthy communities and hopes to pursue a career in city planning and public policy after graduation. The lessons from Hurricane Katrina and New Orleans continue to inform her research.

Erica Dudas has lived in New Orleans since 2004. After relocating from Michigan to pursue a PhD in sociology from Tulane University, her plans changed on August 29, 2005, when Hurricane Katrina devastated New Orleans. She received her masters in sociology from Tulane in 2006, traveled extensively in Africa, Europe and the Caribbean before returning to New Orleans to work for the non-profit community. Erica currently works with several New Orleans organizations that focus on local workforce development, cultural advocacy, education and healthcare access, in addition to serving as an adjunct lecturer of gender and sexuality at Tulane University. She also works for a local jazz club and has contributed to several documentaries about post–Katrina New Orleans, her most recent was Shell Shocked, a documentary about New Orleans's youth gun violence epidemic. In her current role as managing director of the New Orleans Musicians' Clinic & Assistance Foundation, she helps keep the city's music culture alive by providing resources to local musicians in obtaining comprehensive healthcare, mental health services, and social services as they return to New Orleans to live and work.

James R. Elliott is associate professor of sociology at Rice University where his current research focuses on interactions of urbanization, social inequality, and the environment. Recently published work examines the accumulation of hazardous industrial wastes in U.S. cities, sociodemographic responses to natural hazards, and local drivers of carbon emissions. He was on the faculty at Tulane University from 1999 to 2006 and at the University of Oregon from 2006 to 2014. Prof. Elliott has served as an advisor to the sociology program at the National Science Foundation and is currently co-editor of *Sociological Perspectives*, the official journal of the Pacific Sociological Association.

Elizabeth Fussell is associate professor of population studies (research) and adjunct professor in the Sociology Department at Brown University in Providence, Rhode Island. She studies international and internal migration in the Americas, population change in New Orleans after Hurricane Katrina, population and environment, and the life course. She was on the faculty at Tulane University from 2001 to 2007 and at Washington State University from 2007 to 2014. She has published her research in *Demography*, *Population & Environment*, *Social Forces*, *Annual Review of Sociology* as well as other journals and in edited volumes. She is currently working on a book titled, *Katrina Stirs the Gumbo Pot: The Arrival and Reception of Latino Immigrants in New Orleans after Hurricane Katrina.*

Dana M. Greene is a research fellow in the Institute for the Environment at the University of North Carolina, Chapel Hill. Dr. Greene specializes in the sociology of disasters and environmental sociology. She is a frequent peer reviewer for academic journals, and is presently working on two book contracts (in addition to her other academic journal article writing). In the "disaster world," Dr. Greene often volunteers with relief agencies to assist with rebuilding post-disaster, while concurrently engaging in fieldwork to learn more about the social, political, and economic impacts of disasters on vulnerable populations.

Timothy J. Haney is associate professor of sociology at Mount Royal University in Calgary, Alberta. He also serves as director of the Centre for Community Disaster Research at MRU. His work focuses on the sociology of disaster, particularly how families and communities prepare for, evacuate from, and recover from disasters and catastrophes of all kinds. Currently, he is undertaking two projects on the devastating 2013 Southern Alberta flood, both funded by the Social Sciences and Humanities Research Council (Government of Canada). His work has appeared in outlets such as *Social Science Research*, *The Sociological Quarterly*, *Journal of Urban Affairs*, *Critical Sociology*, and *Teaching Sociology*. Dr. Haney lived in New Orleans during Hurricane Katrina and was a graduate student at Tulane University.

Andrea Wilbon Hartman is a doctoral student in sociology at the University of Illinois at Champaign-Urbana. She received her masters degree in sociology from Tulane University in 2005 writing a thesis titled "Casinos and Crime: A Sociological Investigation of the Relationship between Gambling and Crime Rates in Louisiana." Hartman was a New Orleans resident at the time Hurricane Katrina hit the Gulf Coast, forcing her to temporarily relocate to New York City. Upon her return to New Orleans, she taught urban sociology at Tulane University and participated in a National Science Foundation (NSF) funded study called the Neighborhood Change Survey, which investigated the social impacts of Hurricane Katrina on the New Orleans metro area. In 2007, Hartman published an article entitled "Filler Up Please: Coping With Racial Stigmas after Hurricane Katrina" in *Narrating the Storm: Sociological Stories of Hurricane Katrina*. Additionally, she published an article titled "The Evolution of Erykah Badu: From Musician to Third Wave Feminist?" in the *Race, Gender & Class* journal. Her research continues to focus on issues pertaining to race, class, gender, and urban redevelopment within the context of neighborhood change.

Jeannie Haubert is associate professor of sociology at Winthrop University in Rock Hill, South Carolina. She studies racial and ethnic relations, social stratification, and immigration. Dr. Haubert did her graduate work at Tulane in New Orleans from 2001–2006 and received an NSF dissertation grant to study Latinos and housing discrimination following Hurricane Katrina. More of her Katrina-related research can be found in the journal *Organization and the Environment* and in two other books, *Through the Eye of Katrina: Social*

Justice in the United States, and *How Ethnically Marginalized Americans Cope with Catastrophic Disasters: Studies in Suffering and Resiliency*.

Danielle Antoinette Hidalgo is teaching assistant professor of sociology and women's, gender, and sexuality studies at Montana State University. She received her PhD (2009) in sociology from the University of California at Santa Barbara and her MSc (2001) in sociology from the London School of Economics and Political Science. As a graduate student at Tulane University, she lived and worked in New Orleans for three years (Fall 2003–Spring 2006). In summer 2006, Danielle and Kristen Barber pitched a Katrina book project to publishers and one year later, they co-edited and published *Narrating the Storm: Sociological Stories of Hurricane Katrina* (2007). She currently lives in Livingston, Montana.

Pamela Jenkins is research professor of sociology and faculty in the women's studies program at the University of New Orleans. She is a founding faculty member of UNO's Center for Hazard Assessment, Response and Technology (CHART). Before Katrina, her research interests were diverse, but focused on how communities respond to a variety of problems. Her research interests post–Katrina include documenting the response to Katrina as part of a national research team on Hurricane Katrina evacuees. She has published on first responders, faith-based communities' response to the storm, and the experiences of elderly during and after Katrina. Throughout her career, she has evaluated a number of national and local efforts focused on community sustainability. At a community level, she is involved in several projects that work directly with best practice for violence prevention including domestic and community violence.

Jessica W. Pardee is assistant professor of sociology at the Rochester Institute of Technology. Dr. Pardee earned her degree in 2009 from Tulane University in New Orleans, LA, where she was enrolled at the time of Hurricane Katrina. In 2014, she published the book *Surviving Katrina*, a study of the survival strategies of low-income, African American women during and following the hurricane. This book and related research investigates the intersection of race, class, gender, and geography, in relation to disaster preparedness, lived experience, and recovery. Dr. Pardee also devotes time to examining the meaning of conducting research on traumatic community events from a reflexive perspective. Additional projects include assessing the disaster preparedness of childcare facilities in the greater Rochester, NY, metropolitan area, and using agent-based modeling to forecast the effects of family evacuation patterns on decision making and timeliness.

Mimi Schippers received her PhD in sociology from the University of Wisconsin-Madison and is associate professor of sociology and gender and sexuality studies at Tulane University. Her research focuses on gender and sexuality with an emphasis on alternative practices, relationship forms, and cultures. She is author of *Rockin' Out of the Box: Gender Maneuvering in Alternative Hard Rock* and is currently working on her next book titled *Polyqueer: Masculinity, Femininity, and the Queer Potential of Plural Relationships* (forthcoming).

Bethany L. Van Brown, an assistant professor in the Department of Criminal Justice at Loyola University, New Orleans, earned her doctorate from the University of Delaware. Brown's areas of expertise are social vulnerability and disasters, organizational perspectives involving community-based groups in disasters, and crime during disaster events. She is currently researching crime patterns leading up to, during, and following disaster events, along with working to better understand the link between animal abuse and domestic violence.

www.ingramcontent.com/pod-product-compliance
Ingram Content Group UK Ltd.
Pitfield, Milton Keynes, MK11 3LW, UK
UKHW041632031026
15587UKWH00001B/231

9 781498 501200